The *Incredible* Yanqui

Lee Christmas (left). From a snapshot made about 1901 near Puerto Cortez, probably taken after Christmas had ridden single-handed into the mountains to capture the assassin who had blown an American railroad man through the corrugated iron roof of his home with dynamite.

The *Incredible* Yanqui

The Career of Lee Christmas

Hermann Deutsch

Pelican Publishing Company
Gretna 2012

The word "Pelican" and the depiction of a pelican are trademarks
of Pelican Publishing Company, Inc., and are registered in the
U.S. Patent and Trademark Office.

ISBN: 9781455615766
e-book ISBN: 9781455615773

Printed in the United States of America
Published by Pelican Publishing Company, Inc.
1000 Burmaster Street, Gretna, Louisiana 70053

TO A STAUNCH FRIEND AND GALLANT SOLDIER

GUY R. MOLONY

LIEUTENANT COLONEL, U. S. R.

THIS BOOK IS VERY AFFECTIONATELY DEDICATED

Prescript:

FOR THE tale that follows I claim no virtue but honesty. It is a story that had to be written. To be quite frank, it had to be written twice.

The first time I set it down, I began unwittingly the biography of a myth, and as the tale progressed, the facts I encountered did such violence to the aura of legend that at the end there was no fable left at all, but a creature of flesh and blood who was in no sense the same being whom I had started out to portray.

Thus I learned just how unreal was the Lee Christmas of whom I had heard and read in the past; and it seemed to me a pity indeed to destroy for others the glamour I had lost. Then it came to me that the real Lee Christmas I had found deep in that thicket of pinchbeck tinsel was a far more remarkable person than any the Sunday Supplements of two decades ago had been able to conjure up, and I went back to the beginning and set down a new tale, in which I offer you, in place of a mannequin " hero " an amazing vagabond, a failure, if you will, until a capricious Kismet focused upon him the absorbed regard of a wondering world, showered him with fortune for a brief space — and then sent him back, broken, to obscurity; a failure who had been touched fleetingly with splendor.

It is pleasant to acknowledge that the work involved in this task would have been far beyond my unassisted powers. Without Col. Guy R. Molony, and his memory for details in the days of Christmas' success — a success to which he contributed so large a share — an account of the bizarre events of 1910 and 1911 along the Caribbean would have been a mere routine catalogue of dates and places.

Without the patient help of Frans Blom, head of the Department of Middle American Research of Tulane University, in selecting from that Department's magnificent library those pamphlets and records which had a direct bearing on the times and changes in whose development Lee Christmas was so intimately associated; and without his no less patient assistance in translating smudged and faded Spanish letters, battle orders, and other documents, it is doubtful whether an adequate background for what lay behind a dozen major and minor revolutions in Central America could ever have been pieced and fitted together.

This applies as well to the brief but intensive seminar in the history of Honduras conducted for my particular benefit by my friend Sr. Jorge F. Durón, now vice-consul of Honduras in New Orleans, who used as a text the volume of which his illustrious father, Dr. Rómulo E. Durón, of Tegucigalpa, is the author; and to Dr. Durón additionally is due my special appreciation for the intimate personal account he gave me of the scenes amid which the Paredes-Knox "Dollar Diplomacy" treaty was disapproved by the Congress of Honduras of which he was a member.

There have been many others who have given much in the way of assistance. Mrs. G. F. Hanson, of Memphis, who was the first Mrs. Lee Christmas; Dr. Sydenham M. Waller, John T. Griffin, Charles Jeffs, Ricardo López, Federico Girbal, and Coronel Francisco Cleaves of San Pedro Sula; Col. E. T. Mc-

Laurie, of McElroy; J. H. Burton and A. Bruce Bielaski of New York; Judge Rufus E. Foster, Miss Alice J. Molony, Anthony Boyd Cetti, Max Schaumburger, Gwen and Bruce Mack-Manning, E. E. Moise, and Don H. Higgins of New Orleans. To these and many others I owe — and herewith tender — my very sincere thanks.

HERMANN B. DEUTSCH

New Orleans, La.
October 17, 1930

Contents

List of Illustrations

To Make a Long Story Quite Short:

In the fall of 1894, a man who was destined to upset various lesser governments — not to mention the dance he led the United States of America — left New Orleans for the tropics because he was penniless and there was nowhere else for him to go.

Thirty years later, almost to the day, he returned to New Orleans from the tropics because he was once more penniless and there was nowhere else for him to go.

But, in the meantime —

Credit was given to Lee

IT WAS all quite as mad as the March Hare's nightmare, and small wonder, when you stop to consider that thirteen madmen were engaged in the business of capturing a nation. The fact that the hot tropic sun beat down upon a barricade of clear gray ice, which mirrored the lush green of the jungle and the flaming colors of the orchids, was sheer delirium in itself.

And from behind that wall of ice (they had built it of massive, 200-pound blocks) came the heavy concussion of ball-and-black-powder cartridges, dealing dreadful execution among barefoot soldiers in dun-colored cotton uniforms, so that the straggling charge across the narrow-gauge railroad trestle faltered and disintegrated. Limp bodies sprawled queerly upon the cross-ties before that thick ice barrier in the steaming jungle, and sooty buzzards flapped, unhurried, from the tiled roof ridges beyond the lagoon to investigate.

This was the fourteenth day of April, and the year was 1897. The Battle of Laguna Trestle was under way, where the Chamelecon river reaches the wide bay in which Hernando Cortez had landed his horses and his Iberian mules nearly four centuries before. Though it was less than a skirmish to all save the poor devils whose bodies lay so queerly sprawled before that insane breastwork, the Battle of Laguna Trestle was shifting history in and for all of Central America.

True, the victors of Laguna would enjoy a triumph of scarce a fortnight's duration, after which they and their brief " government " would fade forever out of the political picture in

3

Honduras. None the less, no battle would leave a deeper impress on the nation's subsequent record, for at Laguna Trestle was born the myth of Lee Christmas. Here it was that a ruddy, wide-shouldered gringo* was pitchforked into such far-spread fame as a warrior that he ceased for three decades to be a tramp railroader and became the most noted "*aventurero yanqui*" the Spanish Main has ever known.

For the chronicler, the charm of history lies in the fact that —if only he waits a sufficient time before setting down his tale—he can always trace the fall of an empire to the loss of a horseshoe nail. Thus the failure of the most famous of America's "dollar diplomacy" treaties really began with the Battle of Laguna Trestle which, in turn, had its roots in a tumbled little heap of many-hued skeins of silk floss on the work-blackened desk of a roundhouse superintendent in New Orleans one sultry October night of 1894—the year that cast up Lee Christmas at Puerto Cortez, as engineer of what was then the only railroad in Spanish Honduras; a ninety-kilometer narrow-gauge system wavering inland from the sea to Pimienta.

For three years, now, Lee Christmas of New Orleans, Memphis and elsewhere, had made that run three times a week — up from the coast one day, with empty box cars to be dropped off at plantation spurs and at San Pedro Sula, the metropolis which boasted the only ice factory in Central America; back to the coast the next day, picking up loaded banana cars at the plantations and two carloads of ice at San Pedro. Three round trips a week with a toy engine and a toy train on a toy system for one who had once known the thrill of lording it at the throttles of the Illinois Central's huge Moguls; three years of strange

---

* The term "gringo" has not quite the same significance in Honduras as in Mexico, where it is applied exclusively to North Americans, being derived, through the easy slurrings of folk-etymology from the opening words of one of Robert Burns' poems, which was one of the favorite songs of the soldiers of the United States during the Mexican war, to wit: "*Green grow* the rashes, O; Green grow the rashes, O; the sweetest hours that e'er I spend, are spent among the lasses, O." In Honduras, a gringo is any white foreigner, European or American; not merely, as in Mexico, the "green-grow" of the United States.

chatter in an alien tongue at the *cantinas* where he gruffly ordered whisky *cocktaileys* while he longed for the homely cheer of Tom Cook's saloon on Poydras street, midway between the I.C. yards and the roundhouse; incomprehensible talk of *Conservadores* and *Liberales,* of *colorados* and *azules,* instead of the familiar political gossip of the Third Ward, of Regulars and Goo-goos and Y.D.'s and the jobs that would be parceled out to the faithful when Remy Klock was elected sheriff and John Fitzpatrick was made mayor.

Lee Christmas knew nothing of the glorious victories through which Manuel Bonilla, Policarpo Bonilla and Terencio Sierra — a new triumvirate of young Liberal leaders in Honduras — had broken the tyrannical hold of Domingo Vásquez; and cared less for the fact that these victories had been won with the aid of President José Santos Zelaya of Nicaragua. Though he had been nearly three years in the tropics, his political interests still lay in the Third Ward of New Orleans, and not in any considerations of Honduras as the buffer state of Central America.

The mythical Lee Christmas would have taken this into account, of course, but the mythical Lee Christmas was not yet born, and the real one was just a tramp railroader who couldn't make a living back in the States, and to whom it meant nothing at all that of the five Central-American republics, three — Nicaragua, Honduras, and Guatemala — were the largest, and that Honduras lay between the other two. It had never occurred to him that whichever one of the others was allied with Honduras held the balance of power in all of Central America. By consequence, the moment a government friendly to Nicaragua came into power in Honduras, Guatemala began to give aid and comfort to any one who cared to promote a revolution that would put in an opposition regime there. This was no sooner achieved than Nicaragua busied herself to upset the new *entente* in favor of one with herself. All of which made for plenty of administrative variety in Honduras, and kept official tenure from falling into the rut of stability.

Thus, as long as the new Big Three — Policarpo Bonilla, Terencio Sierra and Manuel Bonilla — who were friendly to Nicaragua, controlled Honduras, the focus of revolutions would lie in Guatemala. So it was from Puerto Barrios in that country that young Enrique Soto's thirteen madmen set out in April 1897 to capture an entire nation. By sailboat they crossed to Puerto Cortez, and dropped anchor near the inland base of the sickle-shaped promontory that forms one side of Cortez bay.

Along that promontory runs a single street — the *Calle de Linea;* along the middle of the street run the narrow-gauge tracks of the railroad. At the outer point of the promontory is the banana wharf; at the base, where the broad lagoon that is the mouth of the Chamelecon river empties into the bay through a narrow channel that is bridged by the railroad trestle, is Laguna. The single street is Puerto Cortez and, practically in the back yards of the homes on the seaward side of the street, near Laguna, Enrique Soto's thirteen madmen dropped anchor.

General José Manuel Durón, who had been a political exile since his espousal of the lost cause of ex-President Domingo Vásquez, was their leader. Among them were at least two *Norteamericanos* — General William Drummond, who is still enjoying a peaceful and wealthy old age in Guatemala City at the time these lines are written, and General William Jeffries. The names of the other ten generals have been forgotten.

General Durón's campaign to seize Honduras with his twelve sub-generals was nothing short of inspired. Always at dawn the long native *cayucos* come out of the Chamelecon and Ulua rivers into the bay, laden with plantains and casavas and papayas and oranges and alligator pears and other market vegetables, to be huckstered along the single sickle-shaped street of the port. Just before dawn of April 13, 1897, General Durón's madmen possessed themselves of the first of these large canoes that came along. Swiftly they jettisoned its lawful cargo of vegetables, lay down in the bottom, covered themselves over with banana leaves, and arranged a few bunches of ripe plantains atop.

Upon pain of instant death, the luckless native owner of the vessel was ordered to paddle slowly along the bay shore of the town, offering for sale his supposed wares with the customary, long-drawn huckstering call of *"Plátanos! Plátanos!"*

General Durón knew his native soldiery. Their government ration was slim, and their pay — when they got it — slimmer still. By way of compensation, they levied upon the local peddlers under a thin guise of "inspecting" cargoes. As the cry of "Plantains!" arose from the waterfront, a good half of the garrison of Puerto Cortez swarmed from their *cuartel* on the inland side of the street, across the railroad track and through the gardens on the opposite side, to the shore of the bay, commanding the peddler to bring his *cayuka* alongside to be "inspected."

He obeyed, of course; but even as the eager hands of the inspectors were reaching for the ripe plantains so temptingly displayed, the canoe erupted thirteen armed and determined generals. The soldier-inspectors had left their weapons back in the *cuartel* on the other side of the street, and they were immediately taken prisoner.

Leaving their captives in charge of two guards, the remaining invaders slipped through the gardens and rushed the *cuartel* itself. The *comandante* — a consumptive — surrendered in the hammock to which his illness confined him, and the rest of the garrison followed suit. Half of them, and possibly more, having no other means of livelihood in prospect, immediately re-enlisted under the victorious banner of Provisional President Enrique Soto, as represented by his commanding general, José Manuel Durón.

Thus, twenty minutes after the start of the Sotoista revolution, the revolutionists were in possession of an army, a garrison, a Hotchkiss gun, two old brass Spanish muzzle-loading cannon, rifles, munitions, the largest seaport in Honduras, the terminus of the country's only railroad, and a treasury — for quite naturally, the first prize, after the garrison had capitulated, was the Puerto Cortez customs house.

The real metropolis of the Atlantic section of Honduras, however, was San Pedro Sula, sixty kilometres inland. It was General Durón's next objective. His campaign plans were quite complete, and, had there been in his forces a single person who could run a locomotive, he would have proceeded at once. As it was, he marched his men three miles from Puerto Cortez to Laguna to await the arrival of the down train that afternoon. As a result, when Engineer Lee Christmas of New Orleans, pulled up at Laguna siding, he and his asthmatic little wood-burning engine, and his string of loaded banana cars, and his two box cars of ice — one for Puerto Cortez and one for Puerto Barrios and Guatemala City — were seized as prisoner and prizes. Moreover, it was made quite clear to him, incredible as it might be, that he was either going to pilot a trainload of revolutionists into battle, or that he would be shot. Not merely figuratively shot, or anything of that sort, you understand; but completely and definitely killed.

In a curious five-page autobiography which he penciled a month or two before his death, Christmas gave the following version of the incident, and it is only fair to remark that the palliative dashes with which he sought to temper the vigor of the written record, are his own. So, by the way, is the orthography.

". . . a Revolution Broke out on the 13 of April 1897 where he was captured by the Revolutionist and forced to handle an Eng at the point of a Bayonet, he applied for Protection from the American Consul which of course he did not get. he was then taken a Drunken General and given to understand that he would be Shot. this of course was a Bitter pill for Lee so he said to the Gen all Right if I have to be made a target of give me a Gun so I may kill some S— B— while they are pluging at me he received all the Guns he could use. then the Goverment forces attacted the Port of Cortez the fight was won by the Rev-forces and credit was given to Lee and he was promoted to a capt. in the Honduras army likeing the new game. . ."

Thus forcibly committed to a " new game," Lee Christmas called on all the ingenuity at his command to insure his survival of it. He had no illusions whatever about what would happen to him if he were perched out in the cab of his locomotive, in front of a trainload of *revolucionarios,* while they debated the issues of the day with the armed forces of the federal government. Learning that the sortie was to be made at dawn, he put in the balance of the day and a good part of the night, rigging a traveling fort which would go ahead of his engine.

About the edges of a flat-car he built up a double wall of sand bags, and in between the two layers of sacks, he sandwiched a filling of scrap three-quarter-inch boiler iron from the railroad yards. At the front of this traveling redoubt, he mounted the Hotchkiss cannon the revolutionists had captured. About the rest of the walls, revolutionist sharpshooters — *tiradores* — were placed. Thus if Lee Christmas actually had to go into battle, he would at least have a cannon and a guard of riflemen in front of him. In any event, that was the general idea, and Lee Christmas might have become, in this fashion, the first to employ an armored train in warfare, had not Colonel Carlos Girón — federal *comandante* of the garrison at San Pedro Sula, which was the point of attack — been a brave and reckless soldier himself.

The moment Colonel Girón heard of the outbreak of a revolution on the coast, he left San Pedro, without waiting for orders from his government at Tegucigalpa. All night Giron and his men rode from San Pedro toward the sea, and when, on the following morning, Generalissimo Durón's troops made ready to entrain at Laguna, runners brought them word that the federals were hard upon the port.

General Durón at once chose the defensive, and ordered a barricade thrown up so that the federals would have to charge across the trestle into the defenses. The only material close enough at hand, at the moment, consisted of the 200-pound blocks of ice in the two box cars at the siding; and so a thick wall of ice was thrown up across the tracks there in that sweltering jungle. General Girón was evidently too impetuous to order a halt so that the beating tropic sun might breach this fortress — a task which it unquestionably would have accomplished in a few hours. He gave the word to charge.

Lee Christmas had been sitting back in the cab of his locomotive all this while, quite aloof from all this feverish military activity. Actual combat had been no part of his bargain. But with the ragged volley that met the first charge across the bridge, something happened to that tramp railroader who hadn't been able to make a living in the States. Possibly a wild shot or a ricochet had come uncomfortably close, and had roused his quick temper to resentment. Possibly he was just thrilled by his first contact with the sheer martial stir he later grew to love. Possibly, indeed, a dormant heritage from a father who had stormed the heights of Chapultepec with Scott, was suddenly quickened into life.

The fact remains that on the moment Christmas left the cab of his asthmatic little woodburner, and joined the front rank at the barricade, rifle in hand and fighting. Not one of the revolutionists exposed himself more carelessly to enemy fire. Not one took a more reckless part in repelling the federal assault, so that the charges that were launched across that narrow trestle withered and fell away.

Short and sharp was the engagement, for early in the battle General Girón himself fell, badly wounded, and the federals drew off, leaving the field at Laguna to the thirteen generals who had set out to capture the country the day before, and to a wide-shouldered, ruddy *gringo,* who was embraced on the spot by the chief of the thirteen generals, and then and there promoted to a captaincy.

Since the victory had to be celebrated, the invasion of the inland territory was put off for a day, and by the time Lee Christmas, with that flat-car-fortress in front, finally moved his train up the Chamelecon valley toward San Pedro, the government had issued orders, and the revolutionists met no resistance.

For the three shrewd young liberal politicians who were at the head of the government rather welcomed the Enrique Soto revolution as an opportunity to show power. Policarpo Bonilla's term as president was drawing to a close, and it was Terencio Sierra's turn to succeed him. Sierra was Minister of War and Commander-in-Chief of the armies. A decisive victory over a revolutionary force would make him a national hero, whose choice by the people at the ensuing election would be a foregone conclusion.

During the week or ten days which it would take Sierra's army to organize and march on San Pedro from Tegucigalpa, the revolutionists could do no harm whatever, since they, on their part, could not organize a march from the railhead up the continental divide to the capital in so brief a period; and so the only two garrisons along the line of invasion — Choloma and San Pedro Sula — were ordered to draw back into the hills, to save the victory over the Sotoistas for General Terencio Sierra. In the meantime, too, word was dispatched to President Zelaya in Nicaragua, who promptly ordered out a gunboat to steam up the coast to Puerto Cortez, and thus cut off the revolutionists by sea, as well as by land.

During this interval, the revolutionists were having high and merry times, lording it over their particular strip of Honduras, and laying great plans for the invasion of Tegucigalpa. Christmas, smoking his rank native *puros* — the tropically intensified equivalent of a stogie — made daily trips between San Pedro and Puerto Cortez with his train, and drew the pay of a captain. Banana export was not stopped, of course, and the export duties, as well as the customs collections of Honduras' chief port were fed into the Sotoista treasury.

First intimation that all was not well came in the shape of a message from Puerto Cortez that a hostile Nicaraguan boat, crowded with men, had appeared off the point of the promontory. General Drummond was immediately sent to the coast to deal with the situation, and Christmas rushed him down with a detachment of men in a special train. Arrived at the port, General Drummond ordered one of the ancient brass muzzle-loading cannons — a heritage of Spanish domination — trained out to sea toward the gunboat which was standing discreetly off the coast. General Drummond was no artilleryman, and his theory of ballistics seemed to be an avoidance of anything that smacked of half-measures.

The normal charge for one of those cannons would be about five pounds of coarse black powder. General Drummond put in the contents of a 25-pound canister. On top of this awesome load he placed not one round cannon-ball, but two. The cannoneer who was standing by with a lighted fusee was so frightened that he could not apply this fusee to the touch-hole, because his hand shook too badly.

Impatiently pushing the man aside, General Drummond bent over the cannon and, puffing his cigar to a healthy glow, squashed the lighted end of it against the touch-hole, with the result that two round shot went screaming down the main and only street of Puerto Cortez, danced in a brief ricochet over the surface of the Atlantic Ocean, and then dropped out of the world. But there was another result. The quintuple charge of powder, with a double load of shot to give it yet further force, vented a fiery stream of candescent gas back through the touch-hole of the cannon, over which the inexperienced General Drummond was still bent. The General dropped to the ground, one of his eyes literally blown and seared from its socket — and the second " battle " of Puerto Cortez in the campaign of April 1897 was over.

Bearing their wounded general with them, the revolutionists fled by train back to San Pedro Sula, only to be met by news of a fresh disaster. At the head of some two thousand federal soldiers, General Terencio Sierra was marching upon San Pedro. Within three days, at the most, he would arrive. So far as the government of Enrique Soto was concerned, that was the end of the party.*

If the Sotoistas remained in San Pedro, they would be annihilated. Escape to Guatemala via Puerto Cortez was cut off by the hostile Nicaraguan gunboat. Securely bottled, the heads of the military government of young *don* Enrique Soto took to their heels, via some sure-footed mules which had been pastured in the broad *potreros* of Señor Charlie Jeffs, which steeds they headed straight up over the mountains—Las Cumbres —whose serrated ridge line reached skyward between Honduras and Guatemala. Singly and in pairs—*el Sr. Capitan don Lee Crreesmas* among them—they escaped overland to Guatemala, where Manuel Estrada Cabrera was just coming into the power that would maintain his tyrannical presidency for twenty long years, and where a fresh plot to overthrow the alliance between Zelaya of Nicaragua and the Bonilla-Sierra-Bonilla entente of Spanish Honduras could be—and was—immediately incubated.

In the meantime, the infant Christmas myth had already assumed lusty proportions. Though he understood little more of Spanish than he needed to order *'ot cakeys* for his breakfasts, and to seek diversion among the cantinas and burdeles where he invariably sought his leisured ease, Christmas was promptly appointed by Cabrera to a place in the secret service of Guatemala—an organization which did much to keep that President's regime secure against assault for two decades.

For it was fighters and not linguists that Cabrera wanted to attach to his service. To him, the fact that Christmas could not speak Spanish was of no more moment than the fact that he was also—

* See Appendix No. I.

Color Blind

THOUGH much that is authentic has come down to us out of the first thirty years of Christmas' life, that span shall be touched but lightly in the present tale of it, for few of the provable details are pretty. Practically all that was subsequently written of these years was confected to fit the later Christmas myth. Much of this he took a delight in inspiring himself, in the days that were to come, when special writers from New York and from Mexico City and from London came to interview him; much there was that he glossed over; and much that he was careful to omit.

Yet there are sources from which the truth can be gleaned readily enough. As these lines are written, the first of his four lawful wives still lives in Memphis. She knew him as a gangling twelve-year-old in a little sawmill town deep in the swamp forests of Livingston parish, Louisiana. Anthony Boyd Cetti, bosom companion of Christmas' early railroading days in and about New Orleans, is still there, as special representative for the L. & A. railroad. The story with which the *Daily Picayune's* " ever alert and enterprising reporter " seems to have scooped the town on March 23, 1885,* gives the details of his first elopement, and may be found in the archive room at the City Hall. Tom Cook, who kept the saloon that was Christmas' favorite hang-out in those early days, is a hale and hearty Chief Deputy Sheriff in Orleans parish. There are still eye-witnesses who saw Lee Christmas' tipsy departure for

---

* See Appendix No. II.

the run that ended in the wreck which drove him from railroading in the United States. We shall get little help here from the five-page autobiography, however, for it was this period of his life which Christmas always touched upon most sketchily. However, we read:

Gen Lee Christmas
was Borne on the 22nd of Feb 1863 on his Fathers cotton Plantation on the Banks of the Amite River Livingston Parish La about 19 miles from Baton Rouge. his Father Winfield Scott Christmas was a cotton Planter well to do up to the Civil war where the Yankees visited and left him only the old Homestead. his father was named Winfield Scott after Gen Scoctt and served as a soldier in the Mexican invasion. in 1857 his father moved to Springfield La where he died in Jun 1879 there were 3 boys & 3 girls Borne to the family all Dead but Lee Started out in Life 1st as a cook on a little Schooner by name of Cileste under Capt Bob Caldwell which Plied bettween Springfield & the new Basin N. O. at the age of 13 years was avanced to a sailor then to the Captain of the Schooner Surprise after to Captain of the Schooner Lillie Simms. in 1880 obtained employment on the New Orleans & Great Jackson R R which after was the Chicago St Louis & New Orleans R R then to the Illinois Central R R today. leared to fire a Locomotive in the days when wood was Burned. went to the New Orleans & Texas R R which today is the Mississippi Valley RR was promoted to a Locomotive Engineer in 1885 where he Ran as such untill Nov. 29-1891. Went to Honduras, C.A.

The Winfield Scott Christmas who had helped to carry the halls of Montezuma was broken in health when he abandoned his cotton plantation and moved to the sawmill town deep in the Livingston parish swamps. It was there that the tall stripling who had been christened Leon Winfield Christmas met Mamie, the young daughter of Fred Reed, the mill foreman, and began a boy-and-girl courtship in which he showed that somewhere about him there was an incurable streak of the romantic. For there was no other reason why he should steal through the town at dead of night, to slip scrawled love-notes beneath the Reed kitchen door where Mamie would find them in the morning.

The death of Lee's father saw what was left of the family — for at least two of the children had also died back there in the swamps — moving to McComb, Miss., where Lee worked for a few months as a waiter in the railroad restaurant, and then, at eighteen, became a brakeman on the run between McComb and New Orleans. There, in the old Planters' Hotel, he met Boyd Cetti and formed one of the very few close friendships of his life. Tiring of his work as brakeman, he served a back-breaking apprenticeship as fireman and became an engineer in 1884. Tiring, in turn, of this, he left his cab and became baggage master at Vicksburg. The following March he received a letter from Mamie Reed. It was the first sign of life he had had from her in more than three years, but the day he received the note he got a leave of absence, and boarded the first train for New Orleans.

As a wooer he was nothing if not forthright. Here is the story Mrs. G. F. Hanson, of Memphis — the Mamie Reed of the eighties — tells of the incident today:

"He come to the door," she recalls, "and right there asked me if I was ready to marry him. I had always said I would, so I told him I'd marry him as soon as pa and ma said. But he wouldn't hear to that. He said he had a house fixed up for us in Vicksburg, and he would come to take me out to Spanish Fort the next afternoon, and instead of we coming back to my house, we would go down to the train and go to Vicksburg to be married. And I told him all right."

But Mamie's mother must have smelled a mouse for, on the following evening, just as the elopers boarded the train, she ran out upon the platform, screaming for the watch. The train had already begun to move, but shrieking at the top of her voice, Mrs. Reed clutched the handrail of the rear platform and was promptly dragged from her feet, so that the train had to be stopped to save her from injury.

The policemen whom her cries had summoned to the scene were a puzzled lot. Mrs. Reed demanded the arrest of her daughter, but would make no charges. Meanwhile the train crew were becoming impatient. The upshot was that Mamie and Lee departed for Vicksburg, where they were married the next day at the home of Lee's brother by Squire M. J. Lowenburg, and became, as the *Daily Picayune's* inspired headline writer put it, a "Merry Christmas Pair."

Seven months or so later they returned to New Orleans, and were duly forgiven by the Reeds. They settled down in a home in the Third Ward, near the combination grocery-and-saloon of Ed. Remy Klock, whose brother-in-law was the fireman on Christmas' engine, and for a time they prospered. Then Lee decided to go in for politics. He was still forthright in such matters. He wanted political recognition in the Third Ward because one of the firemen on the road, himself a minor political figure, had been rewarded by a city job on one of the drainage pumps, which meant that his duties consisted of reporting twice a month to draw his pay, a portion of which he split with some superior. This did not in the least interfere with his employment or his earnings as a fireman, and the whole thing struck Lee Christmas as a decidedly admirable arrangement.

Methodically he purchased the silk hat, the cane, and the " jimswinger " coat which were essential adjuncts of political activity in those days. Just as methodically he started out to mingle with the boys at Remy Klock's saloon, at Tom Cook's, and at the gambling houses. He developed a tremendous appetite for liquor,* a capacity which is still spoken of with awe in Central America. He carried this to such an excess that Mamie, he, and the two babies — Ed and Hattie — ultimately came to live quite frankly on the bounty of the Reeds, for

---

* In Puerto Cortez it is still reported as a fact that Christmas' favorite "light punch " to be served his guests at the Palms Hotel, for *bailes* or similar social gatherings, was a fifty-fifty mixture of native rum and champagne, with various fresh fruits sliced into it. He could never be persuaded that this was a hard drink.

Christmas' money was spent in the dissipation that he regarded as necessary for political success.

At the height of the campaign in which he was helping to elect John Fitzpatrick mayor and Remy Klock sheriff of Orleans parish, Christmas came in from the run one day, donned his silk hat and his jimswinger, seized his cane and fared forth upon the highroads. About the time the carouse reached its peak, he was suddenly called to move a trainload of bananas north in a refrigerator special. He had not slept since his previous run, but somehow they got him into his working clothes and hoisted him into his cab. His father-in-law swung aboard the engine at a crossing with a big pail of black coffee with which it was hoped he might sober up.

The fireman with him was a new man, who did not realize that Christmas was sound asleep at the throttle. They met another train head on at Sarpy, around a bend that was screened by a dense growth of willows.* Christmas later told his wife, who had hurried to the hospital, that the first thing he remembered after leaving New Orleans was the pain of the steam that was scalding him as he lay pinned to the cross-ties beneath his engine.

He was dismissed from railroad service and blacklisted.† For three years he was neither more nor less than a tramp. At intervals he would leave his family for protracted stays, working in lumber camps or cane fields, and would return for equally prolonged sprees in Memphis or New Orleans. He tried to run a railroad men's hotel-and-bar in Memphis for a time, but the venture was a failure. His ambition for place on the public payroll got him no farther than one of the many gangs whose duties it was to clean the open sewers with which the New Orleans of those days was drained.

He was sleeping off a spree in the warden's office at the parish prison over which Sheriff Remy Klock presided when word was brought to him that his wife had just been delivered

---

* A detailed account of the wreck may be found in the New Orleans *Times-Democrat* of December 2, 1891.

† See Appendix No. III.

of a baby daughter. He hurried to see her, promised to settle down, and left to look for a job. He returned four months later, seedier than ever, with no clear account of where he had been in the meantime. It was then that he heard railroad men were being sought for work in the tropics, on the banana trains of the Honduras National out of Puerto Cortez.

Seeking information on this score he looked up the night yardmaster of the Illinois Central, W. B. Baldwin, and was overjoyed to learn that Baldwin himself was looking for men to handle the steadily increasing winter freight rush and that, if Christmas were content to begin with a switch engine in the yards, he would doubtless soon be back on the road. Three years and the need for men had evidently done much to temper the severity with which the old blacklists were being enforced.

There was only one condition attached to the offer of a job. Since Lee had dropped out of railroading, three years previously, the color vision test had been instituted. But the special testing car from Chicago was right in the yards, and he could take his examination that very afternoon.

The night foreman of that roundhouse, Boyd Cetti, was the boon friend of Lee's first railroad days. It was to Cetti that Christmas came that night, in the roundhouse office where his friend was seated at a work-blackened table, and it was really Cetti who exiled Lee Christmas to the tropics.

" He came up to me kind of dragging his steps," Cetti relates, "and not the way he used to walk, swinging his shoulders, quick-like. I asked him what was wrong, wasn't he going to work for us? And he says no, because the so-and-so doctor from Chicago tells him he's got the color blind.

" We were a funny lot, in those days, and all this color blind stuff was new to us. Like a lot of the other boys, I didn't believe there was any such thing as color blind, and so, when Lee told us the doctor said he had it, we went and unlocked Dr. Allport's testing car and got a pile of all that embroidery floss out of it and put it on my table."

Over the tumbled heap of vari-colored silk on that work-blackened table, Lee Christmas, sandy brows puckered, hunched his wide shoulders.

" It was kind of awful to watch that man," Cetti once more takes up the tale. "There he was, and he would pick up a piece of floss as green as the greenest grass and put it with one that was as red as blood and say the color was the same. I finally stopped him. 'Lee Christmas,' I said, 'I want you to tell me and tell me straight. Do those colors look the same to you?' and he looked up like he was kind of puzzled and 'Ain't they the same?' says he. 'The same!' I yelled. 'Can't you see one of 'em's greener'n the greenest grass and the other is redder'n the reddest blood?' He shook his head and then, for the first time, I realized there really must be such a thing as the color blind.

"Well, he looks at us kind of slow, like he couldn't believe it, and 'Before God, boys, you are not fooling me now, are you?' he asks, and it made me feel kind of queer, the way he said it, but I told him before God we were not fooling him. So he straightened up, then, and told us how he heard that morning they were paying big money in Honduras for hoggers on their banana railroad, and he was asking Baldwin about it, which was how Baldwin come to offer him a job, but now it is no use, and he will go to Honduras in the morning or the next day or whenever. . ."

Christmas and his wife sold the furnishings of their home for twelve dollars. Ten dollars of that sum he gave to Mamie and put her aboard a train for Memphis with the three children — Ed, and Hattie and Sadie — for he knew that the free-masonry that exists among the Brotherhoods would see them safely there.*

---

* The tale of the discovery of Christmas' color blindness and his subsequent trek to Honduras has been wonderfully rearranged along divers patterns to trick out the Christmas Myth of a later day. In some of these he contemplates suicide, in others he actually attempts it. One of the more bizarre versions is quoted in Appendix No. IV.

With two dollars left in his pockets he took passage on a banana steamer, and went pitching southward across the Gulf past Campeche Bank and the Yucatan Channel and Mujeres light and Glover's reef, to a cut between two ranges of mountains, and that was —

Puerto Cortez

ON THE hot morning when he landed there in the early winter of 1894, Lee Christmas saw in Puerto Cortez precisely what you would see there today. The same *cantinas* and *estancos*,* the same two-story Hotel Lefebvre, the same girls, their lithe figures swaying gracefully, blue-black hair hanging down over flimsy shawls of black gauze, bearing upon their heads flat grass baskets of mangoes and papayas and *pan dulce*.

Christmas hated it all for its alien strangeness, and sought consolation in white-eye, which made matters difficult for the wife and babies who were finding it increasingly hard to live in Memphis on promised remittances which never came. As a matter of record, Christmas stood it less than a year and then returned for a few months to the States. But once more he failed to make a go of it. For one thing, Mamie had at last decided to assert herself and informed him that unless he provided for his family, he and that family would have to part. For another, the monotony of the labor with which he tried to comply with the uxorial edict — he ran one of the tiny trains of cane cars while they were "taking off a sugar crop" at a plantation near Burnside — drove him frantic.

So he chucked the job, and Mamie was as good as her word

* "White-eye" is *guaro*, which is short for *aguardiente*, which in turn may be freely translated as "water that has teeth" from which even the uninitiated may be able to form some estimate of its mettle. It is a rum made from native sugar cane, and the sale of it is a government monopoly, permitted only at licensed "*estancos*," which are thereby distinguished from the "*cantinas*," where only other liquors, and no *aguardiente* may be sold. Incidentally, another derivation for the word *aguardiente* is "agua" and "ardiente" which is "water with fire" — a definition which is no less a gauge of its potency.

and took herself and the children back to Memphis while he made his way to New Orleans and hung about the bar-rooms and did occasional bits of day labor. For a time he worked in the wood and charcoal yards of the Sullivans on the New Basin canal, where the lake schooners on which he had sailed as a boy discharged their cargoes. But he couldn't stick that, either, so he returned to the tropics after writing a bitter letter of denunciation to Mamie in Memphis — a letter which still bears the punctures of the yellow fever fumigation to which it was subject.

And in Puerto Cortez he gave himself over to the revels that obtain most freely in garrison towns and in seaports, Puerto Cortez being both, so that the trollops and the blisters there came to know him as a generous patron whom almost any member of their craft might profitably address as " switt'eart "; and naturally, during the sobering interludes of remorse he blamed Mamie for it all, and in the following year he wrote still another letter to the girl beneath whose kitchen door he had slipped his earliest writings.

Puerto Cortez Honduras, Feb 8 1897

Dear Mamie
No Doubt you will be surprised to get a letter from me I have just wrote to Hattie of course you will see her Letter sometime no Doubt you have began to beleive by this time what my intentions are if you will sue me for a Divorce it can be gotten I will pay all Expenses and agree to Divide all I ever make with my children now I hope you will think the same as I Do it is best for me and best for you as I know the way we have Lived the Last 5 years you could not Live Happy your mother has tryed on several occasions to seperate us so now will be the time to get in her work of course should you Refuse me a Divorce and should I Ever want to marry in this country not being Divorced would not interfere in the Least but for our childrens sake I think you should agree with me I am willing for you to make any charges you may care to I will shoulder all hoping you are well and that you may Give me a favourable & Early Reply I am yours

Leon. W. Christmas.
Puerto Cortez Honduras C.A.

While he was still waiting for his " favourable & Early Reply," the affair of Laguna Trestle pitched him into "the new
game" and exiled him to Guatemala, where he fell ill for a
time. So great had grown his repute as a proven *valiente,* that
the funds for the new revolution were entrusted to him, and
he was sent to New Orleans to make arrangement for the
shipment of the requisite *elementos* — arms and munitions.
But he bungled the job handsomely by talking too much, for
he could not resist the temptation to swagger his new wealth
and importance before the companions who had witnessed his
failure to become a political figure, however humble, in the
Third Ward.

When his indiscretion had completely boggled all chance
the new revolution might have had for success, he was informed that his services were no longer needed, and was left
stranded in New Orleans without funds. For a time, apparently, he worked as a laborer in the Chalmette harbor slip, and
it was here that he received word from Mamie that inasmuch
as he was still failing to provide for his family, she would
accede to his own request and sue him for divorce. So he
wrote her:

Port Chalmette, Jan. 7/98

Mrs. M. Christmas,
226 Kentucky Ave.
Memphis Tenn

Dear Madam Yours of Jan the 6th to hand in Reply will it is with
much pleasure that I Grant your Request for a Divorce I will sign
all papers or come to Mps and sign if necessary please sue as soon
as convenient

Yours Respectfully
Leon. W. Christmas
Port Chalmette La.

Inasmuch as the usual amnesty had been declared by Honduras for all political exiles of the past Revolution, by this time,
Christmas was re-employed on his old railroad job and set

Lee Christmas as a young man — a photograph taken when he first came
to the tropics in 1894.

Puesto Corta
April 8/78

Mrs. M. Christmas
816 Main St
Memphis Tenn

Dear Mamie I
Just Received your Letter
in Reply to the same I wrote
you inclosed you will find
a Check for $50 = pay for the
Dinner and send me my Copy
I will always Kind you what
I Can Each month And May
God Bless you and May you
always Live a True Life
I have Changed Considerable and
I mean you Past and will
try to Live a Better Life

I would Like to visit my
Children this fall if you
will Consent I Cant write
any more now will write
when I send you some money
God Bless you and my children
are My Prayers
D.C.L. Christmas

The last letter the first Mrs. Christmas received from her husband (see page 25).

sail, the following week, for Puerto Cortez. Evidently he prospered, for within six months he sent Mamie the fifty dollars which she had told him she would need for the divorce, and accompanied the remittance with his blessing.

Puerto Cortez
June 8/98
Mrs. M. Christmas
816 Main st
Memphis Tenn

Dear Mamie I Just Received your Letter in Reply to the one I wrote you inclosed you will find a check for $50.00 pay for the Divorce and send me my coppy I will always send you what I can Each month and may God Bless you and may you always Live a True Life I have changed considerable since I seen you Last and will try to Live a Better Life I would Like to visit my children this fall if you will consent I can't write any more now will write when I send you some money God Bless you and my children are my Prayers

Lee. Christmas

Less than a year later he married Magdalena Talbot of Puerto Cortez, and for a time settled down to such solid domesticity that he gave up his railroad job and acquired a half-interest in the store of Sr. Juan Garvin at Choloma. There the two daughters of the union — Leah and Juanita — were born. There too he asked his wife for a divorce when he became enamored of a beautiful blond Italian girl, one Adelaide Caruso, who lived in Puerto Cortez. And there, finally, an assassin whose very name is forgotten today, one night planted a load of buckshot in Lee Christmas' breast and brought him literally within one pulse beat of the grave.

Various motives have been mentioned in subsequent accounts as prompting the attempted assassination: jealousy on the part of the heirs of Juan Garvin, who had lately been gathered to his fathers; commercial rivalry, inspired by the fact that Christmas stood unaccountably high in favor with the new administration, although he had once aided a revolution against it. Many believed the affair was over a woman, and this may well have been the case. Whatever the cause, Christmas certainly rubbed shoulders with death on that occasion, according to the description given by Dr. Sydenham Waller, who is still one of the best-loved figures in Honduras, and who was summoned to Choloma by handcar to attend the wounded gringo in what were confidently expected to be the latter's last moments.

"I had a loaded syringe of nitroglycerine in my kit," Dr. Waller tells the story today. "As I entered the room where they had lifted Christmas to a cot, I saw the man was just about gasping his last. I listened to see if his heart was still beating, and I heard it contract feebly once or twice. Then it stopped.

"'Clinch your teeth,' I told him. 'Clinch your teeth and don't breathe. If you open your mouth now, you're dead.'

"I couldn't tell whether he could hear me, for I was working fast to get that syringe of nitroglycerine into him. I did it—right into his breast—and then listened again. And finally I heard his heart take up its beat.

"'All right,' I said. 'You can relax now.'

"The man must have heard me, because the moment I said it he relaxed and started to breathe. It was as remarkable an instance of sheer grit as I have ever witnessed. The man was as good as dead. His heart had stopped. Yet even in that extremity he had the courage to obey my directions, and it pulled him through. That was a man, that Lee Christmas. Of course, when it came to women. . ."

Magdalena nursed him through his slow convalescence and as soon as he could be up and about he gave up the store, moved back to Puerto Cortez where Adelaide Caruso lived, and renewed his request for a divorce. He did not return to railroad work, and what his means were—for he was in funds throughout this time—no man knew save Christmas alone, and the newly inaugurated president of Honduras, who was

Terencio Sierra

WHEN the reign of Domingo Vásquez over Honduras was abruptly ended in the early nineties, the leaders who captained that victory were, as already noted, three in number: Manuel Bonilla and Terencio Sierra, young planters and soldiers; Policarpo Bonilla, young attorney and scholar. Popular idols, these, who helped to found the Red Party — the *Partido Liberal* — and dedicated it to high purpose.

In token of that dedication they convoked a convention, summoning the delegates to write a real constitution of liberal reforms for the nation. Chief of these was the clause which forbade any president of Honduras to succeed himself in office. Revolutions would then be a thing of the past, for at the end of each quadrennium, the president would necessarily have to step down, without the necessity of unseating him by armed revolt.

Dr. Policarpo Bonilla was named by the convention as first president under this new constitution. Manuel Bonilla was chosen vice-president with him and Terencio Sierra became Minister of War. It was an understood thing, among the *Liberales,* that General Sierra would be the candidate of the party to succeed Dr. Bonilla as president, and that General Manuel Bonilla would fall heir to the presidency thereafter.

Long before this political cycle had run its course — in fact, hard upon the heels of Policarpo's accession to the palace — the friendship between himself and *don* Manuel was ruptured by a bitter personal enmity, the true cause of which to this

day remains unknown. There has been published one story *
to the effect that the two Bonillas (who were not related for
all that their names were the same) had paid court to two
sisters, and that Policarpo, who was of pure Castilian descent,
objected vigorously to having Manuel, in whose veins flowed
an admixture of Indian blood, marry into the same family and
so broke up the match. It is a matter of record that Manuel
remained unmarried.

Whatever the reason, Manuel soon withdrew from the vice-
presidency, and became *comandante* of a small army post —
possibly Yoro. In spite of his personal bitterness toward Policarpo, he remained loyal to the party, and no one worked
harder than he for the election of Sierra, which came off by
an overwhelming majority.

When the latter was inaugurated, there was wild rejoicing
over the true dawn of the new political era. The election had
indeed been peaceful, and the various inaugural addresses were
all pitched upon the theme that for the first time a presidency
had been turned over by an incumbent to his successor without
bloodshed.

Ceremoniously Policarpo Bonilla handed to Terencio Sierra,
in sight of the populace assembled before the palace, a copy of
the Liberal Constitution, in token of the transfer of government. No less ceremoniously Sierra raised the volume high
and pledged that he would turn it over to his successor as
peaceably as he had received it.†

But there was in Terencio Sierra a streak of madness, which
was just beginning to make itself apparent. Frequently he
walked alone in the forest, because he heard voices there, and
the voices whispered to him that it was his destiny to rule Honduras as long as he lived. He made no secret of his voices,
though he confided to no one else at the time the messages

---

* *The Daily Picayune,* New Orleans, January 29, 1911.
† Lest the reader think this rejoicing over the transfer of one administration to
another overdrawn, an excerpt from a history of Honduras is included in Appendix
No. V.

with which they were freighted. But on the practical side he set out, the moment he was safely inaugurated, to attach to himself, by bonds of patronage, men whose valor and loyalty had been proven under fire.

One of these was Lee Christmas. Not only had legend dealt kindly and freely with the courage the ruddy *gringo* had displayed at Laguna Trestle, but Christmas had given subsequent proof of his fearlessness as well. Single-handed he had tracked down and captured the assassin who had blown an American railroad man through the corrugated iron roof of his home with a charge of dynamite. After the attempt upon his own life at Choloma, and while he was not yet recovered of his wounds, he had hobbled to the jail-yard where his would-be slayer was being held, and had all but killed the man himself with a rock as his only weapon.

Though the connection between Sierra and Christmas was kept secret for a considerable time, it adequately accounts for the fact that the latter gave up his railroad job and yet remained in funds. Even today, Sr. *don* Ricardo López, a retired government official living in San Pedro, recalls that in 1900 or thereabouts, when he was a young treasury employe, he was directed by President Sierra to pay to Lee Christmas $2000 for what was never more fully described than as the execution of " a mission in Guatemala."

Oddly enough, it was Christmas' insistence on a divorce which brought his high standing with the Sierra administration to such public notice that the President threw off the cloak, summoned Christmas to the capital, and there installed him as Chief of the Federal Police. Moreover, the President of still another Central American republic might well have devoted to this divorce his very attentive regard, as succeeding events finally shaped their course. That was José Santos Zelaya of Nicaragua. Zelaya was no altruist. He had not helped the *Partido Liberal* to its victory in Honduras because he thought well of constitutional reforms in the abstract. Zelaya desperately needed to maintain a friendly government in Honduras. Along the border, between the two countries, there was a strip of territory whose ownership had been in dispute ever since the two neighboring republics had won to autonomy. In this strip Zelaya had farmed out some rich concessions to American capital. He could cash in on those concessions only so long as his claim to the territory was not actively gainsaid; in other words, only so long as an administration friendly to him in Honduras conceded his rights thereto.

Once more we may trace the loss of an empire back to the lack of a horseshoe nail. Lee Christmas' current marital difficulties transferred him to Tegucigalpa; that transfer had a definite effect on the outcome of President Zelaya's claim to the disputed strip of territory.

Under the laws of Honduras, the matrimonial ties which bound Christmas and his second wife could be loosed only by mutual consent except for cause. Quite naturally, he could not allege his sudden infatuation for Adelaide Caruso as grounds on which he could be granted a divorce for cause.

One of Magdalena's brothers — an employe of the railroad with which he is still connected as roadmaster — took Christmas' attitude in particularly ill grace, and it was generally expected in Puerto Cortez that when these two — Christmas and Talbot — met, the bad blood between them would come boiling to the surface at once.

That is how matters stood one night when Lee left his home and went, as was his custom, to the Hotel Lefebvre bar, joining a party of five or six about the round table there. Among them was a cattle-buyer from Belize who was one of Christmas' friends, and who, with the request that his own name be omitted, tells the story today.

"There was still one vacant place after Lee sat down," runs his account of what transpired. "Just about that time, Talbot came in. There weren't any words or anything. Talbot sat down in the vacant place, and when I looked over at him, he had his pistol out loose in his lap. Christmas was talking right along, but he kept his eyes on Talbot, and he was sitting tipped back in his chair with his knees against the edge of the table, so if Talbot made a move to pull the gun he could up-end the table at him. Anyway, after a while, Lee got up, like he hadn't a care in the world, and sort of sauntered around the table, and then like a flash he lunged, grabbed the gun out of Talbot's lap, and put it away. Talbot jumped up too. Christmas left the gun there and said for them to go outside and talk because this was a family matter. They went down toward the banana wharf and stayed about half an hour, and when they came back there wasn't any more trouble between them."

Had this been all there was to the affair, it would certainly not have been worth the chronicling. But the Talbots had friends, and one of these, learning what had occurred, came down to the Lefebvre barroom and, standing in the doorway, began to unburden himself. This time Christmas acted without finesse. He jumped up, kicking back his chair so that it went clattering across the floor and brought up with a crash against the bar.

"You'll put your oar into a family matter, will you?" he shouted, and plunged for the doorway.

Because of the injuries he had received at Choloma, he still had but one serviceable arm, but before the luckless intruder could dodge, Christmas delivered an open-handed slap with such force that it sent the man spinning out through the doorway into the street. Blind to everything but his rage, he followed after and lashed out once with his fist. The man went down, striking his head against one of the rails in the roadway and opening a cut in his cheek that bled profusely. Once more Christmas followed after but, by the time he had recovered his balance, the man had scrambled to his feet and was sprinting down the track. Christmas returned to the bar, grinning sheepishly, his anger gone.

"Best runner I ever saw in a fight," he chuckled as he righted his chair and seated himself once more at the table.

However, on the following morning, Christmas' victim appeared before the *juez* at the *juzgado,* and lodged formal charges of assault and battery. Christmas was summoned to appear that afternoon for trial. He did so, swaggering into the court room with his pistol belted at his side; for by special dispensation from the president of the republic, he was permitted to carry arms at all times.

His victim and other witnesses were the first to testify. Then Christmas was called to stand up before the judge and give his version. Evidently the judicial mind had already settled upon the verdict, and evidently the judicial mind was also prey to acute misgivings as to how that verdict would be received.

"Before you can testify," said the *juez,* therefore, "you must lay aside your weapon."

"I need not take off my gun," Christmas replied. "I have permission from President Sierra."

"That makes no difference here. You cannot give evidence unless you lay aside the pistol."

Christmas shrugged his broad shoulders good-naturedly enough. He seemed to think the whole matter more or less of a joke. So he pulled the pistol from its holster and laid it on the table before him. Then he began to tell his side of the story. While he was thus speaking, the judge leaned casually across the table and pushed the gun out of Christmas' reach. At the same time, an armed guard stepped behind the witness and trained a cocked pistol on his back.

All unaware of this, Christmas continued his story, when a sudden movement of the guard at his back caught his eye. He turned his head swiftly, saw the cocked gun, and realized at once that his own weapon was beyond reach. It was to the intense surprise of all present that he suddenly laughed aloud, but obviously he felt flattered by all this evidence that he was considered so dangerous.

Then the incredible thing happened. At least, it sounded incredible to Christmas. The judge abruptly found him guilty and ordered him lodged in the jail. When it finally penetrated his consciousness that these people were seriously proposing to put him in jail, Lee Christmas' good nature and patience forsook him simultaneously. Leaving his gun and brushing by the open-mouthed guard as though he were non-existent, he turned and walked out. He did not run. He walked away from that court room simply to indicate the completeness of his disapproval.

After him swarmed the judge, the clerk of court, the chief of police and others, trying to lay hold of him. He flung them off with great sweeps of his one good arm. They tried to argue with him; to convince him that he had been duly sentenced and that it was now his plain duty to accompany them to jail. His only response was to walk up the track the faster. Then they resorted to their clubs. Some of the blows he warded off with his one serviceable arm. The pith helmet he wore deadened the impact of others. Those that landed on his back and shoulders he simply disregarded. And thus the little maelstrom went seething up the one street of Puerto Cortez.

Señor Federico Girbal, now a *comerciante* in San Pedro Sula, but then a resident of Puerto Cortez, tells the rest of the story:

My wife was out in front of our house [he relates] when I heard her cry out that many men were beating Christmas there in the street. So I stepped outside. There was the judge, there was the chief of police, there was an American named Morris, there was the secretary of the judge, there were two policemen, and they were hitting him with sticks, and trying to catch him, and I saw it was not right. He was defending himself with but one hand, and as I rushed up to them a policeman hit him on the head with a stick, and only his helmet, which was of cork, saved him. Christmas said he was going to send a telegram to the president, and the judge said Christmas could not go to send the telegram but must go to jail. So I told the judge I would go bond for Christmas if he would let him stay at my house until we heard from the President, to whom

I myself would send a telegram. The judge agreed. So I took Christmas into my house, and Magdalena his wife came there to see if he was hurt and an American friend of his came too. They stayed there for some time, and Christmas wrote a telegram which he asked me to send to the President, and he and his wife and friend went home to his own house then.

Later that evening, however, Lee Christmas and his friend — the same anonymous cattle-buyer from Belize who had been in the party the night before — began to drink. As he downed glass after glass of spirits, Christmas became correspondingly dissatisfied with the course of the afternoon's events. The more he thought of it, the more it occurred to him that people might come to believe he had run away from the judge and the secretary of the judge and the two policemen and the chief of police and the American named Morris, whereas in reality he had merely tired of such nonsense as being ordered to jail.

He talked the matter over with his friend, and that worthy was inclined to agree that thoughtless persons might indeed believe that Lee Christmas, with one arm in perfectly good working order, had actually run away from this young army. For a while, they discussed what had best be done about the matter, and then Christmas had an inspiration. He and his friend armed themselves. Each took two pistols and a rifle. Thus accoutred, they went down to the scene of the opening of hostilities — the Hotel Lefebvre. Posting themselves before that famous inn, Lee Christmas announced on behalf of both, to the world at large, that he was now ready to have somebody — anybody at all — try to take him to jail, and would one of the bystanders please be kind enough so to notify the judge, the secretary of the judge, the chief of police and all his officers, the garrison at the *cuartel,* and possibly the United States Marine Corps as well. Even if this message was delivered, which is rather more than doubtful, no cognizance, judicial or otherwise, was taken of it. From eight in the evening until ten, that truculent pair swaggered back and forth in front of the Hotel Lefebvre, and then they quitted the field with all the honors of war.

The next morning, long before Christmas had slept off the effect of his previous night's potations, a telegram from the palace at Tegucigalpa was delivered at the port, directing upon the order of President Terencio Sierra that the charges against Christmas be dismissed forthwith, and that he be released at once from custody.

The message caused a notable stir, of course; but gentle Magdalena Talbot thought none too well of such goings-on, and when Dr. Waller, of San Pedro Sula, some time later came to her again at Christmas' request, to see if she might not agree to the divorce, she finally consented.

"I loved my husband when I married him and I still love him," she told Dr. Waller. "But if he really wants a separation, I will agree if he will provide for the schooling of our two children. For myself I want nothing, but if he will do that, I will agree to the divorce."

And so Christmas promised to pay to Magdalena, his wife, the sum of a thousand pesos, and Dr. Waller endorsed a note declaring that if Christmas failed in his payments he would make them good himself, and the divorce was granted and Christmas was free. This was early in 1902, the closing year of President Sierra's term. The political cauldron was just beginning to simmer ominously in response to the gradually rising heat of the campaign for the Sierra succession, and though, according to the old agreement, it would now be Manuel Bonilla's turn to run for the presidency, mad Terencio Sierra began to lay his plans to retain the governmental reins. Thus, if Sierra were ever to need Christmas at the capital, now was the time. And on May 24, 1902, Captain Lee Christmas, late of New Orleans, Memphis, Guatemala, Choloma, and Puerto Cortez, was appointed chief of police of Tegucigalpa, with the rank of —

Coronel

A WORD of explanation: The position which President Sierra
had conferred upon the one-time — and not so long since, either
— tramp railroader from the States was, at least technically,
not that of a municipal guardian of the peace. He had appointed Christmas *Director de Policía,* a federal post. In
theory, he was now supervisor of all the police departments of
Honduras. That is to say, every incoming president appoints
local chiefs of police in each municipality, and over them all a
national *Director de Policía,* who is also commanding officer of
the police department at the capital; just as every incoming
president appoints departmental and sectional *comandantes,*
over whom, nationally, is placed the *Ministro de Guerra.* In
practice, however, the *Director de Policía* exercises supervision
only over the police force at Tegucigalpa — a body of about
185 men.

Christmas found this force nondescript and raggedly uniformed, without much in the way of organization, equipment,
or discipline. This was only natural, because in reality the
Cuerpo de Policía at the capital was an anomaly. Tegucigalpa
was about as free from the sort of crime which falls within the
province of police prevention as any spot on the habitable
globe. The duties of the police force comprised little more
than the taking to jail of those drunks who were fighting, and
escorting to their homes those who were merely drunk.

The only special talents Christmas brought with him to cope
with the demands an executive position might make upon his

36

abilities were physical courage and a sublime confidence in himself — both boundless. Out of sheer vanity — for he would scorn to appear before his new world as the head of a rout of ragamuffins — he had his men smartly uniformed, provided them with shoes, junked their ancient rifles, and equipped them with side arms. Something of discipline he instilled in them, too, though he did not take his duties in this regard too seriously.

For the most part he was content to lord it about the capital as a high government official, in his colonel's uniform. So far as other duties were concerned, he was not too deeply concerned. He had wit enough to comprehend that President Sierra had not conferred this fat political plum upon him as a tribute to his looks, or even to his reckless courage, and that the real work which would be expected of him ultimately had nothing to do with uniforming or drilling his men. Of the actual political mess that was brewing in the presidential cauldron he understood, in all likelihood, rather less than nothing.

As a matter of fact, there was little enough that even an initiate could have told him for, on the surface, all was still quite calm. The administration campaign to back Manuel Bonilla for the presidency to succeed Sierra, just as the latter had succeeded Policarpo Bonilla, was apparently quite unruffled. The personal bitterness between the two Bonillas, seemed not to affect their party solidarity for the present, though in the early days of Sierra's term Policarpo had sought to keep Manuel out of a prominent place in the government.

Don Manuel, at that time, was still *comandante* in the small garrison town to which he had retired during Policarpo's administration. There he calmly began to develop the plans for his own presidential campaign and, being well liked, found such popular favor that there was grave danger the *colorado* faction would suffer an irreparable rupture unless it joined the crowd on the Manuelista bandwagon. Sierra's friends — one of them in particular — urged the President to prevent such a schism by according *don* Manuel governmental recognition more in keeping with his real political status.

This Sierra was a queer mixture of shrewdness and credulity, generosity and insensate rages, *camaraderie* and megalomania. He always carried a machete at his side and it is said of him that he frequently beat his cabinet ministers out of his office in the *palacio* with the flat of his weapon, when they had done or said something to displease him. Other visitors, too, were treated in the same cavalier fashion, when his ungovernable choler got the upper hand.

None the less, when his friends pointed out that it would be shrewd politics to weld the tremendous personal popularity of the little *comandante* of Yoro into the administration, he had more than sufficient acumen to agree out of hand.

"I will appoint him *comandante* at Amapala, if he will accept," Sierra declared.

Amapala is the one port on the Pacific coast of Honduras. It is a fortress on Tigre Island, and all vessels land there, the passengers and freight being lightered in across the shallow bay to the mainland at San Lorenzo.

The friend who had suggested *don* Manuel's appointment to Sierra immediately went to General Bonilla with this assurance from the President. But *don* Manuel shook his wise little head and smiled.

" Why should I accept any other *comandancia* and thus perhaps obligate myself to a course which would affect my future unfavorably? " he asked. " I am planning bigger things than that, my friend, and my plans are progressing very well right here."

"True, but if you remain outside the administration," replied the intermediary, " there will be four years of bickering and strife instead of four years of good times and peace in Honduras. It is a duty you owe to your country and its people."

Don Manuel was nothing if not a patriot. Strange as it may seem to the *politicos* of other republics farther removed from the equator, the argument that he faced a public duty, even though this might redound to his personal disadvantage, carried full weight.

"Tell the President," he declared abruptly, "that I accept." And there, perhaps, you have the secret of *don* Manuel's overwhelming personal popularity. Even today, in Honduras, when a dyed-in-the-wool *azul* wants to show how staunch and unswerving a blue partisan he has been, he boasts: "*Yo soy Manuelista!*" It is the equivalent of our: "I've voted for every Republican candidate since Grant!" or "I'd vote the Democratic ticket straight if they'd put a yellow dog on it for candidate!"

No swashbuckler, this Manuel Bonilla; yet his courage had been proven time and again on the battle-field, and the wounds he received at Tatumbla and elsewhere lent glamour to the record. Moreover, in a land where oratory was little practised, and where political campaigns were waged with pamphlets, he was a fiery and magnetic public speaker. Above all, it was known far and wide throughout Honduras that once Manuel Bonilla passed his word, he kept it. Take it by and large, that combination is a pretty sound recipe for political success in any age and country.

So the intermediary who had sought him out, hastened back to the palace to inform Sierra of the success of his mission. The appointment was made at once. On the following morning, early, Dr. Policarpo Bonilla hurried in to see the president.

"There is a rumor about the capital, General," he said in considerable agitation, "that you are going to appoint Manuel Bonilla *comandante* at Amapala."

"That is not true," replied Sierra, chuckling maliciously, for this was the sort of jest he knew well how to relish. "I am positively not going to appoint him."

"I am glad to hear that."

" No, I am not going to appoint him because — well, because I have already appointed him."

Dr. Policarpo, the story goes, turned on his heel and quitted the presidential office. However, he did not bolt the party; not even later, when Sierra exalted Manuel still further by appointing him minister of war, which was the portfolio he held at the time Lee Christmas was summoned to Tegucigalpa as *Director de Policía.*

It was then, in May of 1902, that the two men — Christmas and Bonilla — first met. Between them there sprang up one of those instantaneous friendships that are based upon mutual liking and understanding. These, for example, were two men whom Terencio Sierra, in the blackest of his tempers, did not threaten with the flat of his machete. Disparate as they were physically, Sierra well knew that any such move toward either of that pair would have meant kill or be killed — and that at once.

Of course, President Sierra still looked askance upon Manuel Bonilla's expressed determination to run for the presidency that fall. The spirit voices still counseled him that this was his destiny, and he believed those voices implicitly. But, on the surface at least, he resigned himself to Bonilla's candidacy, and, a short time after Christmas came to the capital, the president took *don* Manuel and an official party on a sort of triumphal tour of the country, introducing Bonilla everywhere — and notably along the North Coast — as his special *protégé* and the favorite of the administration. At town after town they were feted. Everywhere it was understood that General Bonilla was being " brought out " as the administration's candidate for the presidency.

Yet it was toward the end of that very journey that there came the open break which had so long been imminent. There are, naturally, a number of versions of what evoked it. The one most generally current is that Sierra's wife had a sister, between whom and *don* Manuel the President sought to promote a marriage. The proposal found no favor with Bonilla who lived and died a bachelor. Another version is that on the return journey, after the party had left the North Coast and turned inland, a quarrel was precipitated by some wholly trivial discussion over the wine after dinner.

Sierra's paroxysms of fury are still the subject of gossip. One can well imagine him as, crossed in some trifle of no moment whatever — or it may even have been the matter of the rumored matrimonial plans — he would reach, out of habit, for his machete. In that event *don* Manuel unquestionably would have drawn his pistol and warned him: "If you move to strike me, General, be ready to protect yourself."

Moreover, in the light of subsequent events, it seems rather more than probable that Terencio Sierra may have provoked a break deliberately, to provide a pretext for rescinding his real and implied pledges to support Bonilla's candidacy. So the great triumphal tour came to an abrupt end, and Sierra returned to the capital alone and *don* Manuel continued his campaign independently. There was another independent candidate, too; a Dr. Marco Aurelio Soto who was an uncle of that young Enrique Soto who had fomented the uprising of 1897.* In this, Sierra saw an opportunity to throw the campaign into such a condition of ferment that he might be continued in office at least temporarily.

Forthwith he brought out as the administration candidate of the *Liberales* Dr. Juan Angel Arias. The moment this announcement was made, Bonilla formally resigned his post as Minister of War, and headed a fusion party, known as the Nationalists, composed of his own personal following among the *Liberales* and practically all the *Conservadores;* this in opposition to the liberal administration of which he had hitherto been a part.

---

* Dr. Soto was of course something more than merely the uncle of Enrique. He had been president, and his administration of Honduras was so successful that it is still spoken of as " *la edad de oro* " — the Golden Age.

That ended political peace and harmony in Honduras. From then on it was hammer-and-tongs campaigning until the ballots were finally counted, when Bonilla was shown to have received 28,850 votes; Arias 25,118; and Soto 4857, while a grand total of 14 additional votes were reported as "scattered."

When the congress canvassed the vote, reporting that the largest number of ballots had been cast for Manuel Bonilla, President Sierra sprang his grand coup* by declaring that no candidate could be regarded as legally elected, since not one of the three had received a clear majority of all votes cast.

Manuel Bonilla, with a number of his friends, immediately left the capital and went to Amapala, the fortress of which he had not so long ago been *comandante*. In governmental circles there was high turmoil and debate for, since the term of General Sierra, under the constitution, expired at midnight of January 31, and since, despite the declaration he had made in his inaugural address four years previously, General Sierra would not turn over the copy of the Liberal Constitution to Bonilla in token of the transfer of authority, and obviously could not turn it over to Arias, there was the wildest speculation as to what was to become of the government.

It was then, at good length, that Lee Christmas understood why he had been brought to Tegucigalpa.† He and his 185 members of the gendarmerie would now be expected to stand by Sierra, come what might. The situation put Col. Christmas in a quandary indeed. True, Terencio Sierra had been a generous patron, and had given him place and power and money. But for Manuel Bonilla he had conceived one of the only two genuine friendships of his entire life. So here was Lee Christmas, faced with a choice as to where he should

---

* *La Gaceta*, Tegucigalpa, Jan. 17, 1903, Serie 225, Numero 2, 249, Mensaje dirigido al Soberano Congreso Nacional.

† See Appendix No. VI.

bestow his allegiance—with his one benefactor or his one friend.

He was given little time to consider. At midnight of January 31, 1903, Terencio Sierra would cease to be president of Honduras. On January 30, he played his ace of trumps. While he was still president, he called his cabinet of ministers into council—they were all his own personal appointees, of course—and said to them in effect: " There being no legally elected candidate to whom I can transfer the government from myself, I hereby turn it over to you gentlemen, as a council to represent the executive power of the nation until a lawful president is chosen."

He said this officially in the form of a *Decreto* formally promulgated in *La Gaceta*. While it was being given out, a motley cavalcade was making an unobtrusive exit from the capital, across the Choluteca river and out along the cart road which had been built by Sierra from Tegucigalpa to the Pacific.

A number of deputies and other high officials had already left the city with Manuel Bonilla, accompanying him to Amapala. A number of others were known to be ready to go out, but hesitated to go alone, and there was apparently no organized armed force to conduct them and act as escort. That is, there was no such body until the night of January 30, when, while the President was going through the formality of transferring the government to himself via his own cabinet, *el Señor Coronel don* Lee Christmas, Chief of Police, was quietly marching his picked coppers out of police headquarters. Each of the men wore a *poncho* of cotton cloth dipped in raw gum, and beneath each *poncho* was a rifle and a bandolier of ammunition, in addition to the pistol with which Christmas had armed his men when he took charge of the department.

There, in the dead of night, Christmas' truant police force was joined by group after group of civilians—the leading *diputados, comerciantes,* and professional men of the capital of Honduras. They made a silent rendezvous at Toncontin, four miles south of Tegucigalpa, under the armed escort of Christmas' gendarmes. The utmost caution was observed as they skirted the base of La Cruz — the hill on which an outpost of federal troops was maintained. After that, they struck off briskly down the San Lorenzo cart road, and pushed south. Now and again they passed the dying embers of the campfires of some bullock train, the drovers huddled in their blankets beneath the carts. Once they passed a train of pack mules which could make no halt; for there was no pasturage in that bleak and arid upland.

When gray daylight stole upon them, they were almost at the crest of *Cerro de Hule* — Rubber Mountain — the highest ridge they would have to traverse. From then on it was down hill to the Pacific, which they reached three days later. By that time *don* Manuel was already provisional president. He had taken the oath of office before the *alcalde* at Amapala on the morning of February 1.

By that time, too, there had been high goings-on back at the capital, and much amusement among the citizens of Tegucigalpa when it was discovered on the morning of January 31 that the city's police force, in command of their chief, had gone over the hill during the night to join the revolution. Sierra's rage was nothing short of murderous. Theoretically Sierra would be president until midnight, but he cared little about that now. Somebody had to be made commander in chief of the Federal forces, of course; Sierra not only was assured, upon the unimpeachable authority of his spirit voices, that he would be invincible, but he had a few private scores to settle as well. At his own request, the council of ministers to whom Sierra had turned over the executive function a few hours previously, now named him, as their first official act, commanding general of the army, and at the head of a force of more than a thousand men he set out immediately for the sea.

Incidentally, Sierra's appointment was validated by a de facto president, too. The congress of Honduras is composed of regular delegates, known as *diputados propietarios,* and of others, known as *suplentes,* who are alternates and who serve only in case illness, death, or absence from the capital prevent the regular deputy from serving. As already indicated, most of the leading *propietarios* were absent for the simple reason that they were out revolutioning with Manuel Bonilla. Organizing a congress composed chiefly of *suplentes* or alternates, Juan Angel Arias — Sierra's defeated administration candidate — had himself declared president of the republic on February 18, and the appointment of Sierra as his commander-in-chief "by land and by sea" was one of his first official acts.

Bonilla and Sierra were encamped with their forces at Nacáome and El Aceituno, respectively. Little *don* Manuel was in no hurry, for his plan was to send separate detachments of his army from the four points of the compass toward Tegucigalpa, while holding the main body of federal troops at bay near the Pacific. Christmas himself had been assigned to one of the mobile inland units.

Not until early March did Sierra and Bonilla finally join the issue in a three-day battle, at the close of which, badly defeated, Sierra drew back to Nacáome to send for reinforcements. Manuel Bonilla, however, had had enough of bloodshed, and under a flag of truce he sent Theodor Kohncke, German consul at Amapala, to Sierra as an ambassador to negotiate a peace treaty. Kohncke was to present the situation fairly. He was to inform General Sierra that the various bodies of Manuelist troops already had Tegucigalpa all but surrounded, and that they had met little or no resistance worth mentioning on their way up various valleys and passes from both seas to the capital. Defeat, in short, was inevitable for the Sierra forces, and much bloodshed could be spared, if *don* Terencio would but recognize that fact and capitulate.

Consul Kohncke returned after a brief parley, reporting that in his presence General Sierra had gone into conference with the spirits, had levitated a small table in his headquarters, and had finally announced that he was informed by the spirits that all the statements which Kohncke made about the Manuelist conquest of the country were untrue, and that he — Sierra — would be victorious.

That decided matters, of course; and *don* Manuel immediately ordered —

The March on Tegucigalpa

LEE CHRISTMAS was a soldier by instinct, and not by training. It was the march he made as second in command to Saturnino Medal, from the Pacific up the San Antonio Valley to Comayagua and thence to Tegucigalpa, that gave him his first experience of organized warfare. This was no single fight as had been that mad affair by the ice barrier at Laguna Trestle six years before. This was a campaign, with various tasks to be carried out concertedly by isolated bodies of troops. A fighter, rather than a soldier, was Lee Christmas. Yet he took to campaigning like some seasoned veteran of countless military actions.

So far as resistance or actual engagements were concerned, the early stages of that business were child's play. In fact, the federal garrisons had all withdrawn before the invaders reached the towns along their line of march. But such a line of march!

Hondo is the Spanish word for deep. Honduras is the place of deeps — many deeps. Along the Salvador frontier, where they began their trek, there is little of Honduras that is not set up on edge; and a sharp, flinty, cutting edge at that. The pack mules were practically useless. Christmas' policemen were transporting one Krupp 7.5 mountain gun, hauled by mules theoretically. In practice there were many stages where the men had to haul not only the gun, but the mules as well. Special breech straps were constructed. Whenever the slope demanded it — and that was often — the men clambered up first.

Then they hauled up the guns, hand over hand. Then they hauled up the mules with that specially devised breeching. After which there was more of the same, and the day was counted well spent that saw the expeditionary force four miles farther on the road at dusk than they had been at dawn.

The shoes which Christmas had worn the night he herded his policemen out of Tegucigalpa — and he was always rather dandified in matters of foot-gear — were by this time not even very recent memories. He was scuffing around in *caites* — native sandals made for him by one of his soldiers from a cowhide chair seat,* and the crude thongs of hard leather chafed abominably. The army fed itself as best it might, and, between towns where provender could be purchased or requisitioned, made shift to shoot game or, if that failed, subsisted on boiled green bananas. But for all that it was a great time in Christmas's life, for it was this campaign which transmuted the hitherto tenuous substance of the Christmas legend into enduring lore, in spite of the fact that little was recorded for him in the way of military achievement, beyond the daring and courage which were his birthright.

Their first real resistance was encountered in the shrub-grown plain before the hill of Lamaní, commanded by slopes on which the federal soldiery had mounted two Gatling guns. They were the oldest vintage of quickfiring weapon, with a cluster of barrels revolving on fore-and-aft bearings in a brass tube, the whole operated by a hand-turned crank. The men under Saturnino Medal and Lee Christmas sought concealment in the brush of the plain, between a deep ravine that circled from behind them toward Lamaní, and the hill itself. Here they could snipe at the federals as occasion offered.

It was an unsatisfactory sort of skirmishing from the point

---

* A favorite raw material for sandals among the natives of rural Honduras today is a piece of old automobile tire casing. Cut into sections of appropriate size, such pieces of casing are now a staple commodity for sale in practically all of the public markets of the nation.

of view of Christmas, whose temperament craved action. So he took to scouting around on his own, and on one such occasion noted a furtive stir at the base of Lamaní. Seeking the highest point of vantage he could reach, he made out that federal soldiers were trooping stealthily into the gully that cut across the plain, growing deeper until it became the ravine at the back of the Manuelista position.

He hurried back to General Medal and reported, asking permission to take fifty of his own policemen and meet the attack which was obviously being prepared for a surprise launching. Sallying swiftly back with this troop, he distributed them flat on the ground, on both sides of the ravine, only the tops of their heads and the muzzles of their rifles visible even to observers who knew they were there. He then gave order that not a man so much as press a trigger until he, Christmas, had fired the first shot. Then they waited. They waited while the federals approached, stealing softly down the ravine, and keeping themselves, as they thought, well concealed. They waited while the head of the line passed the head of the ambuscade and then Lee Christmas drew a careful bead, fired, and shouted *"Fuego!"*

The ambushers let drive, yelling like maniacs, firing as fast as they could load, and viva-ing for Bonilla, for Saturnino Medal, and for Crrreesmas. It was sharp work and short. Within a few minutes the double flanking fire had literally annihilated the attack. Thirty of the federal force were dead. More than sixty surrendered. A few managed to break through to the lower end of the ravine, and made good their escape.

For a time Christmas believed his smashing victory in the first engagement in which he had ever commanded a body of men, had been won without a single casualty on his side. Later he missed six of his men and, having noted no six bodies on the field, swore he would shoot down the deserters with his own hand when he caught them. A search of the ravine, that afternoon, cleared up the matter. All six were found there, on the brink, and apparently all six were just on the point of firing, so lifelike did the bodies appear. The explanation lay in the fact that their position had exposed only the very tops of their heads. Those who were hit at all, therefore, had been shot through the head, and had died instantly, without so much as a muscular spasm.

This discovery was not made until late in the day, however, for immediately after the battle Christmas had hurried back to Medal to make his report. Taking advantage of the confusion which the return of the few who escaped would doubtless spread in the federal ranks, the entire Manuelisto force immediately charged Lamaní hill itself, threw back its defenders and captured both Gatlings. Quite satisfied with this success, Medal and Christmas withdrew that night and pushed south for the general rendezvous outside of Tegucigalpa. That was on February 25. Two years later, on the anniversary of this occasion, President Manuel Bonilla presented Brigadier General Lee Christmas with a sword of honor, accompanied by a card inscribed: " Manuel Bonilla, president of the Republic, greets you sincerely and sends you a sword which the, Government tenders you as a remembrance of the 25th of February, 1903."

The demands of the present, however, left them no time for speculation concerning the possibility of future recognition. Hastily they pushed on to the capital, where they found only one point actively contested. That was the hill of Berrinche, one of the two mountains overlooking the capital. Here the federal garrison of Arias' soldiery * had mounted a 6.5 Asbury mountain cannon and they were shelling out any point within range where they suspected the presence of a revolutionary

---

* There were three sources of governmental authority in Honduras at the time. Sierra, it will be recalled, had turned the executive power over to a cabinet of ministers. Manuel Bonilla had taken the oath of office as president of Honduras in Amapala. Dr. Juan Angel Arias had had a snap session of congress declare him president, and was at least in physical possession of the capital.

force. Christmas, with the 7.5 Krupp which his men had hauled up from the sea along with its mule teams, was dispatched to fight it out with the federals and silence this " battery " if possible.

The Asbury gun used what is known as " set ammunition " — that is, metal cartridges topped by projectiles. Christmas' Krupp, on the other hand, used individual projectiles, backed by a charge of black powder in cloth sacks. In his first shot at the enemy position, Christmas' shell fell short. He ordered the muzzle of his weapon raised and, much to his disgust, the next shell fell shorter still. He made another adjustment, and then another, and found in each case that the resultant hits seemed to have no relation whatever to the previous aiming of the Krupp.

Straightway he ordered his gunners to cease firing, and then sat himself down to try to figure this thing out — for he had had no previous experience with artillery. By eliminating every other possible factor, he concluded that the cloth sacks of black powder used in loading his weapon contained unequal charges. Immediately he had a blanket spread out on the ground, and upon this he emptied the contents of his entire store of little powder sacks. Then he stepped to a convenient tree, and cut one of the carafe-shaped gourds which, even today, serve as the universal water canteens of the muleteers who tramp beside their pack trains from the remote mountain sections to the city markets.

With his machete, Christmas trimmed a gourd to the size which, he judged, would hold approximately one charge of powder. He was not particularly concerned about the precise amount of explosive for the charges as a whole, but, wholly unversed as he was in the science of artillery, he meant to have all the charges, whatever their size, uniform. Using his gourd as a measure, he refilled the cloth powder sacks, and thus made certain that each should contain the same amount of powder as the next. Then he set his gunners to work once more.

The fourth or fifth shot after the ammunition had been thus standardized, struck under the trunnion of the Asbury gun on Berrinche and wrecked it. Not only that, but wrecked it beyond hope of repair, and it is only as a relic of this same battle that the weapon is still on exhibition in one of the government buildings at Tegucigalpa today.

In the main campaign, of course, this was but the merest incident. While the capital was thus completely enveloped, *don* Manuel, at the head of the main body of his troops, had come to a decision with Terencio Sierra. Moving under cover of night, the latter had withdrawn to Coray, near the Salvadoranean frontier, where he owned a *hacienda,* and here he sought to fortify a position. But Bonilla's army was in hot pursuit, and when dawn came, Terencio Sierra, intimate of the spirits that whispered to him he was destined to continue his rule over Honduras, had fled by a short cut along a secret trail across the mountains into Salvador.

With the last obstacle thus removed, the way to the capital was open and, marching steadily northward over the Amapala cart road, *don* Manuel reached the Toncontin rendezvous on April 13. The victorious army under his command numbered nearly 12,000 men. Tegucigalpa was completely surrounded. Bonillista batteries were set up on the heights of Picacho and Berrinche. In addition the beleaguered citizenry in the capital was more than three-fourths pro-Manuel. Small wonder that there was a clamor for President Arias to surrender.

There was really nothing else for that harassed official to do. He demanded a safe conduct for himself and for his ministers to Nicaragua. These terms were met at once and the Arias government promptly evacuated the capital. Bonilla's first official act, during his triumphal entry into Tegucigalpa at the head of his victorious army, was to make Lee Christmas chief of police once more, with the rank of —

General de Brigada!

This was a signal honor; for, just as there are in the United States of America colonels and colonels, there are in Hispano-America generals and generals.

Any officer who leads an isolated body of troops during active service — particularly if these happen to be revolutionary troops — calls himself " General So-and-so " and is thenceforth referred to as The General. But his status with the government is not that of a general officer. Only those who have been officially made generals by act of the " *Soberano Congreso* " are so recognized, and the number of these was, up to six or seven years ago, surprisingly small in Honduras. One of the few was Lee Christmas.

For a time the newly-fledged general had little enough to do. The army of *don* Manuel melted away just as soon as his victory had been recognized as an established fact by the reconvention of congress in extraordinary session on the third day of May, with the regular *propietarios* and not the *suplentes* in their seats. On May 5, this congress declared unconstitutional and invalid the meeting that had seated Dr. Arias as president; a week later — on May 12 — they canvassed the vote of the previous October and declared Manuel Bonilla elected, with General Miguel R. Dávila as vice-president, and on May 17 *don* Manuel repeated at a public festival the oath of office he had taken before the *alcalde* at Amapala, when he first rose in arms against the Sierra usurpation.

For the balance of that year *don* Manuel was occupied with affairs of state; General Christmas, on the other hand, had absolutely nothing to keep him busy, beyond the routine maintenance of his police force. Inaction, boredom, and the thought of blond Adelaide in Cortez drove him almost frantic, but President Bonilla would grant him no furloughs, and as he knew but one way to make wing-broken hours speed their passage, he turned again to drink and affairs of the purse, taking a rather gloomy pride in the renown which was accorded the width of his raffish swath.

Had anyone but his friend, Manuel Bonilla, been holding the reins in those days, there is no doubt but Christmas would have resigned, returning to the North Coast and Adelaide. But there was sound reason behind the president's determination to keep Christmas on hand where he could summon him to action at an instant's notice. That reason was Policarpo Bonilla. Policarpo had been duly elected a deputy from Copán and was now gathering here, there, and everywhere, all the dissatisfied public elements he could find — notably among the *Liberales* — and endeavoring to fuse them into a solid anti-administration bloc. He was receiving help, of course, from José Santos Zelaya, for that perennial Nicaraguan executive had good cause to be fretted, as will presently appear, by the fact that his friends, the *Colorados,* were no longer the undisputed political bosses of Honduras. There was, too, that bitter and unquenchable personal enmity between the two Bonillas, fed fat by the fact that one of them was now an " in " while the other was an " out."

By the end of 1903, Dr. Policarpo Bonilla had assembled what he felt to be all the requisite raw materials for a revolution against General Manuel Bonilla and waited only until chance or design should furnish him a proper peg on which to hang a revolt; for he had to have some plausible pretext which he could carry before the people to counteract *don* Manuel's tremendous personal popularity with the masses before he could hope to enlist general sympathy and support for his own designs.

Prospects for the incidence of such a pretext were undeniably bright. *Don* Manuel had been elected by a fusion of Liberals and Conservatives. The Liberals expected that *don* Manuel would remain a Liberal partisan in his distribution of patronage, for had he not been *vice jefe* of their party since the time when they had overthrown Domingo Vásquez? The Conservatives, on the other hand, now regarded *don* Manuel as their party chief. Had not the Liberal " machine," through President Sierra and all the power of federal patronage, deliberately tried to knife the Bonilla candidacy?

Don Manuel's appointments to his cabinet rather nicely apportioned the plums as between the Liberal and the Conservative elements, and naturally this served merely to dissatisfy both. Loudest in denunciation was Dr. Policarpo Bonilla. Next to him in bitterness was José María Valladares, who edited and published the *Diario de Honduras,* which daily paper had been one of the originators of the Manuel Bonilla boom for the presidency.

The *Diario,* of course, had supported *don* Manuel as a liberal; and its fiery soldier-editor had been one of those that bolted the Liberal machine to march out of the capital with Lee Christmas' escort of policemen on the night of January 30. He had further rendered yeoman service in the field as commander of one of the divisions that routed Sierra at Aceituno and Coray. But the moment the new .president showed any tendency to bestow recognition upon any of the *Conservadores* who had also aided his campaign, the Liberal *Diario* became exceedingly caustic and began to publish front-page editorials boldly labeled " Where are the Liberals? "

Don Manuel summoned editor-general Valladares to the palace and informed him that he considered that sort of heckling off side. They quarreled, which was no novelty for José María Valladares who, years later, when he was an exile, boasted in one of his pamphlets that he had been on the insurgent side of every revolution in Honduras since he had grown to manhood.* When General Valladares declared flatly that he would continue to publish and edit his *Diario* as he saw fit, President Bonilla turned the job over to Lee Christmas.

There is something particularly incongruous in the idea of Lee Christmas being called away from his roistering amusements to execute a mission of such delicacy. Against the commonplace background of his early years, a playboy fate had splashed in gaudy tints the image of a mythical gallant, a veritable soldier of fortune. Lee Christmas had been pitched to eminence, and wore a gold-weighted uniform in token thereof. Had he been interviewed for the inspirational type of magazine, he would doubtless have attributed his rise to hard work and a willingness to fight anybody at any time and at any odds. His idea of the proper way to get the upper hand in any controversy was to lower his shoulders and charge. Having developed such a philosophy, it is not difficult to see how he would apply it in a debate with a newspaper editor who had given offense to him or to his friends.

The typesetters of the *Diario* had just come to work on a special New Year's edition on the afternoon of December 31, 1903, when there came into the establishment what José María Valladares, in a subsequently published pamphlet, described as "the chief of police, Lee Christmas, Yankee adventurer, accompanied by two officials and twenty policemen, to require me to leave and to turn over to them the keys of the building, on the order of President Bonilla. Before the brutality and [numerical] superiority of this force, I could not do other than what was demanded of me."

General Valladares immediately became Policarpo's right bower as an official malcontent. In his own words, "*con-*

* "*Política Hondureña, Hechos y Deducciones*" — a pamphlet privately published at the Tipografía de Avelina Alsina, at San José, Costa Rica, in 1911. There is a copy of it in the magnificent collection of similar works in the library of the Department of Middle American Research, Tulane University, New Orleans.

spirábamos con actividad" — "we were conspiring actively " — meaning himself and the other dissatisfied *Liberales;* and the only factor that kept their conspiracies from maturing then and there into a ripe revolution was that their leader, Dr. Policarpo Bonilla, was in prison as the result of another diplomatic mission executed by Lee Christmas as mediator; of course, Christmas saw nothing discrepant in the fact that one who had failed to carve a niche for himself in ward politics should now invade the legislative halls of a palace and there arrest an ex-President. And just by the way it had been Lee Christmas who precipitated the national crisis which reached such a radical denouement.

There had been a *fiesta* in Santa Barbara at which two prominent *Liberales* — the Deputy Pedro A. Trejo and a Coronel Ezequiel Romero — came to blows and started a general fight, which the federal police were called to quell. In the course of the *mêlée,* Trejo and Romero received wounds of which they died. Dr. Policarpo Bonilla, always on the lookout for an opportunity to heckle the administration and place it in an unfavorable light, made this the text of a bitter address on the floor of the *salón de sesiones,* charging that the administration had had the two men assassinated because of their activity in the liberal party. Dr. Bonilla's speech was seconded by Dr. Miguel A. Navarro.*

Christmas heard of Dr. Bonilla's charge, for it became the principal topic of political discussion about the streets of the capital at once; the idea that anyone should impute so foul a crime to his friend, the President, infuriated him. It happened that on that same afternoon he encountered Miguel Navarro, who had seconded *don* Policarpo's speech. Applying his own peculiar diplomatic philosophy, Christmas promptly unbosomed himself in what he conceived to be the most natural fashion in the world, stating with a wealth of detail just what he — Christmas — would do to Navarro if

---

* Dr. Navarro is today one of the best-known contributors of political articles to the press of Honduras.

that statesman so much as dared to open his mouth regarding such a charge again. This declaration was pointed with what even Latin America must have regarded as something noteworthy in the way of profanity.

Navarro lost no time in reporting to the Congress, at the next sitting, that "*el aventurero yanqui,* Lee Christmas" had threatened physical violence to a member of the Chamber by way of seeking to influence his legislative course. There was a prompt halloo, and Policarpo Bonilla rose at once to a question, put to Sotero Barahona, Minister of War, concerning these reported efforts at intimidation by an administration official. In fact, the Congress promptly adopted a motion to remain in permanent session until the issues raised by General Christmas' latest diplomatic move had been satisfactorily explained.

Congress had no sooner adopted this motion, than an incredible thing happened. Into the sacred precincts of the *salón de sesiones,* there marched an armed force, headed by General Lee Christmas, and this force arrested Dr. Policarpo Bonilla and eight other members, haling them unceremoniously from their seats to the common gaol.

In his first fury at having a base "*aventurero yanqui*" lay hands upon his patrician person, Dr. Bonilla resisted, and Christmas struck the ex-President several heavy blows. Ultimately the nine captives were confined in the penitentiary at Tegucigalpa, iron leg shackles and all. Dr. Bonilla, once his first rage had cooled, congratulated himself and his confreres upon the turn of affairs. Here, indeed, was just the "cause" he had been looking for. Incarceration by so tyrannical an assault upon the freedom of speech and thought could not but make a martyr of him, and thus neutralize *don* Manuel's personal popularity, alienating from the little President a good share of the following which had hitherto rendered him to all intents and purposes invincible, so far as revolutions against him might hope to go.

Imagine Dr. Bonilla's surprise, therefore, when no charge was filed against him or his colleagues on the basis of anything that had been said or done by any of them in Congress; but a charge of treason and sedition, founded upon evidence which *don* Manuel had been gathering for months of the activity with which "*we veritable Liberales*" had been conspiring. For mark: On the warrant of the uncovered plot, *don* Manuel immediately suspended the constitution, dissolved Congress, declared martial law and installed himself as dictator. The conspirators were therefore tried not in the civil courts, but before a military tribunal, which found them guilty of the charge of treason and sedition, and sentenced them to ten years of military incarceration.

The sentence was only a gesture, of course, in so far as eight of those nine prisoners were concerned, and they were pardoned and released within a few months. Dr. Bonilla, however, suffered the confiscation of his estates and passed almost two years in that penitentiary, while *don* Manuel further entrenched his own position against internal aggression.

As the initial step in this direction he called a constitutional convention which first formally approved the declaration of martial law by the President, and then rewrote the entire Liberal Constitution of 1894, changing, among other things, the term of the presidency from four years to six, and installing *don* Manuel as first president under the new regime. That gave General Bonilla a nine-year lease on the presidential suite in the *palacio* — the three years he had already served, and the six years of the new term.

Finally, suspecting quite shrewdly and quite correctly that the nipped Liberal revolt had received aid and comfort, to say the least, from President Zelaya of Nicaragua, *don* Manuel revived the ancient boundary dispute concerning the territory on the Rio Segovio, and had it submitted through an international court to young King Alfonso of Spain as mediator. It will be recalled that this concerned lands whose Nicaraguan sovereignty had been tacitly acknowledged by Honduras as long as administrations friendly to Zelaya were in power, because the Nicaraguan president, who had farmed out some rich concessions in the disputed territory, would have been deeply embarrassed if his claim to the lands were ever invalidated.

Figuratively speaking, don Manuel then dusted his finger tips lightly against each other, called it a good day's work, and at length gave ear to General Christmas' unremitting plea for a change of scene. Having no prospect of immediate need for the services of his valiant *gringo* at the capital, he appointed him *comandante* at Puerto Cortez, and on behalf of the grateful republic of Honduras presented him with the magnificent dress sword to which reference has previously been made.

Lee Christmas had already sent to Paris for a uniform that showed dark blue here and there through a crusting of gold braid. This, the dress sword, and other effects were stowed on a couple of pack mules. The General himself bestrode a great white horse and headed his steed toward the Atlantic, and Adelaide. They crossed the continental divide and journeyed down the Valle de Sula to San Pedro, where he was royally entertained by the military and civil authorities and welcomed by his friend Dr. Waller, and had his photograph taken wearing the gold-crusted uniform and the sword of honor; and after that he took train for Puerto Cortez, where he had been given his first taste of the new game that he had found so much to his liking, and whence he had departed for Tegucigalpa leaving behind him a fair repute as a good bad-man, a divorced wife, two children, scores of left-hand loves — and Adelaide.

Straight to the *cuartel* he went, to doff travel-stained campaign togs for the new dress uniform, the ornate cap, the custom-fitted boots, the glittering spurs and the new dress sword with which he proposed to dazzle the Puerto Cortez of his humble beginnings — and Adelaide.

But he found her not alone. Another Italian family had

In the new uniform, ordered from Paris, with the dress sword presented on behalf of the Government by President Manuel Bonilla. (Photograph taken in 1905.)

General Lee Christmas (on the white horse next to the bugler) leading a file of officers during a ceremonial review before the Palacio Nacional in Tegucigalpa.

moved to the port during his absence; the family of Peter Culotta, a retired sea captain. One of the Culotta daughters, Erminie Gilda, and her little seven-year-old sister Ida, were visiting Adelaide when Christmas paid the first call of his formal suit for her heart and hand. The General, ever partial to children, made a great fuss over Ida. She was an accomplished little miss, and no whit abashed by the impressive splendor of the big officer's trappings. So he sat her on his knee while he listened with frank delight to her recital of school " pieces," and her rendition of little Spanish, English, and Italian songs.

Thus the General, who had been divorced by the first Mrs. Christmas in Memphis, Tennessee, and who had divorced the second Mrs. Christmas in Puerto Cortez, Honduras, entered upon the courtship of the third Mrs. Christmas while, all unwitting, he dandled on his knee the little girl who would one day be Mrs. Lee Christmas the Fourth. However, since the future was shrouded from him, this circumstance quite naturally had no effect whatever upon his honorable intentions of the moment, and so he continued to devote himself wholeheartedly to —

The Third Courtship

ALTHOUGH Lee Christmas was now a power in the land and a man of means, he encountered in his suit for Adelaide determined parental opposition. For the General was by now known as one who did not regard wedlock as a life sentence and who experienced little difficulty in dissolving the theoretically solemn·matrimonial bond at his pleasure. Therefore, while the Carusos were rather gratified to have the great General Christmas paying court to their daughter, they were decidedly opposed to any steps which might place her ultimately in the category of wives whom Lee Christmas had shelved.

In spite of this parental attitude the courtship went on apace. At the *cuartel* there were a number of handcars to be used for official military transportation. There was also a soldiers' band. Shady lanes, drives, or parks there were none. When the military officials wanted to go anywhere, they used one of the handcars, with soldiers to pump the handles. Those handcars played a great role in the 1905 gallantries of Lee Christmas. On fair evenings, he would order out two of them, and enough soldiers to provide adequate motive power. He and his party would seat themselves on the first; the band from the *cuartel* would be placed on the second. Then the soldiers pumped away at the handlebars, and the band played as the General and his inamorata and their friends were driven up and down the valley.

But it was a tepid sort of courtship, and Christmas soon revolted against the stalemate of crowded parties into which it fell. He wanted to get married, let Adelaide's parents say what they might. So he put the matter squarely up to Adelaide, and she consented, at last, to an elopement.

Early the following Sunday evening he went up the line to Laguna, to the railroad yards which he had known so well during his years as locomotive engineer. There he arranged to borrow not only a railroad engine, but the services of a brother craftsman as well. Between them they rigged up a device on the stack of the locomotive which operated as a silencer. A few minutes after midnight this locomotive slid out of Laguna siding and sped quietly down the *Calle de Linea,* past the *cuartel,* past the Palms Hotel, to the Caruso home which was just a few doors farther along. Christmas was standing out on the pilot of the little locomotive, with a lighted cigar.

He had told Adelaide that if he waved the glowing cigar-tip, it would be a signal that the coast was clear and that she should join him at once. The engine was halted. The cigar tip described a series of swift scarlet arcs there in the darkness. Adelaide, whose family's slumbers had not been interrupted by the silent approach of the engine, slipped out of the shadows and clambered to a footing on the pilot of the locomotive. Holding one arm about her, Christmas "highballed" his engineer confrere, and the locomotive conveyed them swiftly to the other end of the line, where stood the squat banana wharf through which the General had made his first entry into the tropics a decade before.

To the wharf was moored a little sailboat with a native skipper and a crew of two Caribs. It was an open cockle-shell; but it was stocked with provisions, there were blankets for comfort, and a 'paulin for shelter. Thus they embarked for the altar somewhere in Belize, British Honduras. Shrouded by the velvety blackness of a moonless tropic night, the boat cast off and, under a steady off-shore breeze, forged north along the coast, across the Gulf of Honduras. At its best, the sail to Belize would have been a two-day journey. As it was, one of the swift storms of those latitudes whirled down upon them the second afternoon, so that the bridal boat had to be put inshore with speed, beaching at Punta Gorda.

In the sluicing rain, Christmas took one of the vessel's sails and improvised a tent for himself and his bride-to-be. All that evening and all that night and almost all the next morning the storm howled and lashed at the gray seas, and the refugees made shift to shelter themselves under their bit of tent, while the high combers crashed rhythmically and sent long tongues of foam hissing up the white sands. They cooked meals as best they could of the provisions the General had stowed aboard in advance of the elopement, and supplemented this fare with such variations as conch stew and broiled *langosta,* furnished by the skipper and his Caribs.

Toward noon the fury of the storm finally dropped, the seas abated, and late in the evening the journey was resumed. They reached Belize the following night, and the day after that they were married by a British magistrate. They remained in Belize nearly a month, honeymooning. Then they returned to Cortez. Adelaide's family was very bitter, and refused to recognize the third Mrs. Christmas as one of their blood. Not until the following year, when a boy was born — Lee Christmas Junior — did they relent.

That was 1906, when, in December, King Alfonso of Spain finally handed down his decision in the old boundary dispute between Honduras and Nicaragua. Politically, the year had been marked for Honduras by certain other events. Policarpo Bonilla, it may be recalled, was still in prison, serving his ten-year sentence for treason. But his friends were not idle. As the perennial insurgent, José María Valladares, put it:

While General Bonilla [*don* Manuel] was consummating his nefarious work [the new constitution which extended his term to nine years], we veritable Liberals were conspiring actively; but we had to be careful, for fear Doctor Bonilla [*don* Policarpo] would be shot while in prison, although he urged us not to consider this, as he found himself disposed to take the risk which it involved.

At the height of the active conspiracy, President Tomás Regalado of El Salvador succeeded in persuading President Bonilla to restore *don* Policarpo to freedom, and Policarpo, to quote once more the writings of General Valladares *"se trasladó sin pérdida de tiempo á la República de El Salvador"* (translated himself without loss of time to the Republic of El Salvador). There he was joined by the other "veritable Liberals," among whom of course was Terencio Sierra, whose spirit voices were still staunch in the assurance that his destiny was to rule Honduras. Plans for an immediate revolution took definite shape, and General Valladares who was still in Honduras began to assemble a force there to launch the revolt from within, marching for El Salvador where he would be joined by the other leaders.

One of the conspirators, however, turned traitor and exposed the entire plot, so that the administration of El Salvador, at whose intercession Dr. Policarpo Bonilla had been freed from prison, promptly interned him and deported the other leaders. Much to his surprise, therefore, General Valladares received hasty orders to march for the Nicaraguan frontier instead of the border of El Salvador, which he did, encountering a body of Bonilla's federal troops there, at Las Joyas.

A detachment of Nicaraguan soldiers had been ordered to the locality too, "to protect the border against invasion" either by accident or design. All three bodies of troops became embroiled in a brief skirmish action in which the Nicaraguans—claiming that Bonilla's soldiers had crossed the line—aided Valladares' men. Bonilla's troops, of course, reported that the Nicaraguans had been the ones who had crossed the line into Honduras.

President Zelaya of Nicaragua was beginning to feel so insecure in his tenure of office that, instead of disputing this claim and declaring war upon Honduras in consequence, he contented himself with interning Valladares and submitting the entire controversy for arbitration to the Centro-American International Court at San José. But just at this time King Alfonso of Spain rendered his decision in the old Nicaragua-Honduras boundary dispute. The verdict was in favor of Honduras. That capped the climax of misfortunes for Sr. Zelaya, for it left him holding an empty sack along the Rio Segovia, with concessions that he had pledged himself to deliver in lands that were now under the control of a hostile administration in Honduras.

Zelaya at once withdrew the Nicaraguan delegates from the San José convention, refused to abide by the Alfonso decree, and focused public attention on the invasion of Nicaraguan territory by the troops of Honduras during that brief border skirmish at Las Joyas.

Manuel Bonilla immediately gave out a fiery message to his people — and he was a flaming little public speaker — declaring that it was Nicaragua whose soldiers had invaded Honduras on that occasion; that it was Nicaragua which was refusing to abide by the arbitrament of King Alfonso; and that it was now necessary for all true patriots to spring to the defense of the territorial integrity of the fatherland.

With both sides thus absolutely in the right, and each the innocent victim of the other's aggression, war was declared according to the standard pattern used a scant seven years or so later by mightier nations.

Allied with the Nicaraguans were all the insurgent Honduraneans who had been conspiring so actively while *don* Manuel was completing his " nefarious labors." Bonilla put two armies into the field: One, under Salamón Ordóñez, which was sent against the Nicaraguans at San Marcos; the other in command of Sotero Barahona, Minister of War, which moved out to fortify the long plain at Maraita against invasion from the south. The president also telegraphed Lee Christmas at Puerto

Cortez to turn over the *comandancia* there to a subordinate, and join Barahona as second in command.

When the army of Ordóñez was routed in its first engagement, *don* Manuel decided to take the field himself, in spite of the fact that he was coming down at the time with a severe fever; a few days later he had to be left behind with a guard at a native hut along the road. His army, without him, met the Nicaraguans — and disaster — at Namasigüe; the result set a grisly sort of world's record, said to be unbroken to this day. In proportion to the number of combatants engaged, and the actual time of fighting, there were more men killed at Namasigüe than in any other battle since the dawn of recorded history — three thousand or more slain in a few minutes of actual combat. Of course the sniping went on for hours after the rout; indeed, for days.

Among those who escaped in¹ that precipitate flight was a young Sr. Pedro Gonzales, who, at the ripe age of sixteen was relishing his first revolution, even though it was laced with the bitter condiment of defeat. Mention is here made of him because his later exploits figure so conspicuously in the Chronicle of Christmas.*

As for *don* Manuel, his guard remained with him in the remote cottage where the little president, of necessity, had been left before the battle. There he passed the crisis of his illness, and by the time the real fighting had moved on to the north and east, he managed to reach the coast of Aceituno, where he reassembled five hundred or so of his followers who had escaped pursuit. With them he crossed the shallow bay to the fortress of Amapala. But the Nicaraguans and their Honduranean allies heard of it and massed their forces at once for a siege. Realizing that his cause was hopeless, *don* Manuel sent

---

* Through a record which included active participation, from Namasigüe on, in every major revolution in Honduras, Pedro Gonzales only once went through a fight without being wounded in action, and he died of pneumonia, after only partially recovering from the effects of a machine gun bullet through the lungs during the fighting at San Pedro Sula in the anti-Bertrand revolution of 1919.

word to the enemy he would surrender the island without resistance or bloodshed; but not to a Nicaraguan. They must
send a Honduranean officer to take over the port. The allies
did it. They sent Terencio Sierra!—the man against whom
don Manuel had launched his great coup from this same fortress of Amapala in 1903.

The transfer of the fortress was arranged by Commander
Robert M. Doyle of the United States cruiser *Chicago,* which
had been dispatched to the Pacific coast of Honduras at the
outbreak of hostilities. Commander Doyle it was who took
President Bonilla aboard the *Chicago* and out of the country,
landing him in Guatemala, whence, with the friendly aid of
President Cabrera, *don* Manuel made his way to the neutral
soil of British Honduras.

About this same time Lee Christmas reached the heights of
Los Coyotes, near Maraita, where Barahona was encamped with
the "army of the east." Adelaide and little Lee had been placed
aboard a steamer for Guatemala City via Puerto Barrios, as soon
as Christmas had received the president's call. The General
then hastened back up the Comayagua valley to the capital.
Delighted to be rid of routine responsibilities, he supposed this
new venture would be as gay and as joyous as that memorable
campaign, now three long years behind him, when he and his
policemen had left their city beats to snatch a presidency out
of a jungle war.

True enough, the battle toward which he rode did bring him
new renown; a tribute he won by three curt words. They were

"Don't Bury Me!"

Sotero Barahona's force at Maraita plain was small and poorly munitioned, made up of cadets from the military academy, fourteen to sixteen years old. They were to be a defensive unit, guarding the long plain at Maraita, ringed by low hills — Los Coyotes. The revolutionists under José María Valladares would have to cross this plain. There they were to be joined by their Nicaraguan allies; there, too, Bonilla's allies from Salvador were awaited.*

The defenders had entrenched three camps at Maraita and had made machine gun strong points in nests of pine logs. By the time the position was prepared, Christmas arrived. With him was an American named Fred Mills, accompanied by a score or so of Indians. Mills had been employed at the big San Juancito silver mine, but, sensing an exhilarating promise of trouble at Maraita, he promptly enlisted "for the duration."

Almost at once Valladares brought up his revolutionists and, without a shot being exchanged, occupied Los Coyotes, effecting a deadlock that was maintained for two or three days. The invaders could not hope to dislodge the defenders from their

* The course of the incidents set forth in this chapter has been reconstructed from several contemporary sources. In general, it follows the narrative Christmas himself gave to his friends, shortly after the battle, notably Dr. Waller at San Pedro, who tended Christmas and treated his grievous wound, and Col. Molony, who was for many years Christmas' most intimate associate. Other details and corroborative accounts were secured from Col. Francisco Cleaves, now chief of police of San Pedro Sula, who was one of the young artillery cadets in the battle of Maraita. No single phase of Christmas' stormy career in the tropics has been more magnificently garbled by the Sunday-supplement biographers, than this "don't-bury-me" affair, and some of the more startling of these versions of the incident will be found in Appendix No. VII.

strong camps, and the latter could not charge the hills from their fortifications. Both sides, in short, were waiting for re-enforcements. The Nicaraguans, with their allied Hondura-nean revolutionists, arrived first.

The defending army had been intended only as a stop-gap; the main body of troops would be brought up later, after Bara-hona had kept the invaders at bay, to strike the decisive blow. But the main body of troops had been virtually annihilated at San Marcos and at Namasigüe, so that provisions and muni-tions were alike all but exhausted when Sotero Barahona called a council of his *jefes* at night to discuss the matter of surrender.

Any possible line of retreat back to Tegucigalpa had been cut off. Direct assault on what were now four surrounding enemy lines was out of the question. There were scarce two hundred yards of open ground between the camp where the council was convened and the slopes of Los Coyotes. Not a dissenting voice was raised when Sotero Barahona pointed out that their posi-tion, strategically, was hopeless.

Brigadier General Lee Christmas rose from his seat by the camp fire, slipped the machete at his side to an easier position, hooked his thumbs into his belt, and threw back the spread of his wide shoulders. Henceforth, of course, this campaign, if such it could have been called, was a matter of individual tem-perament.

"I know what is going to happen to me if those bastards get their hands on me," he said. "I'm the one that arrested their damn Policarpo, and slugged him. With my own hands. And right out there, one of the generals, Señor Valladares, is itch-ing for a chance to talk to me about the time I closed up his print shop for him. Can you figure them doing anything for me but taking me out, with a grand hurray, to be shot for a lesson? And just as long as I've got to be shot, I might as well take it where I've got a chance to get some of those that's plug-ging at me."

His hearers nodded gravely.

"And I'll not be the only one to get it, either," Christmas went on, turning to Barahona. "You were one of the court that sentenced Policarpo, General. They'll pick you. You and me, tied to mules. Up to the capital and into the cells. Back against the wall. Public show. Traitors to Honduras. *Fuego!*"

Another voice was raised — Fred Mills, completely indifferent as to who might be president of any one of the five republics, and having no earthly business where he was.

"Well, how about me?" asked Mills. "Think they'll pass up a chance to use me for a lesson to the *gringos* not to mix in a private war?"

"Hell's bells, Fred, they won't bother you!" retorted Christmas. "Everybody likes you. You're aces with both sides. Don't I know it? Why they wouldn't be bothering me, only for what I did to *don* Policarpo. I've heard some of the things he said were going to happen to me, if they ever caught me."

"All right, have it your own way, Lee," grinned Mills. "I'm going too."

"You mean you will try to break through their lines in the morning?" Barahona asked Christmas. He was an old soldier, this General Barahona, and he knew that where a mass charge was foredoomed to fail, a scattered exodus would be almost certain to insure for a few the chance of safe escape.

"That's exactly what I mean," replied Christmas. "I'm going through — or out. There'll be seven cartridges in my gun and each of the first six will get me one of those rawhides. The last one will be for me, in case they just nip me on the road. But I guarantee they'll never drag me out in front of a mob and make a show over killing me."

"I will ride with you!" Thus Sotero Barahona, signing his own death warrant.

"And I!" That was Coronel Tejeda Reyes, third in command.

"Me too!" And that was Mills, his flashing smile revealing much gold.

"No. Not you," said Lee Christmas. "You'll be safe here."

"Me too," said Mills. "Try and stop me."

"All right. Don't blame me if you get your can shot off. Pass 'em the word, General."

Sotero Barahona passed his subordinates the word. At dawn the four were to be given time to mount and start their charge across the open. Four men, each armed with a pistol, against an army; a securely posted army with rifles and machine guns that would have nothing else to occupy their attention but those four little targets dashing across the plain. After that, the rest might surrender, or flee, or do whatever the occasion might offer as the best course.

A score or so of Indians, incidentally, also knew precisely what they were going to do in the morning. Leave Señor Mills? That gay and lusty *caballero* with the golden smile and the infectious laugh? Not they! If Señor Mills went out across that plain in the dawn, or at high noon, or under the moonlight, his Indians went with him and that was quite definitely that. So, just before the parrots in the lowlands began their shrieking jungle welcome to the sunrise, the four quietly summoned their officers and mounted — Christmas on a gray horse and Mills on a white one, the other two on mules.

Christmas drew the Luger at his belt from its wooden scabbard, gathered the reins in his left hand, booted his horse and swung out of the shelter of the encampment into a ponderous gallop across the plain. As the charge gathered momentum, the crashing advance would have roused the countryside; but the countryside was already up. Sentries had seen the four men mount, and had given the alarm, evidently in the belief that the entire defending force was launching a charge.

Sooty puffs of black powder smoke blossomed on the low slope toward which Christmas and the others were pounding. Bullets clipped crisply through leaves and branches. Then came a volley, and under cover of the volley, a company of Honduranean revolutionists with one General Francisco Rosa at their head, charged down from their slope into the open to close the plain at the left. A detachment of Nicaraguans swept out toward the right. Other volleys. The four who had set out to auction their lives as dearly as possible paid no heed. It was not yet their turn to speak. Back of the others, and at the extreme left, was Mills, for he would not ride off at full gallop and leave the native boys who were committing suicide with him.

Ducking their heads involuntarily, as though this would protect them from the whining swarm of bullets, the other three gave their mounts free rein and went drumming across the open. Then came the beginning of the end. Mills's horse went down, rolling over and over.

Mills, fortunately, was flung clear. He too rolled over, but with the athlete's swift co-ordination of muscles, found his feet, and plunged ahead, unhurt, his Indians at his back. " Fortunately " he was flung clear. Odd, that this word should have written itself. For it really made no difference. Fred Mills had only a few seconds left to live. Close ahead, and at the left, he saw the mighty trunk of a fallen pine. There was a shallow trench behind it, where the cadets of the artillery school, on their first arrival at Maraita plain, had intended to place a machine gun. Straight for that shelter he headed, with his handful of native boys. But General Rosa and his soldiers were there ahead of him.

Had they met a Nicaraguan detachment, they would have been shot down at once. As it was, there was a delay of perhaps fifty seconds, for some of Rosa's soldiers recognized Mills. Mills the big *gringo* who was always laughing and gay. Mills, who had a jovial word for everyone.

" Don't shoot! It's Mills. Surrender, Señor Mills! " There came a clamor of confused cries in front of him.

And:

"Surrender, Señor Mills! They are friends! Surrender!" cried his own Indians at his back.

A madman, this Mills. He had lost his pistol and was unarmed. He had but to raise his empty hands, and perhaps be safely taken captive.

"Don't shoot! Surrender, Señor Mills!"

"I'll be god-damned if I do!" shouted Mills and plunged ahead exultantly, unarmed.

His Indians said afterwards that it was General Rosa himself who raised his pistol and took careful aim at the running figure. A projecting root or a loose rock — something tripped Mills. Perhaps it was the shock of the bullet itself. Francisco Rosa, so goes the story as it was whispered among the natives later, fired again at the prostrate figure. His Indians scattered on the instant, and most of them escaped up the slopes that were glassy with fallen pine straw. It was all confused, by now. The cadets and the soldiers back at the camp were melting away into the scrub-grown hills as fast as they could under cover of the general attention that was focused on the charge of the four leaders. That is, there had been four. There were only three now.

Tejeda Reyes was riding fast on his nimble mule. He was a few yards in advance of the others — an isolated target. Those who were barring his advance were Nicaraguans. The indiscriminate crackle of rifle fire died down and then was followed by the crash of a single volley. Tejeda Reyes and his mule, both riddled with slugs, went down. Two left. Sotero Barahona was no longer firing. He had emptied his revolver and had thrown the useless weapon away. Bent low over his mule's withers, he rode blindly, urging his mount forward, charging for the nearest draw in the low slopes that confronted him. The effort brought him a few yards beyond the point Tejeda Reyes had reached. Two bullets found him almost simultaneously and he pitched to the ground. Only one left now — Lee Christmas.

Christmas had conserved his fire, and so there were three cartridges still left in the magazine. He had kept his tally very carefully, for he must reserve the last one, and even apart from that he wanted each of the others to count. No use throwing good cartridges away. Just ahead of him he saw Barahona go down. He swerved sharply toward the right to see whether the General was himself wounded, or whether his mount had merely been shot out from under him. No—Barahona was hit. Dead, probably. He raised his own pistol and kicked the gray horse, to continue his charge—and then it came. Through his own leg at the calf, first, shattering the bone; and then through his horse, so that he went down almost on top of the fallen Barahona. But his Luger was still in his hand and there were three cartridges left. Three shots. Two for them, and one for . . . he tried to wriggle out to use those last two shots and found that he was pinned helplessly by the weight of the fallen horse. One leg broken, the other caught under a dead horse. Well, after all, what of it? There'd be only a few seconds more, now. Grotesquely twisted, he took careful aim and fired at one of the figures that were swarming toward him. Again! And now—

He pressed the hot muzzle of the Luger to his temple and pulled the trigger. That is, he tried to pull it. Unbelievingly he whipped the gun down and around, and stared at the open magazine. Open! Miscounted! No last shot!

Panic gripped him; no panic of fear, but of sudden realization. All his plans for passing out in a hot blaze of glory, killing as many of his enemies as he could and cursing the balance as sons of all the fallen women of a million Babylons—all that gone for nothing. Executed like a criminal, with staring crowds to gape at the show. Policarpo would see to that. Stand him in the public square. Any last words to say? Newspaper correspondents to pick up the sensational details of the fulfillment of the death sentence. "The condemned man refused to permit his eyes to be bandaged."

Then a soldier was lunging at him with a bayonet. Lunging at his head, the god-damned fool. A contortion twisted Lee Christmas' head to one side, and the descending gun-knife merely grazed the scalp.

"Not in the head, you rawhide bastard! Not in the head."

Christmas poured out a deluge of the foulest epithets he could lay tongue to — and he was a past master at that — in the hope that he might enrage the soldier so that the second thrust would be the fatal one to the breast. That second thrust, though, was never delivered. An officer, a spruce young Nicaraguan *teniente,* came running up and struck the bayonetted rifle aside.

Christmas turned the tide of his profanity upon the officer, who listened dispassionately.

"Oh, you will be shot without doubt," the youngster assured him. "But it will be a formal execution. Here, let me bind your wounds."

There it was. If only he could provoke the boy into killing him out of hand, he could still be spared that final indignity. So —

"Shoot and be god-damned to you," Christmas raged. "Shoot now, if you've got the guts. But do me one favor. Don't bury me."

"Don't bury you?"

Other soldiers were coming up and forming a ring about the fallen. The roar of musketry had died away. There were only a few single shots, here and there, as snipers searched the slippery slopes for fleeing federals.

"No. Don't bury me, you sons of bitches!"

"But why not?"

It was the question for which Christmas had been waiting. "Because I want the buzzards to eat me, and fly over you afterwards, and scatter white droppings on your god-damned black faces."

It was the supreme insult, and it included not only the young *teniente,* but the ring of soldiers as well. Christmas braced himself for the shock of bullet or knife, and closed his eyes. But he was not braced for what actually did follow, which was a ringing, boyish laugh.

"You are a brave man and shall not be executed at all," said the *teniente,* and the soldiers grinned their approval.

They extricated Christmas from beneath his dead horse, and found to their amazement that General Barahona still lived. The two were carried to a hut on the *camino* that angled across the plain toward Tegucigalpa. Dressings were applied to their wounds, and Christmas' shattered calf was bound in rude splints. In that hut Sotero Barahona died before dawn. Carrying Christmas with them, swung in a litter between two mules, the victors marched on the capital.*

Tegucigalpa surrendered without even a show of resistance. Nicaraguan gunboats had already effected the capture of the ports of Cortez and La Ceiba. Manuel Bonilla had already fled to Guatemala, after the slaughter of his forces at Namasigüe. There was really no opposition left, and what trouble the victors might now encounter would be purely internal, over a division of the spoils.

Lee Christmas was taken to the hospital at Tegucigalpa, and was not even kept a prisoner, thanks to the fame which was accorded the insolence of his challenge to death. As soon as his leg permitted him to travel, he made his way by slow stages, on muleback, to San Pedro Sula, where his old friend, Dr. Waller, attended him until his recovery was complete. Then he

---

* It is only fair to point out that the version of the final stages of the siege of Maraita plain as given here differs in a number of particulars from that embodied by Lic. Felix Salgado in his *Compendio de Historia de Honduras* (Biblioteca de la Sociedad de Geografía e Historia de Honduras, Imprenta el Sol, Comayagüela, 1928). Dr. Salgado's account sets forth that the council of the Barahona officers was called in the evening, and that it was agreed a concerted rush should effect several breaches in the enemy lines; that this was done successfully, and that Barahona might have saved himself, but refused to hasten, insisting on being the last to leave the field with the rear guard, in an endeavor to salvage the supply train. Col. Tejeda Reyes, General Lee Christmas and Andrés Avelino Díaz, together with a number of other cadets and officers, remained by their chief to protect him, Reyes being killed and Christmas and Díaz badly wounded. The excerpt from the Salgado Compendio is reprinted in Appendix No. VII.

joined his wife and son in Guatemala City, and became head of the secret service system which President Estrada Cabrera maintained there. Manuel Bonilla was already an exile in British Honduras, where he settled down to a quiet, agricultural existence at a plantation he purchased on Stann Creek.

Meantime one grim sequel to the tale of Maraita plain had been enacted at Tegucigalpa, where General Francisco Rosa — the officer who had shot down Fred Mills — had returned to resume personal charge of his business, a large mercantile establishment.

With all the discharged soldiers and others still in the capital, the shops were reaping a rich harvest. Many of the natives were buying weapons and General Rosa, helping personally to care for a rush of customers, was extolling the virtues of a 38-calibre revolver to an Indian who had expressed a desire to purchase such a gun. Quietly the Indian asked permission to examine the weapon, and General Rosa passed it across the counter. The prospective purchaser turned it this way and that and, under cover of the movement, slipped a single cartridge into the cylinder. Swiftly he raised the weapon and fired. Just once. General Rosa fell, mortally wounded, behind the counter of his store, and in the confusion the Indian escaped. He was one of those who had followed Fred Mills in the mad charge across Maraita plain a week before.

The incident was the last echo of the victorious revolution that had ousted Bonilla and Christmas from Honduras. Their elimination might have been expected to calm the political scene; but the first phase of the new chronicle was the immediate appearance of —

New Discord in Honduras

AT LEAST four statesmen, who had been making common cause in opposition to *don* Manuel, regarded themselves as the logical heirs to his mantle. They were Policarpo Bonilla, Juan Angel Arias, Terencio Sierra and Máximo B. Rosales. Lest internal dissension over their respective claims again rend the newly consolidated Liberals a compromise candidate was chosen in the person of Miguel R. Dávila, who had been elected Manuel Bonilla's vice-president, back in 1903.

Policarpo was pacified by the restoration to him of some 200,000 pesos for losses suffered through the seizure of his properties when he had been imprisoned by *don* Manuel. Arias and Rosales were given places in the cabinet. Sierra was made *comandante* of Amapala and retired to that Tigre Island fortress to consult his spirit voices. Precisely seven days after Dávila had been installed as president, Sierra issued from his island with as much army as he could muster, and proclaimed himself President of Honduras.

Let us say farewell to Terencio Sierra. His little army was *derrotado* — utterly routed — in its first engagement, and Sierra "translated" himself without loss of time into Nicaragua, where he settled down on a coffee plantation with the only allies who now remained loyal to him in the folly of his grandeurs — his Voices. That same year, walking about the *finca* of his exile one warm November morning, he died quite suddenly of a stroke.

The time is almost at hand, too, when we must take leave of another familiar figure. Revolt had broken out in Nicaragua, led by the same Juan Estrada who defeated Manuel Bonilla at Namasigüe, against José Santos Zelaya, "ferocious Cæsar and bloodthirsty tyrant," as Valladares describes him in one of his pamphlets. Christmas took no active part in that revolt, though he harbored an intense hatred for Zelaya; but many a soldier in the cause of the revolution was recruited through his aid. Indeed, by this time Christmas had even left the secret service of Guatemala to go a-railroading once more, and was running a passenger engine for the *Ferrocaril Central de Guatemala,* a position he held until January 1910, when, shortly after the birth of a second son, Winnfield, he resigned to become engineer on one of the new big Shea locomotives purchased by the government railroad to handle the rush of coffee freights.

Back in Honduras, all this while, new seeds of dissension had fallen on fertile ground, sown by negotiations for a "dollar diplomacy" treaty. So insistent were the reports of seething unrest that trickled into Guatemala from Honduras, that Christmas began to importune *don* Manuel, in season and out, by letter and by messenger, to lead a counter-revolution, stressing President Dávila's lack of personal following. Bonilla, however, was a canny little patriot, who realized just how thoroughly any revolution that hoped to succeed needed to be financed, and so he put Christmas off until the fall of 1909, when it became evident that *don* Manuel had found an "angel." In the ensuing correspondence between Bonilla and Christmas this capitalist was never referred to save as "*el amigo*" — the friend. The same discretion shall be observed here.

Through all that Spring and early Summer, the *negocios* went slowly forward. Little by little, the *elementos* were assembled. The *Emma,* an oyster lugger from Gulfport, Miss., finally put in an inconspicuous appearance at Glover's Reef early in July, bringing rifles and ammunition and two brand-new machine guns.

General Marín, in Puerto Cortez, was arranging matters to help Bonilla and Christmas make that ancient harbor their point of initial attack. General Moncada was in the bush with 200 loyal Bonillistas who needed only rifles. At his own urgent request, Lee Christmas himself was named commander-in-chief of the army. Finally, July 21 was decided upon as the day of the attack, and *don* Manuel, in Belize, sent the following letter to his commander-in-chief, who was still " hogging " a freight locomotive in Guatemala:

Belize, July 17, 1910

Sr. Gral. don Lee Christmas,
Punta Gracioso.

My esteemed friend:

The bearer of this is the captain of the boat who is to conduct you and the rest of the friends to the place where we will meet. This captain in reality does not know what he is going to do.

Well: Once you are on board — you, the friends, and all the men — inform the captain that he must pass by Sapotilla cays, where we may meet, and then bring you to Glover's Reef, in which place you are certain to find me.

Perhaps the captain will refuse to take you; in this case you must use good arguments to convince him, so that he will take you; if he still refuses, then offer him money; and if he still will not take you, then impose yourself on him and do as you please. These are my instructions.

In the above I have already told you that we may meet in the vicinity of Sapotilla; you must not deviate from this course. If we do not meet there, we will meet at Glover's Reef.

My affectionate greeting to all the friends who accompany you, and until we meet you must all receive the handclasp of

Your friend and Servant,
Manuel Bonilla

Half a dozen boats were riding at anchor off Glover's Reef when Christmas reached the rendezvous. *El amigo* had not done things by halves. If Bonilla could be returned to power in Honduras, there would be enough concessions to make possible the founding of a new Banana Empire to compete with the existing great fruit company. That is not the sort of game one plays with penny-ante stakes, particularly when one of the cards that will fill the hand is the rising mutter (it will be a roar soon enough!) against dollar diplomacy.

The stir of it all was manifest not only here, but at curiously distant and unrelated points as well. A cargo steamer, threshing southward across the Caribbean, raised a brief smoke-smudge above the horizon. Among its passengers was —

Guy Molony

MOLONY had run away from New Orleans as a boy of seventeen, to join Her Britannic Majesty's forces against the Boers. He was twice wounded during that queer series of surprises that is labeled " South African Campaign " in the military pigeon-holes. One of these wounds was all but mortal. Then he got himself into trouble by stealing his colonel's horse so that he could be photographed aboard that noble charger. He wanted to send the picture home to his mother and sister.

Having no fancy whatever for Military Police duty in the Transvaal after the campaign, he returned to New Orleans and immediately enlisted with a regular cavalry outfit in the American army. He had become Sergeant Molony by the time his regiment was ordered to the Philippines. At the conclusion of his " hitch " he returned to his home by way of Japan, remaining rather at loose ends until by chance he ran into Sam Dreben, an acquaintance of his army days — the same " Jew Sam " whom General Pershing was later to designate as the outstanding hero of the A.E.F.

Jew Sam Dreben knew there was going to be hell a-popping in Nicaragua, with plenty of fighting and drinking and the particular pleasures of conquest. He also knew that Molony was " that quiet kid that's a whiz with machine guns; take 'em apart in the dark and toss 'em together the same way." What more natural, therefore, than the following from Dreben to Molony:

"I'm on the hike to Nicaragua this p.m. How about it, kid? Want to come along and sit in?"

So Molony casually notified his family that he was leaving for an attractive revolution in Nicaragua that afternoon, and wouldn't be home for dinner.

It was chicken one day and feathers the next in that sour jungle campaign; a feast of epic proportions in town, or gnawing raw green bananas in the dank and steaming bush. But the twenty-year rule of the tyrant Zelaya was broken, and Dreben, during the latter stages of the successful revolution, in the early summer of 1910, called Molony and said:

"There'll be a big show pop off in Honduras next month. I'm looking for some soft picking here, but a kid like you, that knows machine guns the way you do, can go a long ways there. A hot shot by the name of Lee Christmas is in charge. They're getting set to knock off this Dávila. How about it? Want to sit in?"

"All right," said Guy Molony.

Dreben scribbled a card.

"Take this to Greytown," he directed.

Someone in Greytown looked at Guy Molony with interest, when he presented that card, and without more ado gave him two hundred and fifty dollars — gold, not silver — and sent him to a certain address in New Orleans, with another card. There they looked at him with interest again, gave him another hundred and fifty dollars and a ticket to Belize, put him aboard the fruit steamer *Cartago,* and told him not to forget he was a hardware drummer.

On the night Guy Molony reached Belize he first met Manuel Bonilla. The little general spoke scarcely any English. With the exception of the few objurgations he had learned during Philippine and Nicaraguan service, Molony spoke no Spanish at all.

"Well, we shook hands, in a way," Col. Molony recalls. "He was a little man and he had been shot through the wrist in the battle of Tatumbla during the revolution when he and his friends overthrew Domingo Vásquez and put Policarpo Bonilla in as president. So he couldn't shake hands very well. Anyway, he asked me something in Spanish that seemed to be about machine guns. I took a chance and said 'Yes.' That seemed to please him. All he wanted me to do was to keep quiet around Belize and not to get drunk. We hung around town for a week, and then they put me late one night aboard a little sailboat named the *M.I.R.* I was the only passenger. We sailed all that night and all the next morning. The only stop we made was about noon, when we landed at some little cay, where the *M.I.R.'s* crew stopped to collect a load of conchs. They made a conch stew for dinner, and I want to go on record as saying it was noble grub. Anyway, we got to Glover's Reef late that evening. There were three ships there already. One was the *Emma,* a gasoline boat they had bought at Biloxi or Gulfport or somewhere on the Mississippi coast, where she had been used as an oyster lugger. Another was a sloop, the *Centinella,* and the third was a schooner named the *Britannic.* They put me aboard the *Centinella,* and I turned in and went to sleep."

Early the next morning a tall, sandy-haired figure came over the *Centinella's* side, keen eyes searching among the soldiers on deck until they came to rest on Molony. Lee Christmas — "the General" as Guy Molony was henceforth to know him — was in a towering and profane stew about his expeditionary force.

"Let's see what you know so much about machine guns," he growled. "Here we got two of 'em, brand new, fresh from the factory, and one of the god-damned things won't work. Let's see if you can fix us up."

The quickfirers were far different affairs from the crude old turn-'em-with-a-crank weapons with which Christmas was familiar. These were high-speed guns, rated at some 450 rounds per minute. One of the essential parts in one of the guns had been broken in shipment. However, Molony set to work, tinkering all the forenoon, strewing the *Centinella's* hot, bare deck with integral parts of machine gun, and apparently just messing around. None the less, by mid-afternoon, he had effected some sort of mechanical compromise. The speed of the repaired weapon had been reduced to some 350 rounds per minute, but it fired, as he demonstrated with a few practice bursts. Christmas was enormously pleased, and made it plain that the quiet youngster from New Orleans had risen measurably in his esteem.

That evening Manuel Bonilla arrived at the Reef. This was the night of July 20. Working with feverish rapidity as dusk closed down upon the tropic seas, one hundred rifles and ten thousand rounds of boxed ammunition were transferred to a Carib *goleta* by the two natives who owned and operated her. These were for General Moncada and his detachment, waiting in the bush near Tela, for the revolution to begin. Under a spanking breeze, the fleet cast off and headed for the Gulf of Honduras, down the coast.

Of the two Caribs to whom Christmas had entrusted the *elementos* for Moncada, the revolutionists never saw anything further. They were to have kept well out of sight of land, beaching their craft half way between La Ceiba and Tela the following night. As a matter of fact, they accomplished this, and met Moncada and about a hundred of his men without mishap, delivering their cargo as agreed. Thereupon, their mission completed, they lay down on the warm sand and went to sleep.

The next morning they began to gather the tops of the ammunition boxes, stowing them aboard their boat to be used for firewood. An *escolta* from Tela, in charge of an officer, came upon them there. The boat had been seen at dawn, and was naturally suspected of being a smuggler. The tops of those ammunition boxes which the two Caribs had so thriftily saved, gave damning and complete evidence of the commission of

President don Manuel Bonilla, from a photograph taken not long before his death, March 21, 1913.

General Pedro Díaz (see Chapter " *January* 25, 1911 ").

a far graver offense. The *escolta* did not even accord the two natives the formality of a trial, but shot them both on the spot.

By this time, however, a far more serious blow had fallen upon the expedition which had set out from Glover's Reef with such high hopes. The fleet of three vessels reached Puerto Cortez at two o'clock in the morning, luffing up below the tip of the slim, outer promontory, on the ocean side of the squat banana wharf. Although Christmas himself was all impatience to attack at once, Bonilla dispatched a scout in a small boat to establish contact first with General Marín, the confederate in the city who was to have everything in readiness for the landing party. With so small a force at their disposal, a garrison town like Cortez could be captured only by surprise, of course. The three boats lay hard by each other, so that when the messenger returned, orders could be given to the entire expedition without arousing the sleeping town.

For an hour, or perhaps an hour and a half, the Bonilla fleet lay thus in waiting: a tense and impatient time for all, since, at any moment, the success or failure of their entire venture might be determined. Finally the messenger reappeared, rowing with haste out to the *Emma*. The news he bore to the *jefes* of the revolution taxed the store of profanity of even General-in-Chief Lee Christmas.

Briefly stated, the report was that General Marín, in exuberant anticipation of the morrow's certain victory, had got himself gloriously drunk, and under this inspiration had decided not to await the coming of the Manuelist forces. Setting out to capture Puerto Cortez singlehanded he had been shot, quite naturally, by the military authorities with the utmost dispatch. Upon his person were found papers giving the complete plans of the next morning's Bonilla revolution, with names, dates and places all neatly tabulated and correct. Since then, several other persons — leaders among the local Bonilla adherents — had also been summarily executed or cast into military prison.

In addition, Puerto Cortez was by now literally bristling with machine guns, the banana wharf was jammed with soldiers, there were soldiers on the housetops and behind barricades in the streets all over town. In short, any attempt to land a force would result in its annihilation.

All things considered, it was crushing news. However, even a man of Lee Christmas' unstable and hasty temper knew better than to waste time now, for, with their plans disclosed, not only had the revolution itself collapsed, but they were all in real and immediate personal peril. They had force and weapons enough to capture by surprise a single town, gather recruits there, capture another town, gather more recruits, and so, growing as they went along, ultimately to take the country. But they were in no sense equipped to fight a war as they stood, nor even to defend themselves against an adequately prepared and organized opposition force. So the *Emma's* noisy gasoline engine was started — there was more need for haste now than for silence — and the one-time Mississippi oyster lugger towed the *Britannic* and the *Centinella* away from shore, straight out into the ocean, until a brisk and favorable breeze was encountered.

There the vessels separated, after an agreement to meet on the coast near Tela the following night, in order to get word to or from General Moncada and, if possible, devise a new combined land-and-sea attack. The *Emma's* motor swiftly chugged her out of sight in the warm tropic night. The *Britannic* and the *Centinella* hoisted sail — an interesting maneuver aboard the latter, whose master, owner and navigator, Woods, commanded a crew consisting of his young son. The boy was stone blind, but knew the position of every cleat, sheet, and halyard on the vessel as accurately as if he had possessed the full use of his eyes. Naturally, the fact that the hoisting of sail was taking place in the dead of a moonless night was no handicap to him. Thus the *Centinella's* sails were the first to fill, and she began to forge off into the night.

But not for long. Misfortune had not yet begun to play out her hand with the Bonilla squadron. In less than five minutes the wind left them. There, where they would be in plain view from shore at dawn — and the swift tropic dawn was now perilously hard upon them — they lay, flat becalmed and helpless. Worse than helpless, as a matter of fact; for the tide carried them gently ever closer to shore, where capture and swift extinction awaited them. Woods, nearly frantic, sent his blind *hijo* out to the bowsprit's end to whistle for wind, but without avail.

The dawn slid over the world's eastern rim, and showed the gentle rise and fall of the lazy ground-swell, but nowhere on the polished surface the dark ruffle of wind. Everybody but Woods' blind son was gazing anxiously toward the southern horizon, where the shore-line, against a dimly blue-green background of mountains, met the glassy sea. Guy Molony had a pair of prism binoculars he had picked up somewhere in his military career. He focused these upon the cut where the harbor slashed inland between Cortez and Omóa. Almost at once he picked up a smudge of smoke across the shifting opalescence of the water.

" General, there's a ship coming out of the harbor," he said.

Lee Christmas was not slow to show his interest — and concern.

" Banana boat? Or what? " he demanded.

" I can't tell. All I can see is the smoke."

From the leather case at his belt Christmas took a fine pair of German binoculars and brought them to bear on the sooty smudge at the harbor mouth. Then he snapped his glasses down, put them away very carefully, and turned toward his men.

" Everybody below," he ordered harshly. As this command was being obeyed, he turned toward Molony and bade him remain on deck. *"Tatumbla!"* he remarked casually, as though that explained everything.

"Yes sir," agreed Molony dutifully, " and — er — what is a tatumbla?"

" The *Tatumbla's* just the navy of Honduras, that's all. She's a god-damned gunboat."

" One of those converted things?"

" No such luck. Made in Germany and mounts two 42 millimetre guns — one forward and one in back, and each one in a lousy excuse for a damn turret. Anyway, those turrets are enough to protect 'em absolute from rifle and machine gun fire."

" Built out of wood?"

" Hell, no! Steel!"

" Steel, huh? Well — I reckon we swim, General."

Christmas stared for a moment at the youngster who held a captain's commission in his army, and then pompously, after the fashion of a stage gold-striper, with broadly burlesqued dignity, tugged his whipcord jacket straight, and replied:

" Undoubtedly, Captain. Oh, undoubtedly, sir!"

They looked at each other and chuckled — that pair who had met two nights before on the white sands of a Caribbean coral reef. Soldiers? Yes, of course. But this was no longer a war. It was now and henceforth a strictly personal adventure.

By this time the clumsy *Tatumbla* * — her best speed in those days was only some six knots an hour, and under almost any kind of wind the *Centinella* could have run off and hidden from her — had come within what her commander evidently believed to be effective range. A slow semi-circle brought her bow-on; there was a puff of smoke from her forward turret. Much later came the shock of the detonation. Later still the harsh rumble of the slow-velocity shell's leisurely approach.

" Christ, what shooting! They ought to kill that louse.

---

* Riding by rail from the town of Puerto Cortez to San Pedro Sula, you may still see today what is left of the *Tatumbla* — two spars projecting above the placid water of the Chamelecon river, where she sank, some years ago, not far from Laguna trestle.

Wouldn't you like to be on there and show 'em how to handle that cannon?" Thus Lee Christmas.

The *Tatumbla* lumbered about and let go the stern gun. Once more the thudding boom. Once more the *adagio* rumble of the approaching shell.

"Wouldn't you think the bastard would at least try to land his shells in the same ocean we're in?" fumed Christmas.

"He'll get closer directly," Molony prophesied. "He's got no more to worry about than if he was out target practising. We can't hurt him."

"You don't savvy these lads like I do, Molony. Bet you a good hat when we get to Teguce—because we're going there; this thing ain't played out yet by a hell of a ways!—that he kicks out a dozen more shells and then quits."

"Boom!"

"Hr-r-r-rsh-sh-sh-sh-sh-shoo-oo-ooo-ooooouhhhh!"

Christmas, Molony, and Woods could see that the approaching shell was, as the General had pointed out, not even falling in the same ocean with the *Centinella,* but there was one among those present who had no way of knowing this, and with the next shot there came a sudden discordant squeak in the plaintive whistle from the sloop's bowsprit. Christmas looked forward, and saw the blind boy's face fish-white with terror. Far more plainly than the others could the blind boy hear the lazy drone of those slow shells. Each one brought to his sightless imagination the picture of being blown into the sea. Swift rage darkened Christmas' ruddy countenance as he turned toward Woods.

"You no-good, lousy, worthless son of . . ." he began. Then, realizing the inadequacies of Anglo-Saxon, he switched to fluent Spanish, and told the *Centinella's* master with unbelievable elaboration what he thought of him for bringing the lad on such an expedition. "And if we do get hit, you start saying your prayers," he concluded, "because I'm going to make it my business to drown you, if it's the last act."

A queer mixture of sentimentality and impishness, this Christmas. No sooner had he in some degree reassured the blind *muchacho* who was still loyally whistling for wind, than he gave heed to the anxious clamor of the men who, by his own order, were forced to remain below, where they too were the same as blind in so far as the bombardment was concerned. They could hear the thud of the firing, and the harsh rasp of the approaching shells. But they could see nothing that would have allayed their anxiety. Incidentally, among those men Christmas suspected the presence of a Dávilista spy.

"How close was that one? Are they coming near? Where'd that one go?"

A dozen questions clamored confusedly up from the hatch down which the men had tumbled a few minutes before. Christmas turned to Molony and winked.

"Passed a couple of feet astern," he called back anxiously.

"Boom! Hr-r-r-r-rooo-oo-ooooouhhhhhhhh!"

"That one nipped through a corner of the sail," Christmas told the men below. "Looks like he's getting closer."

There was a dismal howl from the man Christmas suspected of being a spy. For his benefit, the commander-in-chief of the revolutionary army went on to describe the shells as carrying away part of the rigging or whizzing just across the bow, or splashing water on the deck, until the *Tatumbla* — who had either run out of ammunition or else feared to come close enough to bring her guns into effective range — turned tail and steamed back to Puerto Cortez.

All day they lay there, waiting and whistling for wind. Toward dusk, the *Emma,* with Bonilla still in command, reappeared. The scrubby little oyster lugger from the Mississippi coast must have been a welcome sight. Deftly she took the *Centinella* in tow, cruised on and picked up the *Britannic* in the same fashion, and then hauled them farther out to sea.

At the same time the rendezvous for that night was changed from the Honduras coast to Glover's Reef, for, during the course of the day, Bonilla had at last received word from Moncada; the same General Moncada to whom the luckless Carib boatmen had smuggled rifles and ammunition. Moncada had been attacked by a force of some 600 Dávila soldiers. With his 200 men, only half of whom were armed with modern rifles, he held off the enemy for an entire day, at the end of which time his ammunition was exhausted, his son had been killed by his side, and he ordered his troops to disperse and retreat, breaking through the enemy lines individually as best they might. Coupled with the Marín fiasco in Puerto Cortez, this meant that Bonilla now had no organized land force whatever to co-operate with any invasion he might make against the coast towns from the sea. The revolution would therefore have to be abandoned for the time; a council would be held at Glover's Reef to decide a definite course of action.

Having once more towed the two sailboats out of sight of land, the *Emma* cast them adrift. Woods was a skilled mariner, but the day's hectic events had evidently addled his sense of direction. Head winds made it necessary to do considerable tacking. When the dawn once more revealed the Hispano-American scene, the *Centinella* was back in full sight of Puerto Cortez, at almost identically the same point from which she had been rescued by the *Emma* at dusk the night before.

This was, as may be imagined, a complete bellyful for *Sr. don* Lee Christmas, *General en Jefe,* but after popping the safety-valve with a blast of profanity that must have crisped the very hemp fibers of the sheets, he turned to Molony.

" Know what we're going to do now? " he demanded.

" No sir," replied Molony with absolute accuracy.

Christmas drew himself up in vast dignity, until he became once more the ultra-pompous, gold-lace general of fiction.

" Captain," he boomed, "we are going to capture an island and get something to eat. Make ready, sir! "

" Yes sir," said Captain Guy Molony.

That is how the expedition came to —

Utila

THE " eastern " coast of Honduras — that is, the Atlantic coast — is in reality the northern boundary. Out in the ocean, just off the central part of this northern shore, are three large islands, the so-called Bay Islands. English is spoken there more frequently than Spanish, for they were British possessions until they were ceded back to Honduras under the terms of the Hay-Pauncefote treaty. Many of the island towns still bear English names — Coxin's Hole, French Harbor, Oak Ridge, Red Bluff, Dixon's Cove.

Roatan is the largest of these islands, with three tiny satellites — Barbareta, Elena and Morat — clustered in the sea just beyond. Guanaja (or Bonaco) is the next in size and is the farthest east. Utila is the smallest and the closest inshore. It has but a single town, the village of Utila, with a garrison in which, at that time, there were stationed a *teniente* and six men. This was the island and garrison which Lee Christmas proposed to capture, in part because he was tired of the aimless wandering of the *Centinella* and in part as an expression of impish reaction from the sudden debacle of the great coup to which he and Manuel Bonilla had looked forward through four long years of virtual exile.

Freed from further responsibilities and duties in a war in which he was commander-in-chief of one of the contending armies, Lee Christmas now proposed to enjoy himself in his own way.

94

"We'll get news in Utila, too," he prophesied. "The whole place is just a boatman's village, and they all talk English. Nice people, the bunch that lives there; but I understand the *comandante* is all louse. I hope so. I'd like a good excuse to take a crack at somebody in this damn war, anyway. They'll know all about us and who we are, because they take those toothpick *cayucos* across the ocean to the mainland every day, and back again, just like nothing. I been over there a couple of times, when I was *comandante* at Cortez. If we can only get into that harbor after dark, we'll have the island in no time."

Night had fallen when they slipped into the little harbor at the island's southeastern extremity, with the awkward old *Centinella*. Christmas concealed his thirty men about the deck and behind the sloop's rail, so that, to a casual inspection, the vessel looked deserted. Then Woods was ordered to let the anchor chain go with a crash. The rattle brought immediate results.

Utila's entire garrison — six men and the *comandante* — set off from shore in a rowboat to make official inquiries. The commander sat pompously in the stern of his skiff, while his six *soldados* pulled him out to the *Centinella,* which he believed to be an unusually bold or an unusually ignorant smuggler.

As the skiff swept alongside, the *comandante* rose, but that was as far as he ever got. Among Christmas' men was a giant named Enrique, and it was opposite Enrique's place by the rail that the little officer arose, in all his dignity. Two hairy arms came over the rail. Two huge fists got a hearty grip on the epauletted shoulders. Steadily, without visible effort on his part, the *comandante de armas* of the garrison at Utila rose into the air and slowly floated to the *Centinella's* deck.

"Inform your men that they are prisoners and the island of Utila is captured," Christmas barked at him menacingly. "Get on, you. I'm Lee Christmas and I'm in charge now."

The *buja* that followed was brief and to the point, and at its conclusion the captives quite amiably rowed their captors ashore in relays. Sleep and fresh food were the first requisites, and both were made available by the hospitable islanders. So securely did the invaders believe themselves sheltered, that only the most nominal sort of guard was posted.

The next morning the revolutionists enjoyed an impromptu holiday. They were showered with hospitality by a kindly folk, many of whom had met Christmas before and all of whom knew of the big " *Chele's* " * high and valorous repute. Fresh cocoanuts were sent out to the *Centinella,* and fresh avocados and melons and papayas and oranges in boatloads, while the revolutionists, temporarily relieved of the cares and responsibilities of revoluting, lounged about the shaded doorways, drank cool beer, flirted with the pretty girls and behaved pretty much as soldiers on furlough or in rest camp behave the world over, whether they be members of a crack Prussian regiment, barefoot Latin-American *revolucionarios,* or units in the Punkin Center company of the state militia.

By mid-forenoon, Christmas' prophecy that at Utila they would receive news was fulfilled. A Carib boat arrived from the mainland, and the revolutionists learned with real alarm that in stowing rifles and ammunition aboard their sloops at Glover's Reef, they had made an error — just such an error as had cost two luckless Caribs their lives on the beach near Tela. All the empty rifle boxes and ammunition cases had been left on the white strand in the hurry of departure. Glover's Reef was a part of British Honduras, and His Majesty's battle cruiser, *Brilliant,* was even now searching the seas with a warrant for the immediate arrest of all who had so flagrantly violated the neutrality of British soil by using it as a base for a military expedition against a friendly nation.

The news took a good deal of the spirit out of Lee Christmas. It was a sort of last straw in the way of the ill fortune that had

---

* " *Chele* " was the nickname by which Christmas was widely known among his Hispano-American intimates, and the term was not a reference to the fieriness of his temper. " *Chele* " means red, and its application to a person of Christmas' florid and ruddy type is obvious.

dogged his venture with Bonilla from the outset. Besides, having received no word of *don* Manuel from any of the arriving boatmen, he became convinced that the *Emma* — none too seaworthy at best — had been driven out into the ocean and had foundered; or that Bonilla, seeking to evade the *Brilliant,* had been forced ashore, captured by the Davilistas, and shot.

He summoned his men and hurriedly outlined the situation. "What I want to do," he concluded, "is take a little *paseo* up and down the coast and find out if the old man's been captured. If he has, it'll be up to us to rescue him. If not, we'll enjoy the ride. How about it?"

They were all with him, of course, and so the revolutionless revolutionists went once more a-sailing. Christmas was profanely explicit in his declaration that he hated to set foot aboard the *Centinella* again, insisting that she was the hoodoo who had cast a blight on the expedition. But to guard against contingencies, he ordered a machine gun mounted in the stern, so that if the need arose, there could be a cover of fire for a landing party. As a concession to the demands of theoretical tactics, he even had two sandbags filled, to flank the weapon as protection for the gunner.

Then they pulled slowly out of the harbor, and, under the prevailing offshore breeze, tacked south toward the mainland, until they stood some eight hundred yards off the beach, when they cruised leisurely toward Trujillo. It was as they neared the coast town of Balfate that the fun began. There, on the strand, was drawn up a Davilist force of nearly four hundred men. The *Centinella* was well known along the coast, of course, and the officers on shore had identified her immediately. A Carib *cayuco* with a native paddler was dispatched out to the sloop, bearing a note addressed to Lee Christmas, and signed by Pedro Díaz, general commanding. The message was a curt invitation to come ashore and be captured.

This tickled Lee Christmas and so roused the imp in him that he laughed aloud and announced there would now be a picnic for all hands. To Pedro Díaz, commanding general of the government force in the field at Balfate, he scribbled a Spanish note by way of reply, inviting the Dávilists out to the *Centinella* for a battle to a decision.

Pedro Díaz, commanding general and so forth, sent back a note whose tenor was unmistakably insulting. However, at that game, Lee Christmas was more than a match for him. Moreover, Pedro Díaz was short of stature and monstrously fat — a feature which was not overlooked in the note Christmas sent back, as the *Centinella* sailed on down the coast, slowly enough, but at a pace that was anything but leisurely for a soldier carrying a rifle and ammunition bandoliers, when he was foot-slogging under a broiling sun on the uncertain going of soft sand. Yet that sort of foot-slogging was precisely the only thing for General Pedro Díaz, commanding, and his four hundred commandees, to do, if they wanted to keep up with their supposed quarry.

As they were now sailing under a quartering breeze, which eliminated the necessity for tacking, Christmas ordered awnings spread over the decks. Lolling comfortably in the shade, the revolutionists were wafted along on their excursion, and the soldiers of the constitutional government of Honduras cursed volubly and earnestly as they plowed through the blistering sand in pursuit. Frequently the " fleeing " revolutionists would open ripe cocoanuts, and would line up at the rail, in full view of their pursuers, to sip the cool, sweet juice. In this formation, eight hundred yards off shore, they came to the coast town of Nueva Armenia.

Christmas arose, stretched, and yawned ostentatiously.

" Been a nice ride, hasn't it? " he made comment to Molony. " Let's turn around and go back."

With a slatting of mainsail and jib, the clumsy sloop came about and in just as leisurely a fashion started back up the coast. When the soldiers of General Pedro Díaz saw this, they gave voice to one unanimous bellow of rage, and, as though on a signal, every soldier on shore who had a gun raised it and fired in the general direction of the *Centinella.*

"Give 'm a little taste of the machine gun, Guy," suggested General Christmas placidly. The offshore fusillade had done no damage whatever. But it had been enough for the *Centinella's* master, owner, and navigator. With a yell of fright, the worthy Woods hit the deck, and was presently lying under the tiller, flat on his back, with his arms upraised to steer.

Molony ordered the man to get up, as he was lying just where space was needed to work the machine gun that had been mounted in the stern, but Woods declared emphatically that he proposed to stay right where and as he was. Having absorbed some of Christmas' impish humor by direct contagion, Molony remounted his gun, setting it carefully so that the stream of red-hot empty shells from the ejector should fall as nearly as possible on Woods' upturned countenance. Then he loosed a practice burst; short, for you could see the line of spray. He elevated the muzzle a trifle, and noted that he was long, for there was no spurt on the white beach sand. He closed the bracket delicately. The sand sprang up in swift and tiny jets. An instant later the beach was deserted. The government soldiers had melted into the bush where they were invisible.

Molony fired the rest of the belt, partly because that was one way to relieve the general tedium and partly to observe with undisguised pleasure the behavior of the prostrate Woods as that stream of hot empties cascaded from the ejecting mechanism down upon the doughty navigator's features. At nightfall the sloop came to anchor in a concealed channel between two of the tiny islands of the Cochinos group, and at dawn the next morning repaired once more to Utila.

There, at good last, better tidings awaited them. Manuel Bonilla was safe. He and the *Emma* were at Manabique point, on Cabo Tres Puntas — a triangular island in the bay of Puerto Barrios in Guatemala. Waiting only until darkness had once more cloaked the sea, the *Centinella* sailed direct for Manabique, where an immediate council of war was held. The facts seemed to be fairly obvious.

First, the entire coast of Honduras was alarmed and under vigilant guard. A surprise attack was now out of the question. Second, the *Brilliant*, searching for violators of the neutrality of the soil of Great Britain, was added to their troubles. Third, they had no boat capable of coping successfully with the steel-clad *Tatumbla*. Inevitably the revolution must be abandoned, at least for the present. Then came the master stroke!

They would surrender to the government of Guatemala, and be interned under technical arrest by the more than friendly President Manuel Estrada Cabrera.*

What of the arms and munitions?

"That, *mis amigos,* has already arranged itself," triumphantly reported Manuel Bonilla. "Here are the boxes to be shipped to Guatemala City, where they will be deposited in the *cuartel.*"

"But we're going to need them again, aren't we?"

"Ah yes. True. But the boxes must be shipped. It is necessary to fill them with sand and shells, of course, so that they shall be of a requisite heaviness. The real *elementos* go to our friends in Livingston. Thus, when we return, we will be able to get them right there —" he pointed across the bay to Livingston light "— and as for the boxes, why Estrada may keep them, *¿no es verdad?* "

There was an appreciative chuckle. The boxes were forthwith filled with clean sand, and nailed shut, ready for shipment. Then Manuel Bonilla did one of the gracious things which so endeared him to the hearts of his followers, and held them to him by such unbreakable bonds of loyalty. His revolution was a wash-out. After years of preparation he had not even had the fun of a big show; if there were to be another revo-

* It is amusing, at this date, to examine the press dispatches relative to the "arrest" of Bonilla and Christmas by the authorities of Guatemala, and the difficulties which were overcome in effecting this "capture." What the harassed Dávila administration thought is quoted in a succeeding chapter.

lution, every penny that he could rake and scrape together would be needed to finance it. The three thousand dollars that he had left would be all but indispensable as the nucleus for any come-back he might plan to stage. But with that three thousand dollars Manuel Bonilla there, at night, on the sands of Manabique Point, paid off all hands and the cook. Molony, with his share, would catch the boat at Barrios in a day or two — the same *Cartago,* incidentally, aboard which he had left New Orleans as a hardware drummer. Dawn was breaking when the payroll line was finished.

"Well, my friends, is there any suggestion as to what we shall do next?" inquired *don* Manuel.

"Yes," spoke up Lee Christmas, who had just lost the first army he had ever commanded. "I'm dirty as a pig. Let's all take a swim."

And they did. The revolution of 1910 was over. But they were already planning another, which was in all truth destined to have a sting to it. Most of the preparations fittingly centered, therefore, about —

The Hornet

THE financial backer of the abortive revolution of 1910 was apparently no whit discouraged by the reverses which had brought forth that enterprise stillborn. Manuel Bonilla experienced little difficulty in securing the funds he needed for the new venture. Of course, since he already had the arms and munitions in store, another revolution would not have made its financial demands so exacting save for one thing, and on that point *don* Manuel was adamant. Before he and his forces moved another foot in the direction of Tegucigalpa, they had to have a boat; no decrepit oyster lugger with a gasoline engine whose symptoms the veriest layman could diagnose as tubercular, but a vessel which, while not necessarily capable of coping with the *Tatumbla* in a pitched battle, could at least show that ancient ironclad a clean stern any time the occasion for it arose. The American capitalist to whom this fiat was conveyed, agreed, for there was available, by chance, at that particular time, a craft which seemed veritably to have been made for their purpose — the *Hornet*.

This vessel was built in 1890, for Henry M. Flagler, and was rated at the then dazzling speed of 16 knots or better per hour. She was taken over by the United States government for the Spanish-American war, and became a unit of the " mosquito fleet " at which time a belt of two-inch armor plate was placed about her engine room. In July 1910, she was brought to New Orleans and sold there to Joseph W. Beer for $10,000, represented by two notes for $5000 each. At this point she properly

enters the chronicle of Lee Christmas, for by that time both
he and Manuel Bonilla were in New Orleans, on presumably
lawful occasions, one of which was the supervision of the work
of refitting the *Hornet.**
That the presence of Christmas and Bonilla in New Orleans
was not too lightly regarded in certain high quarters, may be
inferred from the fact that not only they, but the *Hornet* as
well, were under constant surveillance by comparatively secret
agents of the United States government. What President
Dávila thought of the situation may be learned, without in-
ferences, at first hand, for he stated his views fully to the Congress of Honduras in his annual message on January 1, when
he touched on the ill-starred *maquinaciones* of *don* Manuel in
the following terms:

"General Bonilla sought asylum in Guatemala, whence he later
went to the city of New Orleans. During his stay in Belize he
constantly menaced the public tranquillity of Honduras, and he now
seeks to do the same from that American city." †

President Dávila's message was, of course, written some days
before it was delivered. On the very day the Congress of Honduras heard their president's sentiments thus expressed, Bonilla
and Christmas gained their first foothold in the country, so
that Dr. Dávila's suspicions anent the constant "menace to
the public tranquillity of the land" were only too well founded.

* An excellent detailed history of the *Hornet*, from the time of her construction, through her war career, and up to her seizure in 1911, appeared in the *New
York Herald* of Sunday, January 29, 1911. Following her "capture" by American
naval authorities during that month, she was sold by the government, and is at
present reported to be engaged in towing crude-oil barges from Mexico to refinery
ports in the United States.

† "*El General Bonilla buscó asilo en Guatemala, de donde posteriormente salió
para la ciudad New Orleans. Durante su permanencia en Belice amenazó constante-
mente la tranquilidad pública de Honduras, y lo mismo pretende hacer ahora desde
aquella ciudad americana.*" From the *Mensaje dirigido al Soberano Congreso-
Nacional en sus sesiones ordinarias de 1911 por el Dr. don Miguel R. Dávila,
Presidente de la República de Honduras.* Printed in pamphlet form in 1911, by the
Tipografía Nacional, Tegucigalpa. A copy of this pamphlet is included in the collection of the library of the Department of Middle American Research of Tulane
University.

However, at that time President Dávila still cherished hopes of North American intervention against the revolutionists by way of what became the famous Paredes-Knox " dollar diplomacy " treaty — a document which evoked merely caustic comment in the anti-administration press of the United States, but was brewing sheer riot and insurrection from the *Costa Norte* to Amapala throughout Honduras.

The intensity of the bitterness that swept Honduras goes back half a century. The construction of the government railroad was financed by three bond issues sold in Paris and London in the years 1867, 1869, and 1870, the bonds being secured by a mortgage on the forests of Honduras — scarcely the sort of collateral to be classed as liquid assets. The funds had fallen short by far of making possible the completion of the projected interoceanic line. The sixty miles which were constructed could not begin to produce revenues adequate to retire the loans. Even the interest payments had lapsed by the time of the century's turn. The foreign debt of Honduras was, in consequence, staggering — somewhere between $12,000,000 and $30,000,000; the exact figures are of little moment.

This was during the Taft administration, in the United States, and the era of " dollar diplomacy." Briefly stated, the United States was offering the Latin-American republics an opportunity to consolidate their foreign debts, through new loans to be made by American investment houses, which new loans were to be consummated under treaties by the terms of which the United States would have the right to place its own accredited fiscal agents in the customs houses of the borrowing republics. These fiscal agents would turn over to the leading institutions, out of the customs revenues, payments sufficient to meet the interest and retire the principal of the new loans, and would thus unquestionably stabilize the public fisc of the borrowing nation. A treaty of that sort had already been concluded with Santo Domingo, and had worked a notable success, it being openly said in the United States that the balance of customs revenues turned over to the local government by the American fiscal agents, even after deducting the loan-payments, was greater than the grand total which corrupt officials had previously permitted to trickle through to the national treasury. Similar negotiations were even then pending between the United States and Nicaragua, and in the summer of 1910, following the collapse of the Bonilla-Christmas revolution, President Dávila sent Dr. Juan E. Parcedes to Washington as plenipotentiary for Honduras, to consummate one of these same treaties on behalf of his country.

Anti-administration papers in the United States began to froth at the type fonts and "view with alarm." Obviously here was just the sort of material to bring glad, eager cries to the lips of the exponents of what was then still a comparatively new profession — muckraking. How could the government of the United States be so abjectly servile to the Money Power as to place the governmental machinery, backed by the lives of soldiers and sailors, in the position of guaranteeing loans made by private bankers? Why not amend the constitution to give the House of Morgan the right to declare war, and be done with it? What did it all amount to but a cold proposal to sacrifice our brave boys in blue in order to swell the already bloated Morgan coffers?

Others, of course, saw in all this a step toward the preservation of peace, rather than a likelihood of jeopardizing international relations. Most of the Hispano-American bonds were held by French and British interests, and the attempts by foreign governments to enforce the collection of such debts was rather more than likely to involve questions affecting the Monroe Doctrine.

It is quite possible that in sponsoring such a pact with the United States, President Dávila was actuated solely by a conviction that therein lay the financial salvation of Honduras. But the very conch shells along the shore knew that once the United States had affixed its seal to a covenant of that sort with the Dávila administration, no revolution would be permitted to overthrow the workings of the treaty, which meant that Manuel Bonilla and Lee Christmas, and the American financier who was backing them, could kiss their proposed campaign a tender but very definite farewell. Undoubtedly this motivated Dr. Dávila in trying to force upon Honduras a treaty which embodied the very essence of civil war. The focus of that resentment was the provision of the proposal whereby the government of Honduras pledged itself to name a general customs administrator *from a list of names which had been submitted by the lending agency (Morgan and Co.) and which had further been approved by the president of the United States.*

"National autonomy is in dire peril . . . Honduras will have to ask the permission of a foreign country before daring to appoint an official to conduct her own financial affairs . . . we would have to cede our independence to *yanqui* gold lust." The Latin-American would far more cheerfully starve in independence than feed himself fat at any table that smacked however remotely of vassalage. And — be the reason what it might — there were suspicions abroad to the effect that no foreign banking institution offering such a loan was actuated by motives of unalloyed altruism.

Dávila, who had risen to the presidency as a "compromise candidate" rather than an overwhelmingly popular choice, had hitherto merely failed to win general esteem. But he became definitely and desperately unpopular now, what with the national bitterness against the treaty which he was sponsoring, because its enactment would secure him against the rising tide of Bonilla sentiment and the inevitable revolution.

Bitterness? José María Valladares — publisher, fighter, and ever-ready insurgent — had been made *comandante* at Amapala, after poor mad Sierra had left that fortress to proclaim himself president. Valladares had earned the appointment by leading the army which routed Sierra's revolt on that occasion. His state of mind, regarding the "*infame traición*" which Dr. Dávila was trying to bring about, bordered on the rabid. In giving vent to the utter blackness of his disapproval of the loan treaty, he overstepped what even Latin America might regard as the proper bounds to political procedure.

In the fortress at Amapala, he picked up a yellow dog. He bought for the animal a collar and leash, led him forth into the streets of the city and there publicly named him "Taft." The press got hold of it, of course. The story was cabled to the United States, and its publication there was followed by a swiftly rising mutter of resentment. That was early in October 1910.

Dávila, frantic lest his careful plans for placing the entire United States as a bulwark between himself and Bonilla's inevitable "menace to public tranquillity" be given to the winds by a subordinate's maladroit truculence, demanded an immediate public apology from José María Valladares, and when this was not forthcoming, summoned the offender to the capital and relieved him of his position. With rather statesmanlike tact, Dávila made no reference at all on this occasion to the dog incident, but based his dismissal of the *comandante* on "offenses of word and deed against the French subject, G. Schang." Valladares was ordered back to Amapala with instructions to turn over the *comandancia* there to Coronel Baltasar Alegría. Instead of complying, *don* José María called out the military force of the garrison, proclaimed himself President of Honduras and went into active rebellion.

As revolutions go, the latest Valladares uprising was nothing to deepen the frontal furrows of any governmental brow. He had made no provision either to feed or to pay his soldiers, and these had no academic interest whatever in their Editor-Commander's views on international fiscal relations. The revolt was declared on October 20, 1910. In the next annual message of President Dávila — the same one to which reference has just been made in another connection — appears this report of the incident:

> Fortunately this abnormal condition endured only twelve days, and terminated without the shedding of blood. The troops abandoned the rebel, who had to submit himself to the forces of the government.

Not wishing to inflict the death penalty, Dávila exiled José Mariá Valladares, who went to El Salvador, and then to Costa Rica, where he later inscribed two fiery pamphlets in which he classed both Dávila and Bonilla as infamous traitors who were selling poor Honduras down the river to the *yanquis*.

Such fagots of internal unrest kept the home fires burning in Honduras through all the late fall of 1910. Meanwhile two missions from the Land-of-Deeps were being prosecuted in the United States at the moment. One was being conducted by Dr. Juan E. Paredes with Secretary Knox in Washington. The other was being less publicly handled in New Orleans by the *Señores* Bonilla and Christmas, and because of the manner in which the information has come to hand, this chronicle is not at liberty to set down the names of any of their associates.

No hanger-on in barrooms, but a lordly patron therein, was Lee Christmas on his return to the scene of his first efforts to carve a be-it-never-so-humble place for himself on a public payroll. For now Lee Christmas was in funds, as all who cared to come from the old Third Ward to let him buy them drink might see. Well set up, well groomed, and well heeled — that was Lee Christmas these days.

"You know what they can do with their god damned rules and their color blind now, don't you?" he asked one of the cronies of his railroad days. "Them and their rules! See what the boys'll have on this round. It's on me again."

For Lee Christmas felt that he was now rightfully come into his own. On every hand he was being regarded, not as a bravo

whose limitless courage had catapulted him to mythical renown, but as a great soldier and an imposing figure in vast
affairs of state. He accepted such regard graciously, too, and
expressed his new grandeur-complex in the fashion he best
understood — by the imperial lavishness of his entertainments
in barroom and bordello. It is hardly an occasion for surprise,
therefore, that the new revolution reached its North American
climax at a —

Rendezvous in a Brothel

CAPTAIN GUY MOLONY of the revolutionary armies of Honduras was working as a laborer for the Otis Elevator Company in New Orleans at a wage of two dollars a day in the fall of 1910, when Manuel Bonilla and Lee Christmas came to take over their newly acquired navy, the *Hornet.* That was during the first week of November, while the excitement — such as it was — over the Valladares revolution was at its peak. He was still working there at two dollars a day on December 21, when General Christmas telephoned the Molony home to "tell Guy tonight's the time." The sole interruption in this industrial program had been the half-day which Molony took off from his time-check in order to welcome his president and his commander-in-chief at the dock on their arrival. That day he received but one dollar, sacrificing the other on the altar of Hispano-American patriotism. Christmas grinned when he saw Molony in the crowd on the wharf.

"Get ready, Guy," were his first words. "We're going to hit 'em again. Remember, I told you we was going to."

Bonilla said nothing, but he embraced Molony in true Latin style, much to the amusement of the waterfront loafers. Both Christmas and Bonilla wanted Molony to quit his job at once, and spend the ensuing weeks with them; but for no very clearly definable reason, Molony insisted on remaining on the Otis company's payroll. Bonilla took a private apartment in Royal street, while Christmas lived with friends or what he vaguely described as relatives. Both of them set to work immediately, after their fashion.

Christmas supervised in person the work of refitting the one-time *Alicia,* which had been rechristened in honor of the *Hornet,* victor in the encounter with "*The Wasp*" in the War of 1812. Not only her engine room, but her hull showed sad signs of the passage of the years. While Christmas was thus engaged, *don* Manuel maintained contact with his American financier, and with the *emigrados* of his cause in Nicaragua and Guatemala, not to mention those who were still "conspiring actively" in Honduras. Caution was essential in such communications because, from the time Bonilla and Christmas set foot on the New Orleans riverfront, they were under constant watch. Agents of the secret service trailed them incessantly. Florián Dávadi, who had come up from the tropics with them, and Joseph Beer, the ostensible purchaser of the *Hornet,* were also subjects of unflagging surveillance. For no vessel flying the American flag might engage in landing troops, arms, and munitions in a friendly country by way of invasion.

It was quite a task for any agent or set of agents to keep up with Bonilla and Christmas, particularly at night, when they invariably "sallied" as the Spanish has it. Almost always they headed for what, in those days, was known as The District. The buildings there ranged from mean little one-room hovels to stately mansions where magnificent furnishings had been prodigally scattered. It was to one of the latter that Bonilla and Christmas usually repaired. Sometimes they went alone. Sometimes Molony went with them. Sometimes Beer or Dávadi accompanied them. Always on those expeditions there was much merrymaking of an ostentatious sort, and much deep drinking. It must have been a strain on the secret service agents to watch these apparently aimless revels night after night, and to trail their subjects back to their respective lodgings just before dawn. Those who were assigned to this duty probably had reason to envy the other agents who merely had to watch the *Hornet*.

About the middle of December the refitting of the *Hornet* was completed, and she began to take on cargo. Her bunkers were filled with coal. Her cargo-holds were filled with coal. Sacked coal was finally stowed upon the deck itself. If those loads were searched once as they went inboard, they were searched dozens of times. It was in all good faith that every searcher could swear that nothing but coal, and coal, and more coal had passed from the fuel barges to the *Hornet*.

That was the situation when, under command of Captain Charles Johnson and a crew of eight men, the *Hornet* cleared for Nicaragua on December 20, and dropped down the ninety-and-odd miles of muddy water that meander from New Orleans to the Gulf. Not satisfied, federal agents went downstream with her until she dropped a river pilot at Pilot Town, and took on the bar pilot who would see her beyond the jetties into the open sea. The *Hornet* was not going to tie up to a levee for "repairs" this trip. Still not satisfied, the federal agents stayed aboard until the bar pilot was dropped, some miles beyond the mouth of the passes, and then at last they left. Not one of them but could swear there were no guns, munitions, troops or anything else in the way of military "*elementos*" aboard the *Hornet;* not one of them, however, who wouldn't have taken his Bible oath that over the whole proceeding there hung like a pall the faint but unmistakable odor of fish. That was December 20. It was on the afternoon of December 21 that a telephone message was received from Christmas at the Molony home.

"Tell Guy it's tonight!"

When Molony returned from work that evening, he was given the message by his sister. He took it casually, went to his room, packed a few belongings and wrote out a pencilled order.

"Take this," he told his mother and sister. "It's for eight

Lee Christmas and Guy Molony, in 1922, when the latter was Chief of Police of New Orleans, and Christmas paid his one-time home city a visit while en route to New York from Guatemala.

The *Hornet.*

dollars I've got coming to me at the plant. I won't be here in the morning to collect."

Mrs. Molony and her daughter made no protest. In just such a fashion had this same youngster left for the Transvaal, for the Philippines, for the jungles of Nicaragua, and for Glover's Reef. He joined Christmas at Canal and Royal streets. Bonilla, Dávadi, and Drew Linard, special correspondent of a New Orleans newspaper and a former member of the consular corps, were already there.

"Wait a minute. Let's hang around," directed Lee Christmas in the hoarse growl which passed with him for a whisper. On the Old Town side of Canal street — that thoroughfare which still divides the French and the American cities of New Orleans — they stood before the cigar store that was then the rendezvous of all the Crescent City's sporting element. Finally Christmas spoke once more.

"I see them. They're watching us. Let's go."

He had spotted the government agents who, now that the *Hornet* had dropped on down the river, were redoubling their vigilance. Casually the five strolled back through the crowd on Canal street, past Bourbon, Dauphine, Burgundy, and Rampart to Basin, which formed one boundary of The District. There, at the house where they had spent many an ostentatiously care free evening of revelry during the past weeks, they rang a bell and passed in under the red rays of an overhead lamp.

No sooner had they entered the ornate and mirrored "parlor" than Christmas summoned a young man who had been waiting, and, taking him to a shuttered front window, pointed to a group of three men, passing slowly along the opposite side of the street. The messenger left without further instructions, and then the evening's orgy began. A stranger sought and gained admission shortly thereafter, and him they welcomed too, just as though they had no idea that somewhere about his garments he wore a polished nickled badge.

Bonilla was heavily in funds and, though taking no part in the revels himself, he began to buy champagne lavishly at brothel prices. Christmas drank glass for glass with any one who cared to join him. His copper-and-steel constitution could not be upset by so mild a tipple. Dávadi drank too. The girls drank, as part of their job. Molony, sitting by himself in a corner, soon went to sleep. A casual observer might easily have thought him in a besotted stupor, but it was just a boy's sound sleep. He had been working all that day as a factory laborer.

The real rioting fell to Christmas, Dávadi, and the stranger. The general shouted and laughed and sang and danced and cracked broad, goatish jokes. He was in his element, for such a party was always much to his liking. Incessantly he fed quarters into the tinny mechanical piano of the period. Incessantly he ordered more wine. No one could have guessed what tenseness underlay all this jesting, for this night was to be a test of the value of their weeks of preparation. The previous sowing of wild oats had been carried out with a purpose, and tonight they would discover what the harvest was to be.

Midnight came and passed, and still the picture was unchanged. There was the swart little man who had been President of Honduras and who, in less than a fortnight, would really be President once more. He was sitting in the corner, apparently overwhelmed by the noisy gaiety, but smiling a bit shyly and urging his followers on with a frequent " *Muy alegre, amigos! Muy alegre!*" There was the commander-in-chief of the revolutionary armies, drinking with half a dozen painted and kimono-clad girls, feeding quarters into the insatiable maw of the piano, and dancing like some cornfield roué, come to the Big City for the devil and all of a time. There was Guy Molony, a boy, but veteran of four wars and soon to be a *coronel* in a fifth, later still to hold a colonelcy in the A.E.F., later still to be chief of police of this same city of New Orleans, and now sound asleep, with the healthy, tired sleep of youth, in a corner of the garish, noisy room. And there was the stranger, beginning to look a trifle disgusted and weary, although the fate of the most famous of America's dollar diplomacy treaties was being decided there in the parlor of that bawdyhouse.

Until two-thirty that morning the stranger stuck it out, and until two-thirty Manuel Bonilla sat smiling in his chair, saying "*Muy alegre, amigos!*" now and again; and Lee Christmas jested broadly and danced and drank and laughed, and Guy Molony slept and Florian Dávadi tippled conscientiously and Drew Linard watched, and the girls sang and danced and plied the revelers with ever more and more champagne. Then the "stranger" abruptly took his departure. The merrymaking ceased as though a switch had been thrown, cutting off the current. Christmas quietly stationed himself by the front door and waited. In a moment or two the young man he had sent away upon the party's arrival at the bagnio came hurrying back.

"I'm hiding behind the shutter, Cap, right on the corner where they're waiting," he reported, "and then this bird that was in here comes out just now and says: 'Hell, this is just another one of those drunk parties like they been having every night for I don't know when. I'm getting sick and tired of it. It's a cinch they ain't going nowheres tonight.' So they all hightailed out of there and I come right over to tell you, like you said for me to do."

Christmas returned to the parlor where *don* Manuel was still seated in his corner. Reaching into his pocket for one of his villainous native *puros,* he bit off the end, lighted it thoughtfully, and clasped his large hands behind his back. Gravely he teetered back and forth from heels to toes a few times.

"Well, *compadre,*" he observed pensively, "I've heard about 'em rising from rags to riches, but this here's the first time I've ever heard tell of somebody going from the whore-house to the White House." He mused for a moment in silence upon this intriguing conceit, and then added: "Well, that's how we're bound. Let's get going."

By the time Molony had been awakened and such outstanding scores as had not yet been paid were settled, two automobiles had drawn up in front of the establishment. Out toward the old Spanish Fort, where Bayou St. John debouches into Lake Pontchartrain they sped; the same Spanish Fort where Christmas had spent the afternoon with Mamie Reed on the day of his elopement a quarter of a century before. Somewhere in the darkness at their left were the Ferris wheel and the shooting gallery and the tintype parlor and the old brick gun emplacement that once had commanded the very Lake channels by which the new government of Honduras now planned to reach the Gulf of Mexico. In those days, of course, there were no such things as paved suburban highways; at least, not around New Orleans. The pits and bumps of the rutted road that flanked the bayou's low levee were exaggerated by the level rays of the headlights, and the speed at which the two motor cars negotiated that stretch was not considerate since this was the first automobile ride Christmas or Molony had ever taken. Both of them vowed, when the cars jolted to a stop at the Bayou's mouth, that it would be the last.

Etched by the headlight rays sharply as a cameo against the black water, the voyagers saw moored at a little wooden pier a forty-foot cabin cruiser whose engine was already turning over. Without identifying this vessel, it may be set down that the engineer was the magnate whose private fishing yacht she was; that the navigator was his brother; and that the tall, spare deckhand of the occasion was a multi-millionaire.

Everybody was hurriedly bundled below, and with popping exhaust the yacht headed across Lake Pontchartrain, across the shoals of the Middle Ground where the dawn overtook them, through the tortuous passage of The Rigolets where they ate breakfast and went back to sleep, and east in Mississippi Sound with Grassy Isle and long Cat Island on the right and the Bay of St. Louis and Pass Christian on the left, until they came, by afternoon, off Biloxi which had been the first capital of Louisiana Territory.

As unconcernedly as any other fishing cruiser on pleasure bent, the yacht made her way across the sparkling waters to Ship Island, which screens the Mississippi Sound from the open Gulf at this point; and there, at dusk of December 23, they dropped anchor and a multi-millionaire cooked an excellent supper for the next president of Honduras, for the commander-in-chief of that president's armed forces, and for the boy who, with half a dozen companions, would, one month from that day, storm and take the supposedly impregnable death trench that guarded La Ceiba. They ate, and as they did so, they kept a sharp lookout for any vessel which, in addition to the regulation green and red running lights, would show two white lights from the cross arms of her short signal mast. All that night they waited in vain.

"It's all right. It's all right," the multi-millionaire deckhand assured them when they expressed concern. "She probably saw she could not get here before dawn and she will stay well out of sight of land while the sun is shining. But she'll be here tonight."

So when dawn had silvered the choppy waters of the Sound, the yacht left Ship Island and crossed to the mainland, docking at a private wharf at Pass Christian. The engineer, still clad in the greasy habiliments of his presumable calling, went ashore for provisions. Everybody else stayed snugly below, in the cabin where the time was whiled away with a bout of poker, the gaming table being the top of a case of thirty rifles, and Manuel Bonilla winning all the loose change in the outfit.

As dusk came on again, a raw chill December wind began to churn the waters of the Sound. In the cabin, however, all was warm and snug, and the air was blue and frowsty with the smoke of the *puros* — rank native cigars of pure tobacco — of which Christmas always carried an apparently inexhaustible supply. With the coming of twilight they headed once more across the Sound to the western tip of Ship Island. The rolling and pitching of their little vessel caused them no uneasiness, but all of them felt at least some misgivings on the chances of the *Hornet* keeping her tryst that night. However, these were swiftly dispelled as they rounded the point of the island. Some twelve miles out at sea—a good, safe, legal three marine leagues — they saw the four lights by which the *Hornet* was making both her presence and her identity known.

Sliding greasily up and down the flanks of the long Gulf swells, the cabin cruiser came scraping at last along the *Hornet's* newly painted side. The case of thirty rifles and the ammunition boxes with three thousand rounds, were trans-shipped. No other *elementos* left the United States via the *Hornet* on this occasion.

Manuel Bonilla was shivering in the raw night wind of December, and his multi-millionaire deck-hand took note. Promptly he shed a luxurious overcoat.

"I've shot the roll on you and I might as well shoot the coat too," he observed cheerfully, wrapping the next president of Honduras snugly into the garment's more than ample folds. That was their farewell; just that and a few blithe cries of "Good Luck!" Then, with full speed ahead, the *Hornet* straightened out for the confused seas of Yucatan channel.

The next day, Captain Charles Johnson, master of the *Hornet,* broke out a barrel of bottled beer which had been stowed aboard, and all through the day the *jefes* of the newest government of Spanish Honduras held high wassail by drinking this brew quite solemnly for—even by the calendar—this was

Christmas

JUST before midnight on December 29, 1910, the *Hornet* slipped into the deep channel of Bahia Graciosa. Manuel Bonilla, Lee Christmas, Guy Molony and the others never stepped ashore, for over the *Hornet's* side there swarmed an invasion before ever her engines had lost momentum. Thirty of them, as hard-bitten a crew of seasoned fighters as ever had been assembled in Central America. Not a private in the outfit; no man whose rank was lower than that of captain. But there was scarce a man of the thirty who had not fought before with Bonilla; no man at all who had not been wounded at least once in action.

With the first to swarm overside was little Pedro Gonzales. He had been an officer in the Bonilla army of 1907 when *don* Manuel's forces were wiped out at Namasigüe, one of the few to escape from that slaughter-pen.

With two other youngsters of his own age, he had slipped into the jungle, to make his way across the bush into Guatemala. To cut them off, the victorious Revolutionist-Nicaraguan allies had placed a cordon of men where they could command a bare ridge across which the refugees would have to pass. The three boys approached this deadly barrier at nightfall, and a council of war was called. As senior officer, Mr. Gonzales decided a charge was in order, and so those three youngsters charged the camp, and in the confusion created by their night-time onslaught got quite nicely through, although a bullet nipped the fleshy part of Mr. Gonzales' hip, which was clear gain, for it kept intact his record of never having emerged from a military engagement without at least one wound.

He had complete faith in his invincibility, and it was therefore always necessary, when disposing forces for battle, to put him in the front line, for no matter where he happened to be, he kept on going. Once in a while he was stopped; but he never stopped of his own volition.

A slight, short youngster, probably all of five-foot-six in height, with a beardless face of an almost Japanese cast of feature; at the time of the *Hornet's* arrival he wore a flat-topped blue cloth cap, much like a policeman's,* and this made his countenance seem even more boyish than it was. He worshipped Manuel Bonilla, and his haste to scramble aboard the *Hornet* as she came to anchor in the deep channel that cut into the jungle at Manabique, was actuated by his desire to be the first to embrace his leader. There was small time for ceremonies of welcome, however. Boats had to be dispatched to Livingston across the bay to get the machine guns and the rifles that had been left there that time when sand and shells, in neat ammunition boxes and rifle cases, had been sent to Guatemala City to be solemnly interned in the *cuartel*. Molony fell upon his two machine guns as soon as they arrived, took them down and cleaned them by lantern light, and had them reassembled before morning. One of them was the gun he had repaired on the *Centinella's* deck at the time of his first meeting with Christmas.

They worked through the night, weighing anchor at dawn, after taking in tow the two sailboats that had awaited them. Straight for the open sea they headed. What they needed most, at the moment, was privacy, since they were still flying the American flag. The *Hornet* was under the registry of the

---

* Since the Latin-American military officer is always pictured as a sort of sunburst of gold lace, medals and sashes, it may as well be stressed that Manuel Bonilla never permitted his officers to wear any sort of uniform in the field. " When you are in town, and want to strut before the girls, all right. But when you are in the field — with me — you wear working clothes."

United States, and as long as Dávila held Honduras her registry could not be changed. Not only that, but Bonilla was informed by one of his men at Manabique that a United States cruiser — the *Tacoma* — had been dispatched with the gunboat *Marietta* to Caribbean waters to keep a sharp and suspicious eye out for the doings of the *Hornet.*

It was for this reason that Bonilla had selected the island of Roatan as the initial point of his attack. In the town of Coxin's Hole, which was the capital of Roatan, the governor of the province of the three Bay Islands maintained his headquarters. With these offices of the civil government — not to mention the customs house — in their hands, the revolutionists could make short shrift of changing the *Hornet* from American to Honduranean registry, and thus transforming her from a lawless pirate and filibuster into a legitimate vessel of trade — or war, if need be — under the flag of *don* Manuel's provisional government.

All that day the *Hornet* stood far out to sea, but when dusk slid across the horizon to cloak the Caribbean, she turned toward Roatan and at midnight came to an unobtrusive anchorage in the harbor of Dixon's Cove, around the high headland from Coxin's Hole. As the crow flies, the two places — Dixon's Cove, with a few fishermen's huts, and Coxin's Hole, with the *cuartel,* the *casa de administración pública,* the customs house and other government buildings — are really shoulder to shoulder. By debarking at Dixon's Cove, they could remain invisible, although a short jungle footpath would bring them within striking distance of their objective.

Leaving Manuel Bonilla, Captain Johnson, and a guard detail aboard the *Hornet,* the others went ashore at dawn. Pedro Gonzales, in charge of ten other officers, was sent ahead as an advance guard. Christmas with about ten more — McLaurie among them — came next. Guy Molony brought up the rear with the detail that carried one of the machine guns and its ammunition, and, because of this load, was the slowest on the march. Caution was cast aside. As rapidly as possible they pushed ahead. Within ten minutes Pedro Gonzales sent back word to Christmas that a skirmish party of some twenty-five government soldiers was cóming out of Coxin's Hole toward them. Hard upon the heels of this message there sounded, from up ahead, a burst of rifle fire. Pedro Gonzales, without waiting for re-enforcements, and without so much as troubling to inform General Christmas of his design, had launched a charge upon the skirmishing party and had scattered it. By the time the main body reached the rise from which they had an unobstructed view of Coxin's Hole and the harbor that lay beyond, Gonzales held the position and he and his men had squatted down to smoke. A moment later there was a sullen boom from the cannon at the fort, and Christmas directed his entire force to take cover.

"I know that old gun," he said, "and it's only round shot and they'll never . . ." he broke off, slack-jawed and staring, for the fort was firing not at them, but out to sea where — wonder piled upon wonder! — the fat old *Centinella* was waddling toward the port from the mainland. Christmas began to swear, for the superstitious belief that the *Centinella* was his particular bird of ill omen was deep-rooted in him; but then he broke off to laugh.

"Oh Guy!" he called to Molony, who with his machine gun detail was the last to arrive. "Take a look at this! Remember the time I was kidding and told the boys how the shot was splashing water on the deck? Last summer, I mean, when the *Tatumbla* was cracking down on us? Well, there's the *Centinella,* and I'll be damned if a shot didn't just splash water on her deck for sure enough."

By this time the *Centinella* had come about, and was doing her awkward best to get out of range. Christmas had other things to engross him, too, so he paid the vessel no further heed. Yet when they occupied Coxin's Hole, later in the day, they found the *Centinella* in the harbor, waiting for them with a load of recruits, all eager to join the Bonilla standard.

Christmas and his men were on a crest some eight hundred yards across the valley from the town, beside an abandoned hut built on pilings, three or four feet from the ground. Oddly enough, Pedro Gonzales had awaited them here instead of going right ahead to capture the town with the handful that constituted his advance guard. Christmas placed the machine gun, Molony, and one man to pass ammunition, under the abandoned hut, so that the gun, commanding the approach to the fortress, could cover the advance which he then organized by dividing his men into two groups — one headed by himself and the other by Pedro Gonzales. Knowing the town as he did, Christmas then outlined the routes by which the *cuartel* was to be approached and finally assaulted if it came to street fighting.

At this point in the proceedings there came an interruption in the arrival of Manuel Bonilla in person. He looked over Christmas' preparations disparagingly, ordered the machine gun brought out from beneath the hut and mounted in what seemed to be the most exposed position available, then dragged out from the hovel an old canned-goods box, sat himself down thereon beside the gun, and finally told Christmas that if he proposed to have a battle that morning it would be as well to start. Christmas raged and told the President he would not leave until he — Bonilla — took shelter.

"If you get shot," he argued, "we've had all of our trouble for nothing."

"That is as it may be, *amigo mío,*" replied *don* Manuel placidly, "but I am tired of riding around and I am weary of hiding. There is going to be a battle? Good! I am going to watch it."

To all further arguments, pleas and objurgations he turned a supremely deaf ear, and while the debate was at its height, there came still another interruption — a shout from

Pedro Gonzales who had kept his eyes fixed on Coxin's Hole across the valley. A conspicuously white flag with a considerable escort was leaving the town and coming across to meet the invaders. The emblem of truce was being borne by the *alcalde* himself, and his entourage included the leaders of the civilian population who requested that a man be sent back with them to arrange the terms of surrender! Bonilla immediately commissioned one of his thirty officers to accompany the party back across the valley, and after a parley of about two hours' duration, Coxin's Hole — fortress and all — was turned over unconditionally to the revolutionists.

The citizens of the community took it all quite as a matter of course. Having small fancy for being shot over, they had virtually forced the military authorities to surrender. They realized they had little cause for further apprehension. Bonilla was known for never permitting anything that ever remotely approached looting, and was said, indeed, to have shot with his own hand one of his soldiers who had ravished a girl in a captured town.

The only really disappointed Manuelist of them all was Pedro Gonzales. He had taken part in a bona fide battle — had he not fired upon and routed an enemy skirmish platoon? — and had emerged without so much as a scratch. The long record of which he was so vain was broken at last.

By the time the *Hornet* had been brought around to the harbor at Coxin's Hole, *don* Manuel had already appointed one of his men as *comandante* of the captured garrison, a friendly civilian as *gobernador político* of all the Bay Island department, and a third as collector of customs. No sooner had these appointments been validated, than negotiations were carried into effect to consummate the sale of the *Hornet*. Before leaving New Orleans, Captain Johnson had received from Joseph Beer, the vessel's owner, a formal power of attorney conferring upon him the full agency in the matter of such a sale. This document was now duly produced in the presence of Fernando

P. Cevallos, "chief judge of letters of the Department of the Bay Islands and Notary Public by ministry of the law," and by virtue of this authority the *Hornet* was sold on the spot to Florian Dávadi of Tela, for the sum of $40,000 American, or 100,000 *sols,* the purchase price being represented by a cash payment of one dollar and a mortgage for $39,999 on the *Hornet* herself. Assuming that all parties to the transaction were in the "plain enjoyment of their civil rights," they did "freely and espontaneously" make that sale, with the *señores* Samuel H. Stern, A. J. Ganía, Emeterio Lanza Ramos and Tomás B. McField as witnesses, the latter being a pedagogue by profession and acting as interpreter; for the transaction was consummated both in Spanish and in English because, as the bill of sale puts it, "Mr. Johnson ignores the Spanish language " and — as the bill of sale does *not* put it — it was desired that there be no possible room for doubting the validity of the transfer.*

Whereupon every one connected with the Bonilla expedition breathed a great sigh of relief for, regardless of her previous condition of servitude, the *Hornet* was now the undisputed property of *señor don* Florian Dávadi, and under the registry of Spanish Honduras. Now indeed were those who would henceforth use her naught but honest, hard-working revolutionists, and not *filibusteros* on the high seas.

Over and above that, it might further be borne in mind that the provisional government of *don* Manuel, though not quite two hours old, now had:

(1) a foothold in Honduras; (2) a navy of its own; (3) an army whose thirty officers had nearly a hundred enlisted men at their command. But it was not yet a day's work, for this was December 31, 1910, and General Lee Christmas had just bethought himself that he craved —

---

* The bill of sale became an important piece of evidence two months later when Bonilla, Christmas, Johnson, Beer and Dávadi were all indicted by the federal district court in New Orleans, under charges of having fitted out in America a military expedition against a friendly country. Additional details have been included in Appendix No. VIII.

A New Year's Frolic

THE various appointments, official installations, and other maneuvers took up most of the day, so that it was six o'clock of New Year's Eve when the heads of the new government of Honduras — as just established in the Bay Islands — had time for a breathing spell. Finding himself at length with some leisure on his hands, it occurred to Christmas that, according to the calendar, this was a holiday, an occasion demanding fitting relaxation and amusement. So he strolled along a residence street until he came to the house where he had billeted Molony and McLaurie, and during that walk there came to him an inspiration, which he hurried to share with his friends, whom he found seated on the front gallery of their quarters, smoking contentedly.

"Listen," he burst out, "I've just come down with one hell of a fine idea. I've got a real longing to spend New Year's Eve in Utila. What say if we go over right this minute and capture the joint?"

Molony nodded and put away his pipe.

"All right," he said, and arose to go.

But McLaurie was torn by doubts. He and Christmas were on a more informal footing. They had been fellow engineers in Guatemala. In fact, four years later, when Christmas was to take as his fourth bride the girl he had dandled on his knees as a tot of seven, Ed McLaurie would be best man. So —

"How about the Old Man, Lee?" inquired McLaurie. "Don't you reckon he'll kick at our going off like that?"

" Bet a good hat he doesn't. First place, he just told me I earned a holiday and I could go and do anything I pleased with his blessing. And besides — I was with him this evening when he heard from some folks here that the Dávila crowd have put a regular *hijo de puta* over at Utila for a *comandante.* He's an American — a guy by the name of Jackson that used to work for the fruit company at Tela, and he's been riding the living hell out of those people at Utila because they were decent to us when I and Molony hung out there last July. Got the whole place under martial law, won't let 'em take out their boats half the time, and all like that. And anyway I haven't had any fun in so damn long. . ."

" But Lee, you got to have orders of some kind, to show you ain't just a bandit or something. You got to get the Old Man to give us orders to capture the place, all regular."

" I'll do that, too."

" Well, all right then. Let's go. Who all are you figuring on taking along? "

" You and me and Guy with a machine gun and about seven more. Ten of us ought to be a-plenty. We won't have any trouble there."

" How about transportation? " Molony interposed. " They're so nervous about the *Hornet* I don't reckon they'll let you use her."

" Damn the *Hornet,*" Christmas began. Then he chuckled and the chuckle became a guffaw. " I'll fix that up all right, Guy. I've just come down with another idea, be damned if I haven't. You and Ed be down at the water's edge at seven o'clock. That's about an hour from now. Leave the rest to me. I'll have transportation all right, and it won't be the *Hornet,* either." ·

Discipline was quite naturally left behind when they assembled on the quay an hour later; in fact there was a near-mutiny when the revelers, who were about to embark for the capture of Utila by way of seeing the New Year in properly, discovered that Lee Christmas proposed to make the jaunt in the *Centinella.* Discipline, in fact, was so completely forgotten that they cursed Lee Christmas up hill and down dale, in English, in Spanish, in French, and perhaps in Yiddish and Ro. But the General gave them as good as they sent, and better.

"I'm going to break this miserable old grease-barrel's jinx if it takes a leg," he concluded his remarks. "Git aboard and do your cussin' there. And hurry it up. I aim to have me a pers'nal interview with Governor Jackson."

They "gitted," since they were eager for the lark and had voiced their blasphemies merely *pro forma* as part of the fun. Incidentally, they set sail by virtue and authority of the following official orders, which *don* Manuel had hastily dictated to one of his newly appointed clerks:

Roatan, Dec. 31, 1910

Sr. Lee Christmas, Commander in Chief
of the forces of the North Coast.

Please embark with your forces at nightfall for Utila, where you will encounter a guard of twenty soldiers under Coronel Jackson, and order him to deliver his arms.

If the said Coronel resists, use the force at your command to oblige him to comply, *after exhausting all possible resources to effect a peaceful entry and inform this commandante that his authority over this island has been terminated.* *

Carry on your operations with the utmost orderliness, because the program of this government that we have initiated is to guarantee the peace of the commonwealth.

After taking possession of the said island, appoint a commandant-pro-tem, and other officials, designating such appointees as will be most approved by the local community.

If the local officials have been chosen by the inhabitants with entire freedom, order them to continue to function; but if they are those that have been put into power by the maladministration of Dávila, replace them with persons in whom the citizens have confidence.

* The Italics are mine. — H.B.D.

After you have taken possession of the *cuartel,* send back to me by the Centinella the names of your appointees.

Trusting that all will go as well-ordered as in your previous military operations, I beg to remain your respectful servant

MANUEL BONILLA

Armed with this formal document, they landed at two o'clock in the morning, about half a mile east of the cluster of houses on the hilltop where the *cuartel* of Utila was perched. Christmas threw out an advance guard of three men, and the balance of the party, lugging Guy Molony's machine gun and its ammunition, followed cautiously in the wake of this trio. No lights were showing anywhere in the town, save at the hilltop, where two yellow oil lamps cast a feeble radiation a few feet into the darkness. Between these lamps they could make out the shadow of the lone sentry, pacing his beat before the *cuartel* door.

Then they ran squarely upon their own advance guard, whose members had halted beside the first building they had reached. Signalling the newcomers to extreme caution, they pointed in vivid pantomime to the building — it seemed to be some sort of a warehouse — beside whose corrugated metal wall they stood. From within there came the constant, subdued murmur as of many whispering voices; yet not a ray of light escaped through any chink or crack into the night.

Christmas felt his way along the wall until he came to a door, and then knocked swiftly. The murmur was cut off abruptly by an almost tangible silence. Finally the door was cautiously opened a trifle and a head was poked out into the night. Christmas seized the head like a flash, and a terror-shaken voice inquired in English:

"What is wanted, please?"

"What the hell's going on here — that's what's wanted," Christmas growled hoarsely. He had no desire to arouse the garrison.

"Only a prayer meeting of peaceful folk. Who are you?"

"I'm Lee Christmas. I've landed a force of men here and we're in charge of the island."

"Oh, thank God you have come, sir. Thank God! Our prayers have been answered indeed."

Others inside the building had pushed to the door. There were men and women, boys and girls. Christmas released his grip on the alien head and scratched his own, non-plussed.

"I'll be damned if I get this," he complained. "Why do you have to pray at night, and what's so secret about it?"

"It is the *comandante*, General. He has declared martial law and forbidden all public assemblies, and it has always been our custom to pray the New Year in. We are only the Protestant congregation of Utila."

"I'll be god-damned!" exclaimed Lee Christmas, and he said it in all reverence, too. Then he smacked one big fist into the palm of the other hand and turned to Molony. "Guy, do you remember the lay-out here from last summer?"

"Yes sir," said Molony.

"Do you remember the road that runs a little above the *cuartel*?"

"Yes sir."

"How far do you make it between them?"

"About thirty-five yards, I should judge."

"Good. Now take your machine gun and plant it without getting caught right on that road as close as you can get to the *cuartel*. Prepare your gun for action and then wait for me. Don't shoot, don't smoke and don't talk — none of you." Then he rubbed his hands briskly together and turned to the members of the Protestant congregation of Utila. "Can any of you gentlemen take me up to Mr. Jackson's house and show me where he lives?" he asked softly.

Two or three volunteers stepped forward and Christmas chose one at random, disappearing with him into the night. Molony, with the rest of the detail, crept cautiously up the road, as per directions, mounted the machine gun, and trained it on the *cuartel* door. All unsuspecting, the lone sentry padded back and forth barefoot between the two oil lamps — so near that it seemed the invaders could have reached down and twitched his straw hat from his head. Thus they waited — and waited — and waited — until the nocturnal silence of the new year which brooded over Utila was suddenly rent by an agonizing shriek.

At first that shriek seemed to be a mere succession of amorphous yelps of anguish, but as the sound drew steadily closer to the alert group about the machine gun, words became distinguishable.

"*Viva Bonilla! Viv*.... OUCH!!.. *Viva Bonilla! Viva Bonilla! Vi* ... OUCH!!.. *Viva Bonilla!*" howled a heart-stricken voice.

The sentry, who had been walking slowly back and forth on his post, all but brushing the muzzle of a hostile machine gun at each traverse, stood for an instant in frozen horror while those tortured *Vivas* and *Bonillas* were borne to his ears through the night. Then he dropped his rifle to the stone flags with a clatter and quite literally dived into the *cuartel*.

It was a strange tableau which burst upon the watchers a moment later. First came the *comandante* of Utila, the military governor, if you please, who had placed all that island under martial law. He was in his underclothing, and was being kicked very methodically and very accurately up the hill by General Lee Christmas; and all the while the wretched Dávila governor, under threat of immediate and violent physical disintegration, was being forced to cheer for Bonilla at the top of his voice.

Christmas' party gazed with rapt incredulity upon this pleasing picture, loth to believe that fate could be kind enough to vouchsafe them so splendid a gift from the dawning year. Then they let go all holds and the vast bowl of the night rang to their laughter.

"Stop it!" Christmas finally shouted. "A fine bunch you are! Suppose they make a charge out of that *cuartel*?"

So the laughter was suppressed, after a fashion; but the next time the hapless captive yelled "*Viva Bonilla!*" the troops at the machine gun yelled "*Viva Bonilla!*" with him, until at last, catapulted from the toe of the Christmas boot, the governor scrabbled down a short slope into the arms of the waiting gun crew. Christmas arrived two strides later, seized the figure that looked so plaintive clad only in undershirt and drawers, and fastened a steely grip upon the back of Governor Jackson's neck.

"Now yell it again!" commanded General Lee Christmas.

"*Viva Bonilla!*" bawled the negligé governor. And —

"*Viva Bonilla!*" bawled the officers of the invading revolution.

Then Christmas suddenly recalled that his written instructions from *don* Manuel bade him "exhaust all possible resources to effect a peaceful entry and inform this *comandante* that his authority over this island has been terminated." Without releasing the grip he had clamped on the region of his prisoner's cervical vertebrae, he faced him toward the *cuartel*.

"And now, damn you," he gave order, "go down there and tell them they have surrendered the island to us."

Mr. Jackson was by this time in no mood to debate the point. While walking down the slope to the *cuartel* he was already shouting to his soldiers that they had surrendered. And it was so.

General Christmas hurriedly appointed a new *comandante* on behalf of the revolutionary government, and just as hurriedly formed what was called a small committee on public safety, arming its members with the guns and munitions that had been delivered to him by Mr. Jackson's soldiery. Then he accompanied the ex-governor back to his residence and permitted him to dress. This was at daybreak, and Christmas provisioned his expeditionary force by the simple expedient of

scattering its members among the homes of the grateful citizenry for breakfast; after which he hustled them all, including
Mr. Jackson, back aboard the *Centinella.*

Christmas also amused himself on the return journey by
assuring Jackson, over and over again, that he — Christmas —
had enough influence with Manuel Bonilla to make certain
that Jackson would not be tortured before he was shot; and
don Manuel was in a fine fury, the next morning, when he
heard about it, for of course he set Jackson at liberty immediately.

However, the provisional president had far more serious
matters to engross his attention at the moment. Dávila was
moving heaven and earth to get his treaty signed, and thus
bring himself under the armed protection of the United States
before the revolutionists gained a footing on the mainland;
opponents of the treaty — and their numbers were growing
literally hour by hour — were sending urgent messages to their
champion, *don* Manuel, to make haste so that the negotiations
might be halted.

Across the sea from the Bay Island group lay Trujillo, rich
in the lore of the history of Honduras. There had Columbus
first set foot on the mainland of the Americas. On the dusty
plaza, behind the century-old church, had William Walker
— the Tennessee law student who once sought to unite the
five Central American Republics and make himself master
of them all — been executed. And there at Trujillo was the
issue of dollar diplomacy decided, to the tune of a duet whose
two components were —

Cannon and the Hornet's Whistle

FOR they were busy days that followed the *Centinella's* return from that New Year's frolic in Utila, because that luckless sloop was not the only vessel to make port in Coxin's Hole on January 1. In all the glory of official spick-and-spandom there came also the United States cruiser *Tacoma,* whose commander, Archibald Davis, was rowed ashore in the gleaming gig and demanded proof that the *Hornet* was not engaged in illegal enterprises.

His wishes in this regard were readily gratified. The report, for example, had been that the *Hornet* now mounted two naval guns. It was a simple matter to disprove the story, for all the armament the *Hornet* carried consisted of one machine gun packed in the hold (the other was aboard the *Centinella*), and a few rifles. Under no circumstances could this be construed as transforming her into a vessel of war. As to her registry, there were the papers to prove she had been a Honduranean vessel for at least seventy-two counted hours. But in spite of this patent odor of sanctity, Commander Davis remained at Coxin's Hole with the *Tacoma* to await developments.*

* Ugly rumors about this phase of the activity of the United States were thick in Honduras, and were used freely by anti-administration newspapers at home. The story was that, out of a desire to assist the House of Morgan by consummating the "dollar diplomacy" treaty, the government of the United States was saying to President Dávila, in effect: "Put through the treaty by getting your Congress to ratify it and we will seize the *Hornet* and stop your revolution. If you fail in this, we cannot use you or your administration, and so we will let the revolution proceed." Additional color was lent to this version by the fact that the *Hornet* actually was seized less than a week after Dr. Paredes, on behalf of Honduras, had signed the treaty in Washington — a fact of which the opposition press in the United States made the most.

For a time, this caused the revolutionists little concern, for there was enough to do to keep them well occupied. Women were engaged to make blue denim uniforms, blue-and-white hat bands, cotton *salvagües* for ammunition, and the like. Recruits were being received on every boat from the mainland, and these had to be allotted to newly organized units, armed and equipped. The need for swift action, however, soon made Bonilla impatient of delay. The Dávilists were being given more time to garrison the coast where Bonilla must, of necessity, drive his entering wedge. None,the less, while the *Tacoma* remained at Roatan, the Bonilla forces could make no move. As long as matters maintained their status, the *Tacoma* could find no excuse to seize the *Hornet;* and until a real foothold had been secured on the mainland, the loss of the *Hornet* would be too crippling a blow. As a result, nothing whatever was done by either side from January 2 until January 8, when the *Tacoma* suddenly decided the best thing she could do — apparently her own radio installation was not sufficiently powerful — was to make a flying trip to Ceiba for directions straight from Washington.

The *Tacoma's* smoke was still a faint pastel smudge on the southern horizon, when the *Hornet* left Coxin's Hole, with the sailboats *Centinella* and *Romería* in tow on a bee line for Trujillo. Thirty officers and 150 men constituted the invading force. But they had plenty of blue-and-white hatbands in readiness for recruits. They reached the coast just before dawn. *Don* Manuel wrote in his own proper hand a set of orders for General Lee Christmas to take Trujillo, adding the customary instructions to effect this capture without resorting to force, if possible, but in all events to effect it. There were 75 in the landing party that rowed and waded ashore through the shallows a mile west of the city at five o'clock in the morning of January 9.

President Bonilla remained aboard the *Hornet.* His *jefes* had called a council of war and declared flatly and unanimously that if he went ashore and exposed himself to gunfire as was his wont, they would remain aboard and let him conduct his revolution solo. The little statesman sulked for a time, but finally capitulated when Christmas suggested that before any attack be launched by land, the *Hornet* cruise east in front of the bluff on which Trujillo is perched, in order to draw the fire of the Garrison's only cannon, a Krupp 7.5 with a range of approximately 2000 metres. This would divert attention from the manœuvers of the landing party while they sought and occupied positions from which they could charge and carry the bluffs.

To this end Christmas divided his force into two groups as soon as it was assembled on shore. One group, under Ed McLaurie, was dispatched along the narrow beach to the base of the bluffs in front of the town. The other, led by himself with Molony and Gonzales as aides, cut straight across to the foot of the western bluff. At the base of this 400-foot hill the Cristales river flowed into the sea, and about its mouth were clustered the huts of Cristales village, a Carib fishing settlement. As the land party cautiously made their way, they heard the hoarse blare of the *Hornet's* siren. For a moment they paused in alarm; then they relaxed, grinning. *Don* Manuel was taking no chances of being observed adventitiously. To make certain that the garrison at Trujillo centered its attention on him, he was sounding the whistle to let the world know that the good ship *Hornet* was among those present.

He obtained gratifying results almost immediately. There was a crashing detonation somewhere atop the bluffs, followed by another whistle. As the landing party, under cover of the excitement, made their way unobserved across Cristales ford, a regular toss-and-catch game was played between the Krupp 7.5 and the *Hornet*. The cannon would fire, and *don* Manuel, his own presidential hand on the whistle cord, acknowledged the shot with a derisive blast of the siren.

Thus Christmas' party forded the Cristales without inter-

ruption, and Pedro Gonzales immediately started up the farther slope on the run and quite alone. Christmas knew it
was useless to call him back, so the machine gun was set up
among the Carib huts in the village. By this time the defenders
on the bluff realized what was going on, and there was a burst
of rifle fire from the crest, under cover of which the federals
sought to wheel the Krupp so as to command the western
slope. But Molony had his machine gun ranged, and while
the defenders were still trying desperately to depress the muzzle of their cannon, he loosed his first burst. Two of the Krupp
crew were killed, and a third was wounded. The balance
abandoned the piece and fled back from the edge to the town,
and Christmas with his men swarmed up the slope. Without the loss of a man — save possibly Pedro Gonzales; the Lord
alone knew what had become of him! — they had captured the
enemy artillery which they hastily turned about to face the
town. Molony and his sweating crew lugged up their machine
gun to cover the next advance, from the crest of the bluff to
the *cuartel*. Once everything was set up, they swept in open
order into the city, Christmas in the lead, dodging along walls
to the edge of the plaza, across which they were to charge the
garrison.

But they found the defenses of that stronghold already down,
the gates open, and young Mr. Pedro Gonzales, still quite
alone, accepting the surrender of the entire force. Mr. Gonzales had never stopped after crossing the Rio Cristales. He
was so hot upon the cannoneers that he all but came into the
zone of fire from Molony's machine gun himself, as he charged
into Trujillo after them. He had dashed into the *cuartel* on
their very heels, and with his unfailing confidence in his own
invincibility, had peremptorily called upon the entire garrison
to lay down their arms. Naturally unable to believe that this
youngster in the flat-topped cloth cap had penetrated so far
without a large force at his back, the *comandante* surrendered, and by the time Christmas led in the rest of his army,

the Dávilist soldiers were stacking their arms against the wall under young Mr. Gonzales' stern supervision. As a result, when President Bonilla was landed about eight o'clock, he found his military stores increased by one cannon, 400 rifles, and about 20,000 rounds of ammunition, all of which was formally turned over to him by Lee Christmas, whom he embraced before the populace in the public square while Guy Molony sat on the bare ground in the *cuartel* and took down and cleaned his machine gun.

Bonilla immediately appointed temporary municipal and federal officials, took over the customs house, and set up a functioning administration in general. There was a rush of recruits to the Bonilla arms at once. Those of the surrendered garrison who re-enlisted with him signalized the change by removing the red-and-white hatbands of the *Liberales* and substituting the *Conservador* blue-and-white. Civilians who had been seething privately over the Morgan Loan business, came in to offer their services. As a matter of fact, when Lee Christmas, who had left Manabique less than a fortnight before with thirty men, marched out of Trujillo for La Ceiba, he was at the head of 400 officers and men who were armed with *elementos* and paid with money seized from a defeated enemy. One advantage of a coastal campaign certainly was the fact that the revolutionary treasury got a new transfusion at each captured customs house.

Back in Tegucigalpa, President Miguel R. Dávila was having his troubles. His plenipotentiary to Washington, knowing something of the feeling of Honduras, must have expressed some hesitancy about the advisability of signing the proposed treaty with Secretary Knox. On January 11, Dávila sent to Dr. Paredes the following cable:

Se ha autorizado Ministro Lazo para que firme Convención con Wáshington y contratos con Banqueros ya que Vd. tiene inconveniente para hacerlo. Traspásele poderes. Trujillo en poder de General Bonilla. Gobierno no quiere que se derrame más sangre

Hondureña. Dávila. [Ambassador Lazo has been authorized to sign the treaty with Washington and the contracts with the bankers, provided you hold it inadvisable to do so yourself. Transfer authority to him. Trujillo in power of General Bonilla. The Government does not wish that more Honduranean blood shall be shed. Dávila.]

But President Dávila might have been reassured. The treaty had been signed in Washington the day before — January 10 — by Dr. Paredes and Secretary Knox. Nothing remained to be done to make the treaty operative, but ratification by the Congress of Honduras and the Senate of the United States. If President Dávila could get the document to his congress before Christmas had captured the entire North Coast, he might yet be able to induce that body to ratify; if this were done, he felt sure the United States would put a halt to the Bonilla revolution, in order to protect the integrity of the treaty.

Matters were maturing with a rush. All unaware that the treaty was already on the high road to ratification, Christmas, McLaurie, and thirty men were dispatched by Bonilla in the *Hornet* to Iriona, and captured that seaport with its customs house treasury, its *cuartel* and its ammunition, in a night assault in which the revolutionists lost one man — the first casualty of the war on their side. This swift sortie also marked the close of the *Hornet's* career as *don* Manuel's navy, for on the return from Iriona, as they came in sight of Punta Castilla, the promontory which juts far out into the sea just east of Trujillo, they saw the *Romería* hoist sail and make toward them. The little sloop bore evil tidings, delivered by the skipper. The message read:

Trujillo, Enero 16, 1911

Señor Gral. Lee Christmas:
We are in difficulties with the Captain of the Marietta. It is best to transship all the arms to the boats before entering. Yours affectionately,

MANUEL BONILLA

There was one error in *don* Manuel's message. It was not the *Marietta*, but the *Tacoma* which lay waiting in Trujillo harbor, screened by the jutting headland of Punta Castilla. Had the *Hornet* come sailing unwarned around the point and into the *Tacoma's* arms, matters would have been embarrassing, for by this time there were hundreds of rifles stowed in the *Hornet's* hold, and at least 300,000 rounds of ammunition, not to mention machine guns. As it was, all these *elementos* were transferred to the *Romería* at once, the work being hastened by a lively realization that at any moment the *Tacoma's* ram might appear from around the corner. Not until afternoon did the *Hornet* deem it expedient to come steaming innocently back into Trujillo. She was seized before she could put down her anchor. A prize crew from the *Tacoma* made short work of bundling the *Hornet's* regular complement ashore, tossing a hawser to the battleship, and towing *don* Manuel's navy off toward Cortez.*

President Dávila was still sending urgent cables to his ministers and plenipotentiaries in the United States. Not even the *Hornet's* seizure could tranquillize him; for in Honduras, he who holds the North Coast, holds the country, because he has in his hands the country's main source of revenue. Bonilla needed but one more town of importance to complete his tenure of the entire *Costa Norte,* and naturally all eyes were now turned to —

* See Appendix No. IX.

La Ceiba

Weary and dragging though it seemed — and was — to the participants, you must none the less think of the march on Ceiba as a rather breathless sort of race, in which an amazing vagabond was, for a space, the cynosure of a world's attention. The port that was named for the stately ceiba trees had become key to the revolution on which hinged an international treaty involving millions of dollars, francs, and pounds sterling, the integrity of vast foreign loans held under many flags, and perhaps a crisis involving the Monroe Doctrine. President Dávila was chafing to have his dollar diplomacy covenant ratified by the congress while there was yet time for American intervention to bolster him back into executive security. Battleships of the United States and of England were anchored off Ceiba port, sleek and ready. The moment the congress of Honduras should ratify the *Convención* Paredes-Knox... *Don* Manuel, chagrined but true to his pledged word, stayed behind at Trujillo. Between the treaty and its ratification, marched Lee Christmas at the head of half a thousand men.

That hike in the warm winter rains was a weary job. They were forced to halt at Nueva Armenia, where Christmas received a telegram from Bonilla:

Trujillo, January 18, 1911

Sr. Gral. Lee Christmas,
   Armenia.

According to communications received today from the officers Zelaya and Carbajal, a large number of patriots are gathering in

141

order to take arms; and in order that nothing shall be lacking I have arranged to send you with the officer Barahona those which have been surrendered, together with the troops which he had as escort.

We must see that we arm the patriots who are gathered about Danto, because, according to what I am given to understand, there are many of them.

It would be well to find out how we can cut off communication with the interior.

When the friends who come from Guatemala arrive, I will come to join you in order to share your fate.

Today a mounted troop left for Olanchito, in order to try to cut communication with Tegucigalpa. This would be very important.

The reporter to whom you introduced me in New Orleans came to see me, and asked me to send you his greetings.

Take care of yourself and count always upon the affection of your friend —

MANUEL BONILLA

While Christmas was ready to welcome an increase in the forces at his command, he was impatient of delay. He was also fretted by the conjecture that if the Dávila force in Ceiba, which heavily outnumbered his, reached the conclusion that he was not all eagerness for battle, disaster might overtake him swiftly. However, fortune played into his hands, for at Nueva Armenia there approached, under a flag of truce, an envoy with the following letter from A. G. Taylor, British vice-consul, enclosing a formal note from the commander of the *Brilliant,* and a printed leaflet.

The envelope and the letter were both addressed: "*al Señor Jefe Expedicionario de las fuerzas Bonillista, en donde se encuentre*" — "To the Chief of the Bonillista Expeditionary Force, Wherever he may be Found." Vice-Consul Taylor's letter read:

The bearer of this present goes with a white flag to find you to present a letter which is directed to you by Captain Maurice Woollombe, in command of His British Majesty's cruiser *Brilliant.*

I insist that you kindly acknowledge receipt as promptly as possible, and without detaining the bearer, *don* Carlos Bertot.

Expressing my most distinguished consideration, I am your attentive svt.,

A. G. Taylor
British Vice Consul

The enclosure referred to was a brief letter, typewritten in English, and setting forth:

HMS *Brilliant* at Ceiba
19th January, 1911

Through His Majesty's Vice Consul, Ceiba.
To the Leader of the Revolutionary Forces —
General Manuel Bonillo.

I rely on you, in your best interests, should you contemplate an attack on the town of Ceiba, to prevent your followers from endangering the lives and property of British subjects, who have, of course, been ordered to observe strict neutrality. It will be with regret if I am obliged to use force to ensure the safety of British interests. I consider the accompanying "convention" a satisfactory one, and am supporting it with a force in the neutral zone.

M. Woollcombe
Captain

It was the "accompanying convention" which threw Christmas into a characteristically unbridled fury, not because of the actual terms of the document, but because it had already been entered into between the foreign military detachments at La Ceiba and the commander of the Dávila garrison, Francisco Guerrero, without so much as an abrupt "By your leave" having been addressed to Manuel Bonilla. The details of the agreement were simple enough. A neutral zone was established under its terms, into which all non-combatants would retire during the battle, and if neither party fired on the neutral zone, the American and British naval authorities agreed to keep hands off. The zone, incidentally, consisted of the railroad properties and shops of the Vaccaro Brothers fruit company, and it was additionally specified that if bullets began to pass over this territory, the shop whistles would be blown as a signal to both sides to cease firing. If the signal went unheeded, the *Brilliant*, the *Tacoma* and the *Marietta* would immediately open fire on both contesting armies.

At the height of his rage over this cavalier disregard of the amenities due *don* Manuel as head of the provisional government, Christmas sat down and with the stub of a pencil wrote the rough draft of the following reply:

Nueva Armenia, Jan 21st 1911

To the Commander of
La Ceiba

Dear Sir

I have the Honor to acknowledge Receipt of your valued letter of Jan 19th.

in Reply will say, as Commander of the Forces of Provissional President of Honduras Gen Manuel Bonilla I never nor have I intentions of attacting the Town of La Ceiba. Knowing the danger in which it would place all citizens Foreign and Home. as a convention has been held Bettween the commanders of American and Inglish war vessels with the commander of the Port of La Ceiba, without any consultation with Gen Bonilla I shall consider that we have no voice in the matter. Therefore I shall proceed alone. I have marched within a little over one days march of La Ceiba and the Enemy does not seem disposed to come out on Nuetral grounds. I shall force them to do so or surrender the Port. the convention which you agreet to with the commander of said Port I consider a protection to him. still you declare Nuetrality. you will please consider that the limits which are staked out that the Place cannot be attacked without Endangering lives of Citizens therefore the Enemy can fire on my forces but I cannot fire on them. So I cordialy invite the Commander of the Port of La Ceiba to meet me out of town. *You can rest asshured* I shall not Endanger the lives of any citizens.

I beg to remain yours very Respt.

However, either Christmas himself thought better of dispatching this contribution to diplomatic belles-lettres, or else one or another of his *jefes* dissuaded him. Instead, the Woollcombe note and the accompanying convention were telegraphed back to Manuel Bonilla, who hastily wired the following reply:

From Trujillo, January 21, 1911, received in Armenia 8 a. m. January 22.

Sr. Gral Lee Christmas:

In answer to the message which was sent you yesterday by the Captain of the *Brilliant,* please advise him verbatim the following: —
" In answer to your esteemed official letter, dated yesterday, I allow myself to inform you that in my character as chief of operations of the Northern Coast, appointed by the provisional president of the Republic, General *don* Manuel Bonilla, I have attempted to comply with that which is prescribed by the laws of war, as proven by the conduct which I have observed in the actions which have taken place at the three points attacked by the troops under my command; and in which these have been the victors. The non-combatant inhabitants of La Ceiba should feel completely assured that if the troops which occupy said town should refuse to evacuate it after having been advised to do so, then they will receive all guarantees of safety due them.

" Regarding the neutral zone I can say nothing, as up to the present I do not know if the stipulations contained in the convention, of which you have sent me a printed copy, have been accepted by my government. I have hurried to take possession of the town in order to avoid a repetition of the incendiary activities, killings and lootings which took place in July of last year, and were committed by the troops of President Dávila, as can be proven to you by the same 'bolet.' The above is what I can state to you in my capacity as military chief. I have the honor to sign myself your attentive servant, Lee Christmas."

That is my thought; but if you, after consulting with the second in command, think otherwise, you can modify this answer.

Sincerely,

MANUEL BONILLA,

The message was sent back to the La Ceiba conferees as President Bonilla had dictated it. But evidently Christmas had made some pretty choleric verbal statements which also bore fruit, for upon the occasion of the next interchange of communications, he was treated with the utmost punctilio. In the meantime, however, a formal council of war was held by the Bonillista *jefes*, in the soggy bivouac at Nueva Armenia, to draw up and sign an official plan of battle, which had been put to paper in seven articles. That was January 22, and the next day they broke camp and set off, while the rain drummed down upon them. Seedy and worn and hungry they arrived at the mouth of the Cangrejal river, hard by La Ceiba, two days later.

They were met by an envoy, under a flag of truce, and he bore a letter very formally addressed to General Lee Christmas, commanding the forces of " Hon." Manuel Bonilla in the field; and the " Hon." for *don* Manuel was enough to stamp it as the product of the United States. It was indeed from the American consul at La Ceiba, and read:

General:
    I have the honor to request a personal interview as early as possible.
    I should prefer to meet you at some point on the shore which I could reach by launch, but the bearer, Capt. E. L. Sanchez, has authority to arrange the place and mode of transportation.
    He will be my guide and sole escort, and I shall come unarmed.
    With expressions of my highest consideration, I have the honor to be, General
                                    Your obedient servant
                                        ALLAN GARD,
                                            Consul

The distinguished formality of address was balm to the nettle rash left by the brusquerie of the previous naval correspondence, and, completely mollified, Christmas sent back word to Mr. Gard to come any time he wished, bringing with him anyone he cared to, so long as the entire party approached under a flag of truce. However, the General was hardly prepared for so large a delegation as put out from the banana wharf at La Ceiba in a naval launch a short time later. There was Consul Gard, of course; A. R. Taylor, British vice-consul; Captain Maurice Woollcombe of the *Brilliant,* senior British naval officer; Commander George T. Cooper of the *Marietta,* senior

American naval officer; and an escort of lesser officers and
enlisted men from both cruisers.

The *buja* was carried on with the utmost regard for ceremonial forms, the American and British naval authorities pointing out that there had not yet been any assurance that the
Bonillista force would observe the sanctity of the Neutral Zone,
or heed the whistle signal to cease firing. Besides, there were
other conditions. For one thing, no attack was to be made
that afternoon. For another, no attack at all was to be made at
night.

Christmas shrugged impatiently.

"What the hell! Is this thing going to be fought under
Queensberry rules with a referee, or something?" he burst out.
"President Bonilla is a gentleman. I'm ready to talk things
over reasonably, but god-damn all these rules!"

It was at this point of the discussion that Guy Molony, who
had no interest in the palaver, withdrew unostentatiously from
the group. . . Among the tacticians the story goes that during
the Spanish-American war the forces of the United States, preparing to take Santiago, made as queer a blunder as has ever
marred the record of American achievement in the field. A
plan of attack was laid out which, from the point of view of
strategic technique, was practically flawless. If the various
movements were carried out on schedule, the position of the
Spaniards was already as good as untenable. The attack was
to be launched from the hill at El Caney in the morning. And
in the morning everything was in complete readiness with the
exception of one detail: The Americans were not in possession
of El Caney. They had neglected to take and hold their
jumping-off place. Wherefore the day that should have seen
them in possession of Santiago, with practically negligible losses,
found them waging the costly battle for possession of the hill
from which the attack was to have been started.

Guy Molony joined the United States army no long time
after that. The American military was still smarting from the

sting left by that bitter blunder. Every non-com among the regulars had it drilled into him from then on that before an attack one must not only develop the enemy position, but must be, at the very least, in physical possession of the jumping-off place. It was as a product of this intensive training that Molony accepted the information that he and the machine guns, and Joe Reed with a Hotchkiss cannon were to start their part of the attack by crossing the Cangrejal river at the beach and marching on La Ceiba by that route. The youngest of General Lee Christmas' *coroneles* had made up his mind forthwith that there would be no doubt about his physical possession of the jumping-off place and immediately began to improve the shining minutes in that direction, rather than waste time as audience to a conference, be it ever so formal.

So he called some of his native cadets and set to work with them to dig a small shelter trench on the east bank of the Cangrejal. They worked fast, too, for Molony was in a villainous temper, under the lash of the only set of circumstances that could sour the wonted equanimity of his disposition. He had had nothing to eat for nearly thirty hours.

One of the British naval representatives, also bored by the conference, looked idly toward the river and happened to see what was going on.

"Here! Here! You really mustn't, you know!" he cried, running toward Molony.

In that young man's present mood, this was an incautious form of address. Col. Molony looked up briefly.

"Mustn't what?" he demanded.

"Fortify yourself. I say, we're here under a flag of truce, eh? So you really mustn't."

Molony dropped his spade and stepped from the shallow beginnings of the trench.

"You go," he said precisely, "to hell. Tomorrow morning it's me they're going to be shooting at — not you. And I'd like to see anybody in or out of uniform," he added hopefully, " try to stop me."

By this time the debate had reached a pitch which attracted the attention of the other conferees, and they hurried to the river bank. At once there was a renewed protest. "What's the trouble now?" asked Christmas irritably. "Listen, my idea is those lads in there are the ones we're fighting." He jerked a gauntleted thumb in the direction of La Ceiba. "But don't you see, you're preparing a fortified position while you're under our flag of truce. The federal garrison can't fire on you to stop you while we're out here, and you're taking advantage of it to prepare a trench that is going to be very useful to you tomorrow."

Christmas grinned.

"Who says it's going to be useful?" he wanted to know. "We're not going to be here long enough to use it. We'll be in Ceiba by dinner time."

"Right," retorted one of the visitors. "You'll be there all rolled up in blankets and ready for burial."

"In that case," suggested Christmas, "I'll ask you to pick out a dry place for us, because we're wet enough now to last us all through hell."

Considerably cheered by this interchange of amenities, Christmas then agreed to observe the sanctity of the neutral zone. Later in the afternoon, however, he received another deputy, with still another communication from the naval authorities. It was in the handwriting of Consul Gard, but was signed only by Captain Woollcombe and Commander Cooper.

It read:

Ceiba, January 24, 1911

General Lee Christmas,
    Commanding the Forces of the Hon. Manuel Bonilla.
    In the Field.

General: —
    When we left you this afternoon you seemed to be in some doubt as to whether after surrounding Ceiba you would formally demand the surrender before attacking.
    In thinking this matter over we consider it our duty to remind

you that you have said that you are conducting these operations under the Laws of War.

We would remind you that these rules require the formal demand for the surrender of an unfortified town, which Ceiba is, before attacking it.

In view of the above, and in order that American and British subjects and other non-combatants may have time and reasonable opportunity of seeking the protection to which they are entitled, we have to inform you that we shall expect that such formal demand shall be made.

Very respectfully,

MAURICE WOOLCOMBE,
Captain Royal Navy
H.M.S. *Brilliant*

GEORGE T. COOPER
Commander, U. S. Navy,
Comdg. *Marietta,*
Senior Officer Present
U. S. Navy.

" Tell 'em yes. Tell 'em anything. And get the hell out of here with your flag of truce, so we can go to work without breaking some more of the god-damn rules."

Thus Christmas.

The self-appointed referees of the morrow's battle need have given themselves no uneasiness on the score of a formal request for a surrender. For one thing, the council of officers had already determined upon this two days before in Nueva Armenia.* For another, General Francisco Guerrero — "Chico" Guerrero — was one of Christmas' close friends. For years after the battle Christmas preserved in his scrap book a clipping from a New York paper, in which a war correspondent's dispatch, the day before the engagement, set forth that Guerrero was a renegade from the Bonilla cause and was therefore expected to put up "a traitor's desperate resistance." In the margin Christmas had penciled the words: "False. Never a traitor." Christmas would have been delighted to have his friend Guerrero surrender without a fight, and was therefore determined to urge such a course upon him.

* See the text of the Protocol of seven articles, in Appendix No. X.

Meanwhile Molony's preparations for holding a jumping-off place against the morning's need went forward to completion, just after nightfall. The trench was barely spacious enough to accommodate a machine gun, himself and two native boys to pass ammunition. The rest of the army took shelter as best it might on the highest available ground. Molony morosely draped his slicker over his machine gun and squatted down in the mud of his dug-out to dream of the red beans and rice of New Orleans, rich filet gumbos, and thick steaks; and the drizzle seeped down out of the starless void and the lights of La Ceiba glowed fuzzy yellow through the mist, and the civilian population of the town left their homes — at least a large number of them did — and splashed along the sodden streets to the Neutral Zone; and the official representatives of the mightiest powers in all this whirling world of wonders waited to see what Lee Christmas would do at dawn of —

January 25, 1911

BETWEEN the town of La Ceiba and the Cangrejal River is a thick, matted, jungle scrub, that is virtually impassable. Only two paths, therefore, were open to the attackers. One was the narrow strip of sandy beach from the river-mouth to the city waterfront; the other a road that wound into the town from a ford across the Cangrejal some distance inland. Through the city proper curved the railroad track, running back from the wharf. Half a mile or so back from the beach, on this track, was the neutral zone. Just on the ocean side of the zone was a cemetery, and between the two was a trench into which it would be almost impossible to direct an attacking fire without sending bullets into the forbidden territory.

The beach road was further obstructed by the fact that midway between the river-mouth and the town a soggy salt marsh ran down into the very tide-wash of the sea. Across this bog eight parallel lines of barbed wire, a few feet apart, had been strung as an additional barrier; the wires extended out into the ocean on one side and far up into the swamp on the other. Just beyond this impassé, an amost impregnable trench had been constructed, the ramparts being fortified by huge twelve-by-twelve timbers, set one on top of the other, with sand bags in between so as to leave loop-hole space for defensive gunfire. A short distance beyond this trench, across clear and open ground, ran the railroad track, and beyond that, stood the *cuartel*. Since this line of approach was barred by a bog, eight barbed-wire fences, and a heavy trench in which a Krupp cannon had been mounted, the defenders anticipated little trouble here, because the position was so palpably invincible. The main attack was expected along the road from the inland ford. Across this road, on the Ceiba bank of the river, a trench had been dug, designed according to the latest methods of defensive tactics, with a blunt jog bulging forward where it crossed the highway, so as to give the defenders a perfect field of fire on the ford. Nearly four hundred men — certainly more than three hundred and fifty — were massed here by the Dávilistas.

Christmas assigned the Cangrejal ford and the federal strong point there to General Andres Leiva, his second-in-command, for attack. A Krupp cannon, two machine guns, and nearly two-thirds of his force he gave Leiva when, on the morning of January 25, he divided his army at the Cangrejal bivouac.

"I sent the demand for surrender of the town in last night, but I knew Chico Guerrero would make us fight," he observed. "So that's that. General Leiva, you take your men and follow this bank of the river till you come to the ford, cross there, and go to town. McLaurie, Joe Reed, Molony and Gonzales will come with me to go in along the beach."

Leiva set off, and in the dawn fog he and his men were soon lost to view. Moored in the mouth of the river were a couple of huge banana lighters, clumsy flat-bottomed affairs. Molony had been squatting in the sticky mud of his trench since the night before, all set to cover the crossing, which was accomplished without incident. The Dávila forces had been so confident that the beach road was impregnable that they had made no preparation to dispute the river's mouth.

"Molony and Reed each take a machine gun," Christmas directed when they had all been transferred to the Ceiba bank. "Ysandre Pinto takes the Hotchkiss. Start in along the beach. When the right time comes, we'll follow behind you with the infantry. We don't even know where the Dávila crowd are yet." *

* Comment by Col. Molony in describing the incident today: "All offensive tactics are based on just such moves to make the enemy give away the location of

Molony, Reed, Pinto and their crews made ready to obey. Pedro Gonzales joined them without orders. Christmas laughed.

"All right, Pedro. But give 'em a chance to set up their guns before you take the town."

"When do we start?" asked Molony.

"Now. When the hell did you think?"

"What I mean, don't we get *anything* to eat first?"

Christmas dug his right hand into the side pocket of his corduroy tunic and fished out a moist fistful of crumbled animal crackers.

"Jesus, General. I'm talking about food," complained Molony. But he reached for the crumbs and stuffed them into his mouth none the less.

Christmas laughed and pointed along the beach in the direction of La Ceiba.

"Plenty of good stuff to eat in there. Go get it," he suggested.

A crackle of musketry broke out far inland. Leiva's troops had evidently encountered the enemy. Christmas laughed again. This was going to be good and he — Lee Christmas, commander-in-chief — was certainly cutting a pleasing figure before a world that was a great little old place.

"Get going, boys! Shove off!" he directed.

Molony, Reed, Gonzales, Pinta and their ammunition carriers started off over the delicate wave tracery that marked the beach sand. Almost immediately, from somewhere beyond the brush of the salt marsh, they encountered the first volley from the defenders. Molony wheeled in sudden anger to see who had slapped his face. He put up his hand and brought it away wet with blood, and yet he could have sworn somebody had slapped him across the jaw. The whining bullets were kick-

---

his strong points — that is, 'developing the enemy's position in advance.' I don't know where Christmas got any knowledge of that sort of thing, and I don't think any one else does. I can swear he never studied, or even read, any military books, but nobody could have bettered that as an opening move in the attack."

The beach road into La Ceiba, showing the swamp running down into the sea and the barbed wire entanglements about whose outer posts the Christmas-Bonilla forces waded to charge the trench which the Davila forces had regarded as impregnable.

The "invincible" trench that guarded the beach road from the Cangrejal River into La Ceiba, photographed the day after it was taken by storm in the battle of January 25, 1911. The photograph is taken from inside the trench, looking toward the swamp which, with eight lines of barbed wire entanglements, further blocked the beach.

Machine guns captured by revolutionists at the battle of La Ceiba. The kneeling machine-gunner in the white shirt is Col. Guy R. Molony.

ing into the sand all about. Well, this was as good a place as any. He set up his machine gun, trained it on the far side of the salt marsh, fed the tab and let go, ripping off some fifty rounds in short bursts. The firing on the other side of the marsh was momentarily silenced, and the Reed-Gonzales-Molony detachment advanced during the temporary lull, in which the roll of fire from back by the ford became once more audible. Evidently Leiva had not yet won across, but it was hard to be sure, because you could hear only rifle fire; no boom of cannon or stutter of machine guns.

Then came renewed firing from beyond the salt marsh and a murderous swarm of bullets whining overhead. Christmas, McLaurie and the others, who had advanced a short distance as the machine guns had gone forward, were catching the brunt of it. Firing over a breastwork, the defenders were sending their bullets high; so high that the advance guard was comparatively safe beneath the trajectory. Those of the advance detachment who couldn't stand the gaff, and ran back, really retreated from comparative security into the zone of greatest peril.

Molony's machine gun suddenly stopped. Blistering his palms on the hot barrel — there was nothing else to do — he relieved that stoppage. Pedro Gonzales wearied of inaction. So far, they had not even been able to see what defensive arrangements confronted them, because of the intervention of the screening brush of the swamp. Consequently Mr. Gonzales plunged out into the ocean far enough to take a good comprehensive look. Dodging a spattering hail of bullets, he came splashing back through the shallows to report.

" Their trench is only about a hundred and fifty yards ahead of us," he announced. " The wire fences go right out into the sea, but we can wade around them and then charge their trench."

" Charge hell! " said Molony. " We're supposed to cover the

charge, not to make it. Wait a minute now. A hundred and
fifty yards, is it?"

There were only about a dozen of them left. The fire from
beyond the swamp was deadly. Bodies dotted the narrow strip
of beach. Molony, Reed and Gonzales hauled the Hotchkiss
cannon into the swamp where there was at least the semblance
of shelter. By sheer guess they ranged their weapon on the
invisible objective and began to fire. Mr. Gonzales' impatience
burst its bounds after half a dozen shots had been discharged,
and he decided the enemy trench could now be taken. He
stormed out into the ocean to wade around the outside of the
eight fences.

"For God's sake stay here and watch these guns, Joe," begged
Molony. "There's a part of the belt left. If anything happens,
we don't want them coming over here and grabbing these
guns."

He picked up a rifle and an ammunition bandolier. The
fingers from which he took the rifle had not yet had time to
stiffen. He and four Indian boys, all holding their weapons at
arms' length overhead, galloped into the Atlantic, in Mr. Gonzales' splattering wake, like swimmers bound for a frolic.

Christmas saw them start that charge and interpreting it as
a token that the enemy fire had been silenced, launched all the
balance of his force down the beach, himself recklessly in
the lead. They too dashed out into the ocean to get around the
wire, and some of them stopped to join Joe Reed and carry the
machine gun forward with them.

Meanwhile Molony, Gonzales, and their four native boys
had waded around the outer posts of the eight fences, breast-
ing stoutly against the pull of the water. It was queer that no
one fired on them; but no queerer than the fact that all of
them were dodging imaginary bullets throughout the charge,
when they came splashing up out of the shallows to the firm
sand and hurled themselves tight-lipped upon the trench. It
was deserted. One of the first of the chance shots from the

Hotchkiss gun back in the swamp had apparently dislodged the top twelve-by-twelve timber of the breastwork and tumbled it down into the trench. Panic stricken at the accuracy of this artillery fire, the federals had abandoned the position.

It was a let-down for the six who had stormed the trench, braced for the shock of bullet or for hand-to-hand work. One of the four Indian boys was laughing hysterically. The others, their eyes shining and radiant with the thrill they were experiencing for the first time in their young lives, looked to their weapons. Molony discovered that the fleeing defenders had abandoned their Krupp cannon by the simple expedient of spilling it out of the end of the trench into the sea. He and Gonzales retrieved this weapon and some ammunition for it, and began to set it up so that it could be trained on the *cuartel,* when Christmas swept up at the head of his men.

"Jesus, Guy, I'm glad to see you," he burst out. "When that machine gun of yours stopped, I thought you was killed. Say — they got you in the face, didn't they?"

Molony ran his hand along his jaw.

"Just a slap. And about that gun. You can't fire a gun 'less you got something to shoot in it. We were out of ammunition."

"Ought to have more sense'n to get shot in the face," grumbled Christmas. "Why the hell didn't you duck?"

Molony told him fluently why he had forgotten to duck, but was interrupted by a shout. Around the corners of the nearest houses in the town, troops were drawing into the open.

"Looks like they're coming out to surrender," exclaimed McLaurie.

"No," said Christmas. "They've got their guns. Get ready!"

From the trench they began a haphazard fire upon the approaching soldiers, and these drew back momentarily. Then they reappeared, with an officer on a gray mule behind them, urging them on with the flat of a machete.

" That's Guerrero! " someone shouted, and before Christmas could give the word to charge, a dozen rifles — possibly more — were trained upon the mounted figure. They fired, almost as one. Christmas had already leaped clear of the trench and was racing across the open, with Pedro Gonzales in full cry beside him. Guerrero turned his mule and spurred the animal toward shelter, but they learned later that he had remained in the saddle only until he had turned the corner into the nearest street, dropping to the roadway before the British vice-consulate, mortally wounded. The others had all left the trench and were sweeping across the open space toward the railroad track where they caught up with Christmas and Gonzales who were examining with considerable interest what seemed to be a new machine gun, set up on its tripod and ready for business astraddle of the embankment. Molony gave it a swift glance of appraisal.

" Very first shell jammed on 'em, and they never fired a single shot out of it," was his verdict. He manipulated the barrel deftly with burned and blistered palms. " She'd work now, if we had ammunition," he concluded.

" There'll be some at the *cuartel*," said Christmas.

" Yeh. And it'll only take nine weeks to load up enough belts by hand. We got no loaded ones left, outside this one here."

" I sure wish we could get you something to eat," lamented Christmas. " Nothing suits you today."

So they charged the *cuartel* and found Pedro Gonzales already in possession, with a prisoner in the form of one very badly frightened *guarda de almacén* who had been left behind when the rest of the troops retreated from the building, their General apparently slain. The warden of the arsenal could not turn over his keys fast enough, and with one of them they opened the padlocked door of the ammunition magazine. Molony gave a whoop of joy.

" What the hell's eating you now? " demanded Christmas.

"Look! Santa Claus ain't dead yet. Lookit what he came down the chimney and left for us!"

Christmas stared blankly.

"Belts!" babbled Molony. "Lookit the belts they got ready for their machine gun, and it went and jammed on the first shot. Lookit the belts those babies loaded up and left for us. Say, have you got any idea how long it would take to load those things by hand? And here they are. We got belts for our guns again, I'm telling you!"

They filled the ammunition boxes of one of Molony's machine guns, just as Pedro Gonzales, who had been missing for some time, came trotting back into the building.

"They are all in that trench the other side of the cemetery, right in front of the Neutral Zone," he reported. "Pedro Díaz is with them. I think there are some in the houses beyond the Neutral Ground, too, but most of them are in the long trench back of the cemetery."

"All right then," grinned Lee Christmas. "We're fixed. We're luckier than I thought we'd be. The bunch from the Cangrejal, or leastways some of them, might come charging back the road to recapture the god-damn *cuartel*. So Reed and McLaurie and the others will stay right here with me. We can keep 'em out of here for two years if you, Guy, and Pedro, can take the machine gun and keep Díaz on his fat tail in that trench with his gang. Get going. Remember, Díaz and his outfit can't retreat, because they got their bottoms right up against the Neutral Ground. You keep 'em from coming this way and we'll do the rest."

Pedro Gonzales and Guy Molony slipped along the streets with their machine gun crew. There was rifle fire from snipers, but they paid no heed, because two girls had brought to a doorway an earthen *olla* of water. They drank deeply and gratefully, and then moved on to the cemetery. There Molony set up his machine gun behind a tomb, fed a belt into the appointed slot, and began to work after a fashion one could enjoy at leisure. In the first lull which the deadly tattoo of his weapon produced, he slipped forward to the shelter of another friendly tombstone and repeated. But Pedro Gonzales, dancing up and down impatiently, let his feelings get the best of him.

"Why don't you go up there where you can sweep the whole trench?" he demanded, over and over. The nagging became almost unendurable.

"Aw go take a running jump off the dock for me," Molony advised him callously, and, at the next opportunity, inched his gun across some graves and back of the friendly shelter of another granite block.

"You know what I would do if I had that gun?" fumed Pedro Gonzales, standing up by way of emphasis. "I would take it over to that trench, and put the muzzle of it down Pedro Díaz' mouth till it burned his tonsils." *

There was at this point what Molony naturally regarded as a wholly providential interruption. Some one in the trench had drawn a careful bead on Mr. Gonzales and had pressed a trigger. At very nearly the same instant, a soft-nosed bullet tore off part of the fleshy portion of Mr. Gonzales' upper arm, and he sat down abruptly among the graves.

"There. That's the way it goes," said Molony unfeelingly. "You'll have to go back out of here now and leave me have all the fun. Next time you'll know enough to keep your mouth shut. G'wan back to the *cuartel* now and get your arm fixed up. Leave me do my fighting in peace."

Considerably crestfallen, Mr. Gonzales prepared to retire. There was, of course, balm in the reflection that he had escaped the stigma of taking part in a battle without getting wounded,

---

* A slavish devotion to accuracy compels the admission that the stenographic notes recently made in Honduras of what Col. Molony reports Mr. Gonzales as having said at this critical juncture are so badly blurred as to be indecipherable. Mr. Gonzales' statement, as quoted above, is therefore largely a matter of guesswork. Submission of the moot phrase to Col. Molony for correction has merely elicited the following vague annotation: "Never mind. Just tell them Pedro Gonzales was using very immoral language and let it go at that." This advice is passed on to the reader for whatever it may be worth.

but even so he hated to retire at this stage of the game. It developed that there was no further need for regret. At that particular instant, the defenders boiled up out of their trench and retreated; that is, they tried to retreat, with a derisive swarm of Molony's bullets snapping at their ankles. He was firing low to keep his missiles out of the Neutral Zone.

The attempted retreat failed for the simple reason that there was no place to go. As soon as they reached the Neutral Zone, American and British sailors — the latter in queer straw hats — presented a formidable hedge of bayonet points. So the federals out in the open, with that bristle of bayonets before and the crackling stutter of Molony's gun behind and themselves as a highly uncomfortable filling to the sandwich, raised their hands, 'dropped their rifles, surrendered unconditionally and thus gained admission to the Neutral Zone as non-combatants.

Molony, the wounded Gonzales, and their crew, came trooping back from the cemetery to the *cuartel,* and found Christmas in conference with American and British naval officers. A shade of annoyed anxiety passed over Christmas' features.

"What's the matter?" he barked. "Didn't I tell you to hold those tramps in their trench?"

"Couldn't," replied Molony briefly.

"Why not?"

"They ran out."

"Where to?"

"Neutral Zone. They surrendered there. The damn trench is empty. Want me to go sit in a graveyard with a machine gun pointing at an empty trench, when I'm so hungry I could . . ."

But Christmas had turned triumphantly to the naval officers. "You hear that?" he said. "Now am I right or ain't I?"

The naval officers were obviously impressed.

"I'm telling you facts, gentlemen," Christmas went on. "I'm in possession of the entire town and the *cuartel* and the fortification on the beach. The only Dávila troops that aren't running or surrendered is that bunch in the trench down by the ford. Guerrero is badly wounded and out of the fight. Now what's the use of killing more people when it's all settled? That's why I'm asking you-all to go as a sort of ambassadors to that trench and advise them to surrender. If they don't they'll still have Leiva in front of them, and I'm going to march out with my force and let 'em have it from behind. They wouldn't have a chance."

It may have been a superb bluff; but Christmas had not yet learned how pinched was the plight of Leiva's men back at the Cangrejal. The assault had been practically crippled at the outset by the fact that the first volley from the federal trench had virtually wiped out the revolutionary cannon crew. One bullet in that volley had passed through the stomach of the sergeant in charge of the Hotchkiss gun. Clawing at his belly, fearful that his cannon would be captured forthwith, the dying man took out the breech block of the weapon with one free hand. Using all the ebbing remnants of his strength, he threw that block as far into the swamp as he could. They found him dead beside his gun the next morning, but the missing breech block they did not find until some hours later. Leiva's machine guns had jammed, too, being tricky weapons when not humored. That left the gallant band of attackers with nothing but rifle fire to cover a charge upon the ford and the trench that commanded it.

The Christmas forces had therefore lost something more than a hundred men killed,* all told, and at least another hundred fifty had been incapacitated by wounds. There were more

---

* Only one non-combatant was killed at the battle of La Ceiba. He was an American, Louis Bier, who was ill the day of the fight, and decided to remain in bed in his room. The house in which he lived was one of those looking out on the captured trench by the barbed wire entanglements on the beach.

The remarkable fact of Bier's death is this: During the early stages of the battle, a 42 mm. shell came crashing through the wall, struck just above the head of the bed where the sick man lay, and *exploded there without so much as scratching him.* Consider what happened next: A single bullet from a high-powered rifle passed through the window casing and there stripped off an insignificant sliver of its cupro-nickel jacketing — a tiny hangnail of metal about the size and shape of the butt of a steel pen point. This splinter passed through Mr. Bier's abdomen and killed him.

able-bodied men by far in the single Dávila detachment at the ford, than Christmas had left all in all. The advantage of far superior numbers lay all with the defenders. But Christmas' statement of the situation sounded so plausible that the gold-stripers of two battleships agreed with him, sallied out to the ford, and there put the case so convincingly to the federals that these came in and surrendered. That was about 1:30 in the afternoon, and it closed the battle and — to all intents and purposes — the revolution.

"Molony! Where the hell's Molony?" Christmas was clamoring.

Molony and Joe Reed had apparently vanished into thin air. They were found at last in a house where Reed, who had an uncanny gift for ingratiating himself, had promoted as noble a feast as was ever designed to fill a previously aching void — *tortillas,* goat steak, plantains, *frijoles* and all the trimmings, including a brimming jug of cool milk.

"You told me to go get something to eat in Ceiba, didn't you?" retorted Molony indistinctly. "Anybody tries to drag me away from here now is due to get hurt."

"There's a guy out here wants to take your pictures with the machine guns for the papers," said Lee Christmas. But evidently the ambitious photographer did not go where Molony suggested he should, for the picture was taken and post-card copies of it may still be seen, here and there, in La Ceiba, to this day.

That night General Guerrero died of his wounds in the British vice consulate. He was buried the next day with full military honors and with every able-bodied soldier of both armies in attendance. Just before the funeral Christmas ordered the unconditional release of every prisoner taken during the battle, so that all of them might join in paying the last tribute to the fallen commander. There was only one exception. Pedro Díaz was not set at liberty. This was because he had made himself so bitterly disliked during his official career about

Ceiba that there was real reason to fear his release would result in his almost immediate assassination.

That same night a messenger arrived on the boat that came in from Puerto Barrios. The word he bore was for Christmas, who promptly became jubilant.

"A girl, Ed," he confided to McLaurie. "A girl and she was born the day of the fight. I'm going to call her Ceiba."

To all intents and purposes, the big show at Ceiba closed the revolution. As it turned out, not another battle was fought. *Don* Manuel came posthaste from Trujillo to set up his administration at La Ceiba and direct the course of events which constituted —

The Aftermath

WHEN Provisional President Bonilla arrived in La Ceiba there were left, of the six hundred or so who had marched out of Trujillo a fortnight before, not more than half who were still capable of active service. However, almost overnight, enlistments swelled the Bonilla army to nearly 1000. Moreover, just as soon as Puerto Cortez — the natural point of attack — had been captured, the four largest customs houses in Honduras would be in Bonilla's hands to provide all needful sinews for a continuation of the campaign — Tela, Trujillo, La Ceiba and Cortez, not to mention Iriona, Roatan, Armenia, and the lesser ports of entry along the *Costa Norte*.

For the proposed capture of Cortez, the troops would have to be transported by water, landed somewhere out of direct reach of the garrison there, and then marched along the beach to the assault. That was what Christmas wanted, for he keenly relished the prospect of storming into Cortez as The Conqueror. That was where he had started his career in the tropics with a capital of nothing whatever. That was, quite naturally, where he most wanted to reach the heights.

And so it all came about, too; that is, all but the battle, for Manuel Bonilla received word the day before the attack was to be set in motion that General Tiburcio Carías,* under orders from Tegucigalpa, had retired with the entire federal garrison from Cortez up the railroad to San Pedro Sula.

* Since January 1, 1929, General Carías has been president of the Congress of Honduras. As candidate for the presidency of the Republic in the fall of 1928, he was defeated by Dr. Mejía-Colindres.

Christmas and McLaurie — and by the way, one of the newcomers who joined them there was Jew Sam Dreben — were
at once sent in *goletas* to take over the port, and they did it
royally. One of those who watched the triumphant entry of
the victors was a fourteen-year-old girl. She was that same Ida
Culotta whom he had been wont to dandle on his knees the
while he pressed his suit for the hand of the current Mrs.
Christmas.

Another who received the news of the taking over of Puerto
Cortez at second hand, but whose attention had been centered on nothing else for days, was President Miguel R.
Dávila. He realized fully that if anything whatever of his
crumbling power were to be salvaged, the time for diplomatic
intimations or half-measures was past. So he sent the following decidedly frank telegram to the President of the United
States:

Palacio Nacional, 28 de enero de 1911
Excmo. señor Presidente Taft,
  Wáshington.

El Gobierno está resuelto á aprobar convención y empréstito. Para
ello necesítase suspensión de hostilidades á fin de evitar inútil der-
ramamiento de sangre. Si V.E. puede prestar su valiosa inter-
vención á efecto de que la guerra termine, el pueblo y Gobierno
de Honduras tendrán motivo para agradecer, una vez más, á los
Estados Unidos y á su digno Gobernante, el gran interés que se
toman por la tranquilidad y prosperidad de este país.
  Soy de V. E., con alto respeto, atento y S. S.,
    Miguel R. Dávila

The significant portion of this cabled appeal is: "The government [of Honduras] is *resolved to approve treaty and loan.*
To this end a suspension of hostilities is necessary in order to
avoid needless bloodshed. If Your Excellency can lend your
valued intervention to the effect that war will be terminated,
the people and the government of Honduras will have reason,
once again, to be grateful to the United States and its worthy

chief magistrate for the great interest which they take in behalf of the peace and prosperity of this country."

The appeal was vain. As a final desperate move, Dávila submitted the treaty to his Congress, after calling the entire chamber of deputies into his ante-room, and pleading with them for an hour to ratify it.* Just how potent an influence Dávila was wielding in the affairs of the nation by this time, may be judged by the fact that immediately after his personal appeal, Congress voted, by the overwhelming tally of 32 to 4, to disapprove the treaty. That vote sealed his public career, both at home and abroad.

The very next day, the commander of the American naval forces in Honduranean waters received orders from Washington to "propose" a peace conference. All Honduras understood thoroughly that this proposal from the United States meant that peace must be declared " or else." As a matter of fact, the ensuing negotiations were held, and the treaty was signed, on the decks of the battleship *Tacoma*. By its terms, Dr. Francisco Bertrand was named provisional president, to serve until elections were held in October; and in October Manuel Bonilla was elected president by the greatest landslide of votes in the history of Honduras. He was inaugurated on February 1 of the following year — 1912 — with Dr. Bertrand ultimately installed, as vice president; but as a matter of fact he had been at the capital for practically a twelvemonth already, directing the affairs of government during that entire period from the home of a Dr. Walther, a German physician with whom he lived.

Don Manuel's inauguration precipitated two revolutions, one of which deserves particular mention because it marks the exit

* An interesting statement of what happened during that special session of the Congress of Honduras has been given the writer by Dr. Rómulo E. Durón, one of the foremost statesmen and scholars of Honduras, who has been Secretary of State, Minister of Public Education and President of the National University under various administrations, and who was a deputy in the Congress that defeated the ratification of Dr. Dávila's Morgan Loan treaty. Dr. Durón's account of what took place in the *salón de sesiones,* and excerpts from the published official statements issued by the Congress at the time, will be found in Appendix No. X.

of a familiar figure from the Honduranean scene. The other merited — and received — scant attention even at the time it was begun, which was a day or two after Bonilla once more took up his residence officially at the *Palacio Nacional.* Ochóa Velásquez invaded by way of Salvador, but got only a few miles beyond the border, for lack of recruits.

Shortly thereafter, however, Secretary of State Philander C. Knox made a tour of the western coast of Central America and proposed to include in it an official visit to Honduras.

José María Valladares was still an exile in Costa Rica, but was keeping a watchful eye upon the affairs of his native land. Indeed, the year before, at the time of the peace treaties aboard the *Tacoma,* he had issued the bitterest of his pamphlets, denouncing not only Dávila as the weakling sycophant of the United States, but also Bonilla, as North America's latest *protégé,* selected because he had demonstrated himself a stronger instrument than Dávila to carry out the " *yanqui* " plans for the complete subjection of Honduras.*

Anything connected, however remotely, with the Paredes-Knox treaty was anathema to José María Valladares, and he no sooner heard of Secretary Knox's impending visit to Central America than he sent word from Costa Rica that the moment Mr. Knox set foot in Honduras, he — Valladares — would lead a revolution. Not so much because of this particular threat perhaps, but on account of the fact that the general attitude of the one hundred per cent Honduraneans was still so bitter over the previous year's Morgan Loan *negocios,* Secretary Knox was received at Amapala, on Tigre Island, just off the mainland.

Even this compromise, however, was too much for General Valladares. He left Costa Rica at once by boat for El Salvador,

* Valladares even objected to the choice by the peace conferees of Dr. Bertrand as provisional president, declaring that it was universally recognized that Dr. Bertrand was " *carne de la carne y hueso de los huesos del General Bonilla.*" He further charged that *don* Manuel was being hand picked into the presidency of Honduras by the United States because he had proven on another occasion how well he could dominate his Congress — a reference to the time Christmas invaded the chamber of deputies with his policemen and arrested the leaders of an anti-Manuelist cabal from the floor.

where he gathered about him with fiery eloquence all the *emigrados* from Honduras that he could, crossed the border, and began to pick up recruits. President Bonilla placed General José Manuel Durón in command of the government forces — the same José Manuel Durón who had been leader of the handful of madcaps that had fought young Enrique Soto's revolution back in 1897.

Among the other units in General Durón's command, at this time, was a group of fourteen young machine gun cadets under Col. Guy R. Molony. Valladares withdrew to the heights of El Horno. On that white chalk hill, he made his stand. Moonlight was flooding the white rock when the battle began. In the drenching radiance, which admitted no half tones, but turned everything to silver or sable, the defenders were pitilessly silhouetted against the chalky background.

"They looked," Col. Molony recalls, "exactly like the black blob of a figure printed on military rapid-fire targets."

Even a layman can appreciate that in battle this is no way for a soldier to look to an enemy. The rifles and the machine gun down in the dense shadows of the scrub-grown plain, had no need to speak long. The force of José María Valladares was exterminated. Not figuratively — literally.

General Valladares himself managed to escape, but was shot a fortnight later at Tatumbla, resisting arrest. Thus there was none left to dispute the political supremacy of *don* Manuel, so that in all truth, Lee Christmas could now ride —

The Crest of the Wave

You who have met Lee Christmas before the myth of him had burgeoned, and who may remember what he was in his sorry years, shall find a new Lee Christmas now. Wealth was so easily come by, that he was thenceforth destined to live in an atmosphere of multi-ciphered finance. He and McLaurie acquired a thousand-acre cocoanut plantation by " denouncing " the land from the government. Next he bought the old Louisiana Lottery Building * and converted it into the Palms Hotel. He was receiving salaries as commander-in-chief of the army, *comandante* of Puerto Cortez and Inspector-General of the North Coast. Moreover, he became financially interested (*sub rosa,* of course) in various illicit enterprises which, as *comandante,* he was supposed to suppress.

Naturally, taking himself at face value, he became almost insufferable in his relations with other government officials, notably with Francisco J. Mejía, the Minister of War, who was in theory his immediate superior. Lee Christmas never got over the notion that the government of Honduras consisted exclusively of himself and Manuel Bonilla. Any time Minister Mejía wrote or said anything that displeased him, Lee Christmas resigned by telegram, quite serene in the faith that his resignation

---

* When the lottery was outlawed from Louisiana, its directors erected a fine building in Puerto Cortez, and held drawings there. The results were transmitted from Honduras to New Orleans by specially chartered fast steamers. Christmas used to give away old lottery numbers as souvenirs to the favored among his guests. After he sold the building it was acquired by the late Major Burke, who gave it to the Government of Honduras which converted it into the post office of Puerto Cortez.

would not be accepted — for how could the government of Honduras possibly continue to function without him? And he was invariably confirmed in this faith, for President Bonilla would always summon him to the capital and persuade him to reconsider his resignation.

In his hospitality he was nothing short of princely, and his entertainments — most especially one Fourth-of-July party — were the most lavish affairs ever seen along the North Coast. Upon any occasion of moment — the President's birthday or the anniversary of the battle of Ceiba — Christmas inserted a bold-face advertisement in the newspapers or had handbills distributed, inviting all who cared to do so to come to the Hotel and have a champagne cup in honor of the occasion, whatever the occasion might happen to be. Similarly, he was royally fêted wherever he went. General Andres Leiva, who had been second in command at La Ceiba and who was now *comandante* at San Pedro Sula, tendered an official public concert in his honor, upon one of his visits to that city.

In the fall of the year 1912 he went swaggering back to the United States for the space of two months. He flaunted his new glories before the old Third Ward, and was copiously interviewed by the New Orleans reporters, sending the clippings back to his friends in Honduras. He revisited Memphis where he was no less copiously photographed and interviewed, and where he found that all of his family were married. His first wife was now Mrs. G. F. Hanson. His children had families of their own. All of them came to Honduras within the year, to share his new fortunes.

When he found that a cousin of his, a Dr. William Christmas, had designed a cabin monoplane with lines curiously like those that have developed in the cabin planes of today, his head was filled with buzzing notions about the use of these things in warfare, and quite naturally he realized that he was going to make many millions out of this idea alone by selling fleets of airplanes to the Central American governments, who would thus be secure against revolutions forevermore.

And then his ready cash ran out; but President Bonilla had foreseen that this would happen and had instructed him to call at the consulate of Honduras in New Orleans when it did. He was given his passage back to the tropics, where he once more quarreled violently with Francisco J. Mejía, Minister of War, and promptly resigned. Then he sold an airplane to his friend Estrada Cabrera, President of Guatemala, who eagerly offered to take him back into the secret service of that country; but Bonilla persuaded him to reconsider his resignation, and so he remained in Honduras.

Early the following March, however, over another disagreement with Mejía, he once more not only resigned but announced his intention of quitting the country. Manuel Bonilla was desperately ill of Bright's disease at the time, and he sent Christmas a rather pathetic telegram requesting him to forsake this idea of rushing off into the blue, and " draw $300 which the customs house has been instructed to turn over to you, and come visit me so that we may speak."

Christmas did so, and reached Tegucigalpa on the night of March 20, 1913, when President Bonilla issued the thirty-second *decreto* of his administration, reading: " Finding myself gravely ill and for this reason unable to exercise the duties of the high charge with which I am vested . . . the Presidency of the Republic is hereby vested in the vice president, Dr. Francisco Bertrand."

Bonilla died a few hours later, before dawn on March 21; his passing plunged all Honduras into mourning and completely cut off the cohesive force which had maintained the solidarity of the *partido Manuelisto* — the party which had polled 82,000 of the nation's 86,000 ballots at the election a year before.

However, Christmas' power appeared to be quite unshaken, for when he resigned the next time after a quarrel with Mejía (it was about Christmas' action in arbitrarily driving an army officer out of Puerto Cortez) President Bertrand himself went out of his way to conciliate him and to persuade him to reconsider his decision. The reason for Bertrand's attitude was simple enough. Half a dozen of the leading politicos of Honduras were eyeing the presidency — Policarpo Bonilla, Juan Angel Arias, Máximo B. Rosales, Ochóa Velásquez and others — which presidency Dr. Bertrand was eyeing himself; for he contended that he was eligible to run as a candidate to succeed himself since he had not been elected to the office, but had merely come into it through the death of *don* Manuel. The nimbus of military achievement still glowed about Christmas, and many were those who sought to ally him to their cause, so as to have call upon his services in the event that trouble should accompany the pending elections.

In his domestic affairs, at the moment, Christmas was less fortunate. He had been in the habit of packing off Adelaide and the three children every now and again, when he sought the relaxation of less lawful amour; for Adelaide, as has already been indicated, was no meek and long-suffering spouse, grateful for any favor that her lord and master might show her. And finally, after she had been kept in Guatemala City for some weeks, when Christmas wired her to return, she sent him the three children by boat in charge of a twelve-year-old native nursemaid, and herself ran off with another gallant courtier to Nicaragua, so that, after his first rage had cooled, Christmas instituted divorce proceedings against her.

The year 1914 was marked in personal significance for Lee Christmas by yet two other events, one of which quite naturally followed the other. The first was that he was granted his decree of divorce from Adelaide by the courts, and the other that he began —

Wooing Number Four

WHEN Lee Christmas embarked on this courtship there were living in Puerto Cortez three children of his first marriage, two of his second, and three of his third — a two-year-old daughter among the last-named and a five-year-old granddaughter with the first. He himself was a graying gallant of 52, and the object of his suit was Ida Culotta, just turned sixteen. Very scrupulously he withheld his wooing until after his divorce from Adelaide had become legal and binding. The moment that barrier was down, however, when the honorable nature of his intentions could no longer be open to question, he fired the opening gun. It was on the occasion of one of his frequent journeys to Guatemala. Ida and an elder sister had come down to the dock to see off a girl friend who was leaving for Barrios by the same boat. Christmas adroitly cut in and manœuvered Ida off to one side and away from the party.

"See this pencil?" he asked. "That's the pencil I'm going to write you a letter with from Guatemala."

"That'll be nice," admitted Ida. "What are you going to Guatemala for?"

"I'm going to buy some presents for the little girl I love," replied Christmas with what he evidently regarded as the very Ossa-upon-Pelion of tactful delicacy. "Don't you want to come along and pick them out?"

"I'd like to go to Guatemala — but not today," was the laughing response.

The warning whistle, signalling the boat's imminent departure, put a stop to the budding conversation. But the promised missive from Guatemala arrived by the next boat. It was a picture postal, bearing the single line:

"*Estoy muy triste. No se por que.*" [I am very sad, I know not why.]

A week or so later Christmas returned. He waited until the cool of the following evening, when Ida and her brother's wife strolled past the Palms Hotel on their customary twilight walk. The conqueror of Ceiba asked and received permission to join them. On the way back they stopped for a moment at the Clerici home where Ida's sister-in-law ran in to see the daughter of the house, leaving Christmas and Ida on the gallery. He lost no time.

"Well, I brought back a bracelet and a pearl fan for the little girl I love," he announced bluntly. "Know who she is?"

"No," replied Ida wickedly. "It would be pretty hard telling —with you."

Lee Christmas made short shrift of this sort of fencing. His brows drew down.

"I mean you," he declared unmistakably. "I used to think you were too young, but I don't think so now. You're a very settled girl, and I'll take a chance. Let's go back home now and I'll tell your papa and mama about it."

Swept off her feet as she was by the swift development of the situation, Ida retained wit enough to forbid his making formal entry of his suit with her parents until she should give the word. Reluctantly he agreed, and stuck it out a week. Not having heard from her during that time, he abandoned further irresolution, called upon the Culottas and duly proposed himself before that thunderstruck couple as a suitor for the hand of their youngest daughter.

Mrs. Culotta, startled out of her customary placidity, looked at her husband, frightened. The last time Christmas had visited this home on a matter of domestic arrangement was the

occasion when Captain Culotta had invited both him and Adelaide to take Sunday dinner there, in order to tender his good
offices as peacemaker in the connubial war that was then at its
height between the two. Captain Culotta, therefore, met the
situation just as bluntly as it had been presented to him, and
he met it with a refusal that left no possible doubt as to its
finality. Christmas was more than thirty-five years older than
Ida. He had been married three times before. He was not a
Catholic. He was a fighting man and an adventurer who was
bound to get himself into mortal difficulties sooner or later.
For very propriety's sake, Christmas' notorious penchant for
extra-connubial dalliance was not mentioned, but that this feature of his character was also taken into consideration by the
girl's parents is hardly to be doubted. Christmas would therefore drop his attentions at once. Ida would be forbidden ever
to see him, speak to him, go walking with him, or hold any
other manner of communication with him again.

Despite the prohibition of the parents, Ida and Lee were in
constant communication thereafter. No sooner had Christmas
been forbidden the house than he purchased the Gaborit general store opposite the Lefebvre home, where the Culottas occupied the upper apartment. The management of this emporium
he turned over forthwith to his son-in-law, Robert White. His
own official connection with it consisted of drawing a chair out
upon the shaded gallery, tilting it back against the wall, and
gazing at the otherwise commonplace frame structure on the
opposite side of the *Calle de Linea,* where dwelt his — at the
moment — heart's desire.

He was forbidden to walk with Ida? Very well. Working
at night, with his soldiers, he cut a path through the jungle just
above the town. Cortez consists of a single street, occupying
the approximate center of a long, narrow spit of land, on one
side of which is the bay and on the other side of which is the
blue Atlantic Ocean. A favorite stroll for the young people was
along the bay side to the point, and then along the open ocean

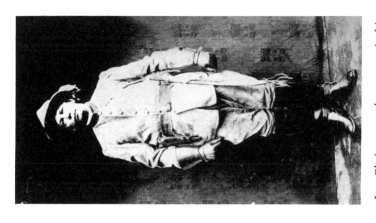
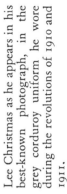

Lee Christmas as he appears in his best-known photograph, in the grey corduroy uniform he wore during the revolutions of 1910 and 1911.

A photograph of Lee Christmas taken at the time he set out on his fourth courtship.

beach. It was like walking along one arm of a hairpin, making the turn at the top, and then walking along the other, the space between the two prongs being made impassable by dense jungle. It was through this jungle that Lee Christmas now hacked a machete-cleared path wide enough to permit passage for himself and his horse.

Thus Ida and one or another of her girl friends — naturally the latter were all in league to further the progress of this thrilling romance — would walk openly down the bay past the banana wharf, turn to the beach and stroll along the fawn-white strand while the General, plain to the most jealously watchful eye, remained seated on the gallery of his newly purchased store. A half hour, or perhaps an hour later, when the girls had long since passed out of sight, the General would rise, call for his horse, mount and ride off past the *cuartel* in a direction that was the very reverse of that taken by the girls. Certainly nothing could be less open to suspicion; yet, once out of sight of the frame houses of Cortez port, the General had but to push through the screen of foliage that hid the opening to his jungle path from casual observation, and then gallop at breakneck speed through the steaming bush. A few minutes later he and Ida were together.

There were other means of even more frequent communication. For example, Christmas began to give little Armando Lefebvre, a boy of eight, champagne corks to play with. Boylike, Armando was intrigued by the gaudy things with their gilt and silvered tops. Yet each of these corks had been craftily hollowed out, and a tender message had been crumpled and stuffed into the recess thus created. So, whenever Ida saw little Armando tossing and catching a new champagne cork, she made her way to him as soon as she could, despoiled the bauble of its letter, and scribbled an answer which was deposited in the same hiding place and similarly delivered. Here is one of Christmas' champagne-cork notes that has been preserved. Surely it is the ghost of the scrawled missives he had slipped

by needless stealth beneath Mamie Reed's kitchen door deep
in the Louisiana swamps nearly forty years before!

                                        P. C. July 3, 1914
My Dearest little Chonchita
    Yours of today Received You cant Imagine how Busy I am on
acct of this quarentine question is my Reason for not answering,
will Darling I did not turn back to Omoa yesterday for the Reason
I dont to see you suffer, if I had gone you would have been Kept in
again What I want and will have is your liberty of course I know
you want to see me and you know I am crazy to see you but we
must stand it for awhile, so don't give ut and dont listen to all you
hear. I am true to you and I have confidence that you are to me,
O god what would I give to be with you this moment.
good night sweetheart a thousand . . .
                    Yours for Ever Pic

    The coltish signature "Pic" was his own idea, though
"Chonchita" (which should be Conchita, of course) is a by
no means unusual form of endearing address among those who
speak Spanish. "Pic" was a reference to the many picnics on
which they managed to meet.
    Then, too, throughout that summer, there were the serenades.
These are — or were — a peculiar institution of Latin America.
As a Northern debutante, at the height of her brief reign, reck-
ons her popularity by the number of invitations and the gross
tonnage of daily orchids she receives, so did the belle of the
Caribbean cast up hers in terms of the serenades tendered her.
The only band in Puerto Cortez was that of the soldiers at the
cuartel, and the ruffling young blades of the town would engage
those musicians to play at this house or at that for an hour at
midnight. Of course, Christmas, as general in chief of the
army, was master of the band; so the leader of that organization received standing instructions that no matter where the
musicians were ordered to play at night, they must first stop
for a space before the home where the Culottas lived, and there
torture old Spanish waltzes and feebly moribund bits of rag-
time from the States. Naturally these serenades could not come

as compliments from General Christmas, or the Culotta elders would have banned them; so they came as expressions of respectful adoration from one Francisco Ávelez, a circumlocution which Ida thoroughly understood. When the music struck up, the young folks would dress and go downstairs to dance. There would be refreshments, and then the whole crowd would troop off to the home of the next fair "honoree." Sometimes, in the dense shadows of a nearby gallery, Ida could see a white blur, and that would be Christmas' tall figure, in his immaculate white dress uniform, and if she found the coast clear, she might slip over there, and they would dance for a few sweet stolen moments, whose dear tenderness not even the orchestra's dismemberment of "*Sobre las olas*" or "Are you sincere?" could blemish.

So the summer wore on and finally Christmas, ever the foe of laggard courtships, decided the time had come for action. He owned a motor launch, the *Maruca,* named in honor of his youngest daughter, and he began forthwith to tinker with the *Maruca's* simple little gasoline engine. Now the Port of Cortez still bore in mind how, seven years before, this same Lee Christmas had doctored a locomotive stack to silence it, and had then used the steam engine for an elopement. So the older heads watched him tinker with the *Maruca's* engine, and chuckled understandingly. Not so the Culottas. They promptly arranged with the Lefebvres, who occupied the apartment below theirs, to spread the story that burglars had attempted to visit their home. On the heels of that report, the elder Culotta promptly had the windows of his upper apartment securely barred, and the doors re-enforced with extra locks. And the population of Puerto Cortez, young and old alike, saw, understood, chuckled again, and sat down to await developments.

Christmas heard of it and lost patience. Yet for once he invoked diplomacy rather than force. Securing a leave of absence he made the long journey to the capital, ostensibly on military business, but in reality to seek out one of Ida's brothers, Salvatore, who was resident manager of one of the fruit companies in Tegucigalpa. To Salvatore he put the case and a fortnight later the twain returned to the coast. Salvatore played ambassador and finally persuaded his parents that perhaps the most certain way to break the attachment was to let the pair see much of each other. And, as he pointed out, even if this plan failed to work, what then? They could not keep Ida a prisoner the rest of her life. Christmas was immensely wealthy, he had tremendous political influence not only in Honduras but in the neighbor republics as well, and so — why not?

Reluctantly at last the parents consented, and once more received Lee Christmas as a guest in their home. In the cool of the evenings he might take Ida out walking, too, provided one of her relatives accompanied them as chaperon; all this, of course, only if Christmas gave his word of honor that there would be no elopement, and that much he promised, readily enough. But he pressed the Culottas to set a date for the wedding and, after he had consented to embrace the Catholic faith, the girl's parents finally ordered carefully ornamented bits of printing which set forth that

CAPTAIN AND MRS. PETER CULOTTA
ANNOUNCE THE MARRIAGE OF THEIR DAUGHTER
IDA
TO
GENERAL LEE CHRISTMAS
ON THE EVENING OF DECEMBER SECOND
ONE THOUSAND NINE HUNDRED AND FOURTEEN
AT EIGHT O'CLOCK
PALM HOTEL, PUERTO CORTÉS, HONDURAS

Though this was his fourth marriage, it was to be Lee Christmas' first ceremonial wedding, and he made preparations accordingly. Expense was certainly not to be spared. He bought diamonds indiscriminately, and sent the stones to New Orleans by an acquaintance with definite instructions which the latter promised to carry out to the letter. A cluster engagement ring, a diamond-set wedding ring, a cake of epic proportions, and flowers were all to be sent to Honduras by the *Saramacca,* which was scheduled to reach Cortez on the day before the wedding. In the meantime, Christmas' daughter Sadie, a skilled needle-woman, was making the wedding dress for the girl — her own junior — who would be her father's bride.

Christmas went up to San Pedro where he was received into the Catholic Church. The priest was to come down to the Port on the afternoon of the wedding day to hear his confession and that of his bride. A string orchestra from San Pedro and a *marimba* from Guatemala City were engaged to aid the band from the *cuartel* in the matter of dance music for the wedding guests. Two ships were specially chartered by the groom — one to go down the coast as far as Ceiba and the other to cross the gulf of Honduras to Barrios, and bring the guests to Puerto Cortez.

Then, the day before the scheduled ceremony, the *Saramacca* arrived, and consternation was all the cargo she bore for the groom. Here was no cake, here were no flowers, here were no rings, here was nothing but black disappointment. The acquaintance to whom Christmas had entrusted the diamonds — and the money — had simply disappeared with both. A local pastry cook was hastily commissioned to bake a plain white-frosted wedding cake. By special messenger Christmas sent two ten-dollar gold pieces to San Pedro Sula to be made into plain wedding rings by a goldsmith there. All of the gardens of the old port were raided for palm fronds and flowers to decorate the altar which Bob White was building in the main ballroom of the Palms Hotel, and to make bouquets for the wedding party. Thus it may well have been that the bouquet which Ida Culotta carried when she became the fourth wife of Lee Christmas held flowers from the garden of Magdalena Talbot who had been Mrs. Lee Christmas Number Two.

On the afternoon of December 2, Lee and Ida were united

by civil ceremony before the justice of the peace, and went then to the Palms Hotel to make their confessions before the priest. Ida was clothed in her wedding frock, save for wreath and veil, and she carried, for the first time, the pearl fan her husband had brought from Guatemala as a gift for " the little girl I love." Lee wore his most resplendent and most heavily gold-laced uniform, and the gold-mounted dress sword. The priest called him into the confessional room first, and there was an immediate scene when the general was ordered to kneel.

" I am in uniform," Christmas haughtily pointed out, " and the wearer of a uniform of the government kneels to no man."

One can imagine, perhaps, how the Lee Christmas who had cadged shamelessly for drinks about the railroad saloons of New Orleans and Memphis must have opened his eyes to stare at this new Lee Christmas whose pride bade him split hairs with the Church of Rome over minutiae of punctilio. None the less, after much arguing, the stiff-necked *comandante* of Puerto Cortez had to yield the point. In all the splendor of his trappings he knelt and made confession.

Then Ida was called in, and there was almost another scene when the priest closed the door of the room on her. Christmas stalked back and forth before the door, pausing now and again to listen, and growing momentarily more angry.

" A damn good thing you came out of there," he growled at his bride when she finally emerged. " I was getting ready to bust in and see what was going on, I was. Fine way to do. When I'm in the room, he keeps the door wide open so's all the world can see me kneeling in my uniform. When you're in there and he ought to keep the door open to show every-thing's all right, he shuts it."

However, the ordeal was over, and they returned to the Culotta home for supper and then walked together back to the Palms Hotel where their union was solemnized by the Church. Ed McLaurie was best man. The groom's five-year-old grand-daughter, Eleonora White, was one of the flower girls. His two-year-old daughter, Maruca, was the ring bearer. Afterwards the hall was cleared for a grand *baile,* and the music played without intermission. The moment the string orchestra finished a number, the *marimba* began one. The brass band followed, and was succeeded at once by the string orchestra again. At three in the morning the guests departed; Lee Christmas and his bride themselves locked up their hotel and put out the lights.

So deeply had all this elaborate courtship and its ceremonial climax engrossed him, that he paid scant heed to the temblors rumbling beneath the scarred surface of Honduranean politics. And besides, how could such matters concern him, in any event? Was he not the Great Invincible, without whom no administration could feel itself secure? Thus it came about that he was quite unprepared for the suddenness with which there now ensued —

The Break

FOR months, Acting President Bertrand had been on the defensive, while a bitter polemic raged about his eligibility to become a candidate at the 1915 elections. Naturally, during this period, neither he nor his opponents in that multilateral controversy cared to strengthen any one of the various oppositions by driving Lee Christmas into some hostile political camp. Therein lay the real secret of the impunity with which Christmas could apparently afford to ride roughshod over the most ordinary proprieties in his relations with other governmental departments.

The constitution forbade any president of Honduras to succeed himself. Yet it was the contention of Dr. Bertrand and his allies that he had never been elected to the presidency, that he was merely serving out the unexpired term of General Bonilla, and that therefore he would not be "succeeding himself" if elected. To make this view of the case still more convincing, he resigned some six months before the end of the current term, so that he would not even technically be violating any provision of the constitution by becoming a candidate. Juan Angel Arias, whom Sierra had run for the presidency against Manuel Bonilla in 1903, Máximo B. Rosales, and Ochóa Velásquez were among those who cried out most vehemently that this was illegal. Dr. Policarpo Bonilla, surprisingly enough, ranged himself on the side of Bertrand.*

* Policarpo Bonilla and Juan Angel Arias engaged in a very bitter public discussion over this issue, and their polemics were published in the following year (1915), in a privately printed pamphlet, under the title: *Documentos Políticos del*

Political disputes of such virulence usually foreshadowed an ultimate solution on the battlefield, and as long as that prospect loomed in the offing, Christmas was obviously regarded as a valuable adjunct to any of the factions that might wish to count upon his services. However, the ferment subsided of itself. Arias withdrew in dudgeon beyond the borders of the country, and left the field clear to Dr. Bertrand, who was now in the position of being virtually unopposed as a presidential candidate at the 1915 elections. And to all this Christmas paid no heed whatever, for he was still blissfully riding the crest, unshakably staunch in the conviction that he was indispensable to any administration in Honduras.

As already noted he had become a silent partner in several of the illicit enterprises about the port. One of these was what was known as a "Chinese Lottery," distinguished thus from the government's authorized monthly lotteries by a name which indicated it was a penny-bit affair of daily drawings, which were and are under the express ban of the law. The merchants of Puerto Cortez were the first to feel the pinch of having this lottery operate. Quite obviously a banana loader cannot lose his petty cash in daily lottery drawings and still spend it for the purchase of goods in the lawful bazaars of trade. So a complaint was made to the government, and — a month after his marriage — General Christmas received a rather peremptory order from Minister Mejía, directing that the daily lotteries in Puerto Cortez be stopped, and at once.

The next steps followed almost as though they had been rehearsed. Christmas flew into a rage and resigned by telegraph, as was his custom. According to routine, this should have been accorded a rather conciliatory reply from the capital, requesting him to reconsider; and indeed, if the political tensions had still been as tremulously adjusted as they had been half a year

---

Doctor don Juan Angel Arias y Doctor don Policarpo Bonilla, Referentes al Problema Electoral de Honduras. A copy of the brochure is included in the collection on the shelves of the library of the Department of Middle American Research, Tulane University.

previously, that is precisely what would have happened. All this, however, was now quite nicely arranged; neither President Bertrand nor anyone else need longer fret about any bravo's attitude. The result was that the reply — also telegraphic — to Christmas' wire read:

Palacio, January 9, 1915

Sr. Comandante, Puerto Cortés:

By decree of this date your resignation has been accepted as commander of this port, with the most expressive thanks for the services you have rendered. Said post should be turned over to the Mayor de la Plaza, Col. Inestroza. Accordingly please turn the post over with the regular formalities.

Francisco J. Mejía

That was all. In that moment vanished the power and the glory that had been Lee Christmas'. Newspapers in the United States, recalling him as "President Maker" and romantic "fightin' fool," printed the dispatches, but a war of considerably greater scope than any Hispano-American imbroglio was now monopolizing the headlines.

Christmas must have been a bit dazed by the realization that the government of Honduras could bear to part with his services under any conceivable circumstances. He remained in Puerto Cortez, doing nothing. He still had more than enough money but was irked by the details of trying to manage the Palms Hotel. So he sold his interest in that enterprise. He had no other occupation than taking his wife and children on frequent picnics about the countryside. Then his son-in-law, Robert White, grew homesick for Memphis and quit the tropics overnight.

That threw the burden of running the store on the General. Naturally, the confidant of presidents had small taste for selling some native crone a yard of flowered calico or a tin saucepan. Besides, there were so many more fascinating schemes whereby he could become a millionaire practically between suns. The *cocal* had prospered under McLaurie's management. It was bringing him a comparatively modest but still quite adequate income. So, early in April, he found a buyer for the store, and left Honduras with his family for Guatemala. He went straight to the capital and established himself with his wife in a suite at the Imperial Hotel. He was very tender with this girl-wife of his, for she was with child.

President Cabrera immediately gave Christmas a place on his secret service, for the tyrant of Guatemala maintained an espionage system that might have shamed that of the Romanoffs. Cabrera was still firmly seated in the palace at Guatemala City, but there were beginning to be ominous whispers about him. Like mad Terencio Sierra, who had sought vainly to perpetuate himself in power in Honduras two decades before, Estrada Cabrera heard voices and held communion with spirits. There were rumors of strange witchcraft sessions in the palace.

None the less, as a government official and an intimate of the president, Lee Christmas was once more a personage, and therefore at peace with himself. The days when he could permit himself to sink back into comfortable obscurity were gone, and he might have become a factor in the government of Guatemala but for his wife's state of health. Physicians told him that unless she were taken from the high altitude of Guatemala City to the sea-level atmosphere to which she was accustomed, she and the child she was carrying might die.

This was in October. Panic-stricken, for little Ida had become very dear to him, he sent her to her parents in Puerto Cortez where, early in November, was born the child of his old age, baptized Dominicio, but never thereafter known by any name save Pat.

He hurried back to Cortez himself, and during the long slow months of his wife's convalescence, stayed on, more or less at loose ends, unwilling to leave her and return to Guatemala. He did develop and casually propose a plan for stopping smuggling and making a multimillionaire of himself, the idea being that he was to be given a monopoly of all liquor importation. Out of the profits he proposed to maintain an efficient coast guard. Fanciful as this scheme was, he set a rough draft of it down on paper, but never carried it farther. Besides, a new and wholly attractive chimera intrigued him at this time, and he plunged into it — a plan for the commercial utilization of the sharks with which the marine waters of that coast abounded. Just where he got the idea that shark oil would prove invaluable for the lubrication of watches and other precision instruments no one ever learned. He always set it out as an inspiration of his own, and he had a trick of presenting it with a plausibility that was almost irresistible.

" The sharks are easy to catch and nothing is wasted. You skin the bodies and sun-dry the hides, and sell them to the United States for leather. You manufacture walking sticks out of the backbone. They're beautiful. You try out the meat and get the oil, which will bring in a fortune by itself, and when you're done with the meat you sell it for fertilizer. There's millions in it — millions! "

With all the enthusiasm of a wholly new interest, he went to work to secure a concession by which his shark-fishing enterprise would be granted a ten-year exemption from taxation. The concession was granted late that summer, and he promptly set about finding capital to finance the industry.

This proved to be far more difficult than he had expected. In addition his funds were beginning to run low. Fond as he was of playing the *grand seigneur,* he had been spoiled by nearly two years of having more money than he knew what to do with. He thought of going back to Guatemala, but his wife objected. So he pocketed his pride and sought a government position and received it — Inspector General of the North Coast. This was merely one of the many posts that had been his in his hey-day, and it carried with it no supervision over the port or the garrison — nothing beyond routine inspection tours of the *cuarteles* in the departments of Cortez, Colón,

Atlántida and the Bay Islands — and the salary was $300 a month.

It was all well enough, as far as it went, but of course his mind was set upon becoming a millionaire via the shark-fishing monopoly, so he put his *cocal* on the market. Many and many an offer he refused, but finally, early in 1917, he struck a bargain with a syndicate of investors. As part payment he took a gasoline boat, the *Taft,* for of course he would need a boat for shark fishing. After McLaurie had been given his share of the balance, Christmas had left about $12,000 in cash.

Before he could begin to organize his shark fishery, war was declared by the United States. That very day Christmas wired his resignation to President Bertrand, packed up his family and his possessions, and came to New Orleans to offer his services to the government of the United States.

And it was this that broke him, for he started off with gay pride to confer himself upon a presumably grateful country. Grateful? Why not, indeed? Not even the United States could go out and pick off the bushes a seasoned general who had served through so many campaigns and had been in supreme and chief command of entire victorious armies. Small wonder he was blithe as he took ship for that northbound journey past Glover's Reef and winking Mujeres Light and Campeche Bank, for it could not occur to Lee Christmas that he was sailing toward —

Disillusion

WHEN it was explained to him that he could not enlist offhand as a general officer in the army of the United States, he went to Washington direct, armed with a letter from Col. Robert Ewing, publisher of the *New Orleans States* and national Democratic committeeman from Louisiana. President Woodrow Wilson was a busy man in those days, but he received Christmas on the afternoon of May 18 and heard him out. The President informed him that these matters would have to be decided by a military board and that his name would be sent to such a board in due course.

And the fact that the Great Lee Christmas had offered his services to the government caused no faintest stir. No reporters rushed to interview him. A wisp of a four-line clipping in a Washington newspaper was all that he could find to send back to his wife. It read:

General Lee Christmas, soldier of fortune and prominent figure in many Central American revolutions, offered his services yesterday to President Wilson. The President told him he would like to talk to him later.

No more. Just that and nothing else, concerning the man whose "military exploits" five short years before had blocked a great dollar diplomacy treaty. But time had moved swiftly. Few there were who remembered, even vaguely, what "dollar diplomacy" meant. None the less he interviewed Senator Robert Broussard and wrote hopefully to Ida that the Senator informed him "he was shure he would land me in a good position. I also seen the Secretary of State and have an other appointment with him Tuesday. Give Pudding my love and kiss my Pat."

However, nothing came of all these high preparations, and so he returned to New Orleans to wait until the government should summon him. He lived in royal leisure with his family for a time, entertaining them largely; for $12,000 was not spent overnight, even though one rented two automobiles — one for himself and one for his family — by the month. Then he thought he might as well improve the interval of waiting by getting his shark-oil company organized, and closing in upon the millions that awaited him in that quarter. So he opened offices in a room above a shoe store on St. Charles street, and interested D. B. Jones and C. B. Webre in the fishery scheme, they agreeing to put up $50,000 to finance the business as soon as it had been proven to have a commercial value, to which end he was to secure for them samples of shark-oil and dry shark-skin as soon as possible.

The agreement was drawn up on September 21, and he was in a ferment to be gone and at it, but he was daily expecting the arrival of his commission in the army, and so had to possess his soul in unwonted patience. Not for long, however. His formal tender of services had been made to the War Department on April 13; on October 1 came the reply which, stripped of official phraseology, was a curt statement that the War Department had adopted a policy of accepting no such tenders unless the applicant had qualified by a course in one of the Officers' Training Camps.

Christmas gave out an interview, printed in the New Orleans *Item,* to the general effect that he was 54 years old and in the pink of condition, and that he could whip any or all of the members of the board that had turned him down for military service. Then he took his family aboard the next boat to Puerto Cortez to become a shark-products magnate.

Once back in the tropics, he set to work in earnest. Each morning he and a native boy would board the *Taft,* go out into the bay and catch sharks. Each afternoon the sharks would be skinned, the hides pegged out in the sun to dry, the flesh stripped from the backbone and cut up into lumps which were tossed into a big iron pot, a sort of open soap-boiler's kettle. All this was out on the beach where, for the rest of the afternoon, Christmas' native helper would feed the fires beneath the kettle while the General himself stirred the mess with a long wooden paddle and contentedly smoked his *puros.* It is an intriguing picture: the former *General del Ejército* and intimate of presidents standing placidly beside his soap kettle, stirring the lumps of greasy shark meat and already spending the millions which the mess would bring; perhaps these visions helped him to disregard the combined reek of drying skins, rendering meat, and bones rancid in the hot sun.

He made several bottles of oil in this fashion and, having thus paid tribute to industry, he sent two of the bottles to his New Orleans associates, and hurried over to Guatemala to secure an exclusive concession for shark fishing in the waters of that republic too in order that he might monopolize this new bonanza. As soon as that was granted, he returned swiftly to Puerto Cortez, but now a really embarrassing problem began to manifest itself. The twelve thousand dollars he had received from the sale of his *cocal* had completely melted away, and it became necessary for him to find gainful occupation and that quickly. Appointment to the military service of Honduras was offered to him. Regretfully he declined this, declaring that as long as the United States was at war he would take military service with no other country. Just at this time, early in January of 1918, Guatemala City was practically destroyed by two earthquakes, and President Cabrera summoned Christmas by wire to take charge of one branch of the relief service. He left for Guatemala at once. When he saw that his duties would involve a protracted stay, he sent for his wife.

" Once a Merry Christmas " was the inscription the General himself scrawled on this snapshot, when he sent a post-card copy of it to Molony.

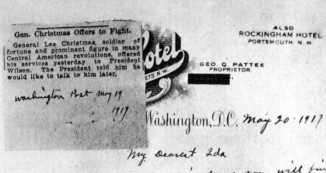

ALSO
ROCKINGHAM HOTEL
PORTSMOUTH. N. H.

GEO. Q. PATTEE
PROPRIETOR.

Washington, D.C. May 20 · 1917

My dearest Ida

inclosed you will find a coppy of my letter to the President which will Explain my delay. My friends here are trying to get the President to put me in Charge of central american affairs during the war Senator Broussard told yesterday that he was shure he would land me in a good position. I also seen the secetary of state and have an other appointment with him tuesday at 11·05 am I never was treated better in my life so have patience if I have to stay here any length of time I will let you come up give Pudding my love Kiss my Pat and the Boys love and Kisses

Lee

The letter and the clipping Lee Christmas sent to his wife from Washington, when he had appealed to the President for a commission in the army of the United States (see pages 190–191).

The same boat brought to Guatemala J. H. Burton, head of a lumber firm, who sought to further a project for erecting a refugee town of portable houses. Upon investigation he concluded that Christmas would be an ideal local representative for his firm. However, only one of the Burton portable houses was ever put up, and that was a little green cottage first used as office, and later as a residence by Christmas and his family. Thereafter the entire project was dropped, but Christmas remained in Guatemala City as local representative of the Burton Lumber interests * and additionally as an agent of the United States secret service. The long-awaited government appointment had been made on May 17, 1918, and at last Christmas had an authentic if obscure part in the World War — at $200 a month.

He still clung to his shark fishing vision, though this bubble had been pricked again when the New Orleans associates declared it impracticable. He was alone in Guatemala at the time, for his wife had been called back to Puerto Cortez because of the death of her father, and she had taken the baby with her. Scouting about for new means to raise shark fishing capital without outside assistance, he worked out a device which was to act as an automatic stopping mechanism for a railroad train the moment the engineer's hand left the throttle — a device which unquestionably every railroad would be compelled by law to install on its locomotives and which would, therefore, make him a multimillionaire. He sent the sketches off to a firm of patent attorneys in Washington and began again to spend millions agreeably, without having any definite way of knowing where he would get sufficient funds to see him and his family through another month.

Then a new interest seized him, one which made his previous dreams of opulence seem like sickly shadows. Petroleum! He

* Mr. Burton has been good enough to give the writer some interesting sidelights on Christmas' connection with this firm. His letter will be found in Appendix No. XI.

prospected for a season for oil in the employment of the W. M. Bancroft company of New York, and heard tales of enormous British syndicates whose resources ran into the billions. After that, as a stay against the pinch of money with which to live, he became a cattle-buyer but all the while he dreamed of oil and fabulous riches. Capital was all that he needed. Here he was — intimate of the presidents of two republics beneath which lay limitless seas of petroleum. With his influence he could secure concessions, special land grants, anything he pleased. Nothing remained but to go North and cash in on his reputation.

So far as Honduras was concerned, however, Lee Christmas was a thing of the past. Dr. Francisco Bertrand had sought to perpetuate himself in office by making a brother-in-law the president, taking advantage of the fact that the country was still technically in " *estado de sitio* " — under martial law — because of the war that had been declared against Germany. But there had been a bloody revolution. Bertrand and his family had fled the country. General López Gutiérrez was president. Christmas? All that political Honduras remembered about Christmas was that he was a brawling foreign trouble maker, and when he came to Puerto Cortez to call for his family and bring them to the States, they would not even let him land. It took action by the American Minister to get him a permit, as an American citizen, to enter Honduras. He remained only long enough to take his family to Barrios by the next coasting vessel, and to wait there for the steamer that would bring them to the United States.

He came to New Orleans bitter and, to all intents and purposes, penniless. The shark oil business was a thing of the past, the patent on his locomotive throttle was hanging fire, and yet here he was, potentially a billionaire if he could only raise a little capital. Guy Molony, now chief of police of New Orleans by appointment of a reform administration, could not finance oil explorations. So Christmas sat down and invented a rat trap which would infallibly kill not only the rats, but all the fleas any rat harbored.

" I'll turn it over to some company to manufacture," he confided to Molony. " The United States Public Health Service will have to adopt it, and that means at least a million of them will be put out. All I want is a royalty of fifty cents on each trap. Of course, when the foreign governments get them too, that'll make it just so much bigger. Anyway, I'll have enough to finance the oil business myself."

So he sent off the drawings of his trap to the patent attorneys and spent the ensuing weeks bewailing his forced inactivity.

" I can get the land denouncements from Cabrera by just saying I want 'em," he said one day to a friend, Forrest Pendleton; and the statement was probably true enough. " Any company that will pay the superficial tax of five cents an acre can go in there and skim the cream off the richest oil lands in the world."

Forrest Pendleton had been head of the New Orleans department of the federal secret service during the war.

" I've got a mighty good friend in New York," said Pendleton. " He's Bruce Bielaski, president of the Richmond Levering Company. Go on up there and talk to him. You used to be in his section of the secret service yourself."

Pendleton lent the General a hundred dollars to enable him to get to New York, where the officials of the Richmond Levering company were sufficiently impressed to make him a cash advance and promise him a contract if he could secure the requisite concessions. Leaving his family in New Orleans, he sailed direct for Guatemala, and began to lay his lines for two things: first, the denouncement, as original applicant, of as much land as possible in the Department of Peten; second, the enactment of certain legislation which would specifically validate land grants to those oil explorers who brought in petroleum on their concessions.

Cabrera promised all this readily enough, and Christmas

jubilantly cabled his backers. Cabrera was ready to promise almost anything in those days, for truth to tell Manuel Estrada Cabrera, who had been president of Guatemala for twenty-two years, was no longer sane. And on April 8, 1920, the Congress of Guatemala met, formally declared the president mentally unfit longer to govern the country, and elected Carlos Herrera head of the Republic.

Cabrera had taken refuge in the fortress of Las Palmas, overlooking the city. When word was brought to him of what had taken place, the mad president ordered his army to bombard the town from the heights. For five days this went on. Among those who took refuge in the American Legation were Lee Christmas and a young New Orleans attorney, Max Schaumburger. The latter, who was seeking to specialize in Hispano-American law, had spent his student vacations in the tropics working for one or another of the fruit companies, had been a member of the United States secret service during the war, and was now taking a special course in law at the national university in Guatemala.*

As the bombardment ordered by the mad president was endangering the lives and properties of Americans, Benton McMillan, Minister for the United States, decided to call for help. Unfortunately the wireless tower was cut off, by shellfire, from the legation, where most of the Americans had taken refuge. A call went up for volunteers. The first man to answer was Lee Christmas. He seemed to have grown years younger over night. His face, a trifle sunken of late, had grown ruddy, and his eyes sparkled, according to Schaumburger's version of the incident. Had not the oil interests been at stake, he would have been in the field. And it was Lee Christmas who took the messages and the wireless operator — a man named Haub —

---

* Schaumburger kept a voluminous diary during those stirring days when Estrada Cabrera's grip on Guatemala was finally wrenched loose, and while Christmas played but a minor role in the affair, the reader may find it interesting to note the amazing way in which the details of Cabrera's case paralleled those of Terencio Sierra's. The entries from the Schaumburger diary for April 8 and 9, 1920, are reproduced, by permission, in Appendix No. XII.

through the city to the tower. The troops on Las Palmas saw them and opened fire on the two little darting figures, but they made it and got through the message that summoned the battleship *Niagara* to a Pacific port. Schaumburger, incidentally, was one of those who drove to Las Palmas a few days later and placed Estrada Cabrera under arrest, later becoming Chief of Police of Guatemala City. Cabrera, the old Czar of the Caribbean, did not long survive his incarceration, and died in prison. Carlos Herrera was chosen to succeed him.

Christmas set to work anew to build, under the Herrera administration, the foundation for the oil denouncements that would make him a billionaire. Seeing Schaumburger's rise to a place of prominence with the government, Christmas employed him as attorney. Together they lobbied for the desired change in the petroleum laws of the country, and together they made good progress; such good progress indeed that in April 1921, the Richmond Levering Company made the promised contract with Christmas, under which he received $500 a month and would be given a large percentage of royalties on production.

But the changes in the laws hung fire, and the company grew impatient. Then, toward the end of the year, at last the new statutes were adopted. Christmas was overjoyed. There was a great banquet at Guatemala City, and among those who sat at the board with him was the same General William Drummond — older and grayer than Christmas himself — who had led the gay two weeks' revolution of Enrique Soto in 1897; for Drummond was one of the group in whose names Christmas had filed his land denouncements. Under the new law it was possible for the syndicate to hold exploration rights for something like 900,000 hectares of land in the Peten.

Christmas' health had been giving him considerable trouble, particularly at this time when almost incalculable riches were just around the corner. An obscure intestinal malady was causing him much discomfort, and he wrote his wife that physicians had advised him to spend as little time as possible in the high altitude of the capital. He added that he would go down to Puerto Barrios for the week-ends. It was while he was there that, in December 1922, his plans collapsed once more. A party of revolutionists seized the Guard-of-Honor barracks in the capital and three of their leaders — José María Orellana, José María Lima, and Miguel Larrave — waited upon President Herrera just after midnight to demand, and receive, his resignation. By the end of January a complete new government, with Orellana as president, had been installed, and this new government ruled that Christmas and the Richmond Levering interests had not been the first to file their denouncements to the rich acreage in the Peten; wherefore, in the Spring of 1922, just after he had turned sixty, Christmas had to begin his campaign to secure the concessions all over again. He had friends with the new government and the Richmond Levering interests kept him on. However, he was constantly checked by increasing attacks of what seemed to be a dysentery. Much of the time he had to keep to his room in the hotel, and he took a mournful sort of pride in his ill health. He sent Molony a snapshot of himself in an old-fashioned nightgown that exposed his shrunken and wasted calves. He inscribed this photograph: " Once a Merry Christmas! " In spite of all this he must have come to some kind of an understanding with the new government, for there is among his papers a letter from an official, cautioning him against the use of the words " The President " in his telegrams, and insisting that under these circumstances he refer merely to " *persona importante.*"

In March, after an attack had confined him to the hospital for two weeks, he decided to go to New York for a conference with Bielaski and for treatment.* On the journey his physical condition took a turn for the worse, and he was carried from the boat direct to St. Vincent's hospital. There he learned that

---

* A brief statement of the Richmond Levering connection with Christmas, by Mr. Bielaski, is included in Appendix No. XIII.

following Richmond Levering's death a short time before, the company, of which Bruce Bielaski was still president, had decided to abandon the Guatemalan project completely. In the event it were deemed wise to undertake the matter again, he was assured his contract would be renewed. For the rest . . .

He wired Guy Molony and the latter sent him $100 with which he returned to New Orleans because he was penniless and there was nowhere else for him to go. He came home to Ida and Pat and Maruca and Lee and Winnfield, all of whom he had not seen in more than a year, and he was helped from the train and driven to the little house in Sycamore street, with no newspaper reporters to make note of his arrival, and no crowds to acclaim his return.

Christmas' illness was diagnosed as a tropical sprue — a disease brought on by a yeast parasite and carrying in its train a pernicious anaemia. There were days when he lay in his bed, too weak to move. There were other days, after the peak of an attack had passed, when he could rise and move about. Something had to be done to provide money for current expenses; anything to tide him over. Within a short time, beyond a doubt, the golden tide would rise and inundate him. There was the locomotive patent and there was the mouse trap, and there was always the shark oil as soon as he should have interested some intelligent capital in it. Then, too, he had written to a lawyer, instructing him to sue the Encyclopaedia Britannica for having slanderously published the fact that he — Lee Christmas — had been killed at the battle of Maraita way back in 1907.* That ought to bring in a little something — a

---

* In its section on Honduras, the editions of the *Encyclopædia Britannica* which have been superseded by the current revision, made the following notation:

"At the outset of hostilities in February 1907, the Hondurian forces were commanded by General Bonilla in person and by General Sotero Barahona, his minister of war. One of their chief subordinates was Lee Christmas, an adventurer from Memphis, Tennessee, who had previously been a locomotive driver . . . *Zelaya* captured Tegucigalpa after severe fighting and besieged Bonilla in Amapala. *Lee Christmas was killed.*"

For no very clearly definable reason, the General regarded this as an outrageous libel, and insisted that huge damages should be wrung from the publishers for maliciously circulating an obvious untruth about him.

hundred thousand dollars or so. And finally, he would write the story of his life. Better yet, he would get some writer to do it for him, and make the writer pay him roundly for the privilege.

On one of these " good " days, he visited the Banana Baron of one of the three big fruit companies. This was not the backer of the revolutions of 1910 and 1911. With that financier, Christmas had long since quarreled violently. For once Christmas made no fanciful proposition to the Baron. All he said was that he, Lee Christmas, was without money and in need. He left the office with a check for one thousand dollars.

It was high time, too, that some such provision was made. As the June heat of New Orleans settled down, Lee Christmas sank into what was apparently a last illness. The physicians looked doubtful. Perhaps a blood transfusion . . .

The story of that transfusion brought the name of Lee Christmas back to the front page and sent reporters swarming out to the little house on Sycamore street, for the man that donated the pint-and-a-half of blood was Guy Molony, superintendent of police. A score of volunteers had clamored for the privilege.

The transfusion put Christmas on his feet for a month or two, and in an aimless sort of way, he became very busy. He secured, for example, the right to sell a gold mine for three million dollars, his own commission to be $300,000 if the sale were consummated. This cheered him immensely, for these were full-flavored figures of a sort he could understand. Under their stimulation he bethought himself of the biography, and called in one of the reporters who had chronicled the tale of the blood transfusion, offering to turn all interviews, papers and other material over to this scribe upon an advance payment of a few thousand dollars.

Flattered considerably, the reporter none the less made plain just how wide a chasm yawned between him and " a few thousand dollars " so Christmas decided to write his own biography unassisted, and dashed it off in a fine fever of creative effort one morning. Not a detail was to be omitted. At the very outset, for example, he set down the name of every little Lake Pontchartrain schooner on which he worked as a boy. But the bright flame he had kindled upon the altar of the muse rapidly died down, so that by the time he reached the point where he told of "liking the new game" that had made him a Captain, he summarized the balance of his career in the following paragraph:

Served as colonel then promoted to Brigadier Gen in 1904 then promoted to a Division Gen the highest Rank in the war of 1911. held the following positions. organized the Police Force three times 1902–1904–1912 Commandante of Port Cortes three times vice President of the Tribunal of War President of the Board of health Comander in Cheif of the Northern Army which Post he held at the time war was Declared on Germany where he Resigned and went to Washington ofered his services to his country was Received by President Wilson May 19–1917 was Recommended by the President for a Commission as Brigadier Gen to war Deportment was passed to selective Board where he was turned down on acct of his age which was 54 Gen Christmas was in the Picture of health with 20 years of Experience in Real active Military Life. so the General has often said when a man becomes my age in the United States he is only good for Fertilizer
so good Bye

His temper was become shorter than ever in that late summer of 1923 for he was impatient of the lingering, dragging illness which grew worse so steadily. During a fit of irresponsible rage he quarreled violently with his wife, and left her, managing to reach the railroad station and take a train for Memphis where, on the point of physical collapse, he appeared at the home of his son Ed and was taken in.

The journey had sapped what little reserve strength was left to him. Physicians were hastily summoned and another blood transfusion was ordered. This time it was a girl medical student who was the donor. The transfusion was successful after its fashion; but he failed to rally from it as he had rallied from the first one. It was at this time that Mamie Hanson came to see him, and the visit marked their first communication, written or spoken, since they had been divorced a quarter of a century before.

"Like to have me do anything for you, Lee?" she asked of the old man who had slipped awkwardly scribbled little notes beneath the kitchen door of her home, in the Louisiana swamps of Livingston parish.

He grinned a ghost of the impudent grin that had been his hallmark in the days when his joyous disregard of consequences had made him a myth of might throughout Central America.

"Might mix me a mint toddy like you used to do, Mamie," he suggested.

"Better let liquor alone, sick as you are."

"Still talk just like your mama, don't you?"

But he would not stay in Memphis, for he was hungry for Ida and Pat and so, with a third blood transfusion to give him strength for the journey, they finally sent him back to New Orleans, where he wept when he found he was so weak he had to be carried from the train, and wept again when he learned that Ida had gone to work in a radio store as a saleswoman, to keep herself and Pat.

The brief New Orleans winter had already set in, for it was December now, and there were raw, chilly days as well as warm and pleasant ones. Hardly a week after his return, physicians decided he would have to be moved to the hospital. He protested feebly, but Ida promised to come there every morning and evening, before and after work.

"How'll I ever get well again and strong on the damn hogwash they feed you in those hospitals?" he asked. "I want you to take care of me. You're all I got left."

"I'll cook the meals and bring them in to you."

So they took him to Touro infirmary and there, day by day, his last remnants of strength ebbed.

"It's only a question of time," said the physicians. " Another blood transfusion would be agony, and might not even help."

Straight from the store where she worked Ida went each evening to a little restaurant near the hospital, and fixed up a tray which she took across the street to his bedside. He would permit no nurse to feed him and he would eat nothing in the way of prepared food that he did not believe Ida had cooked. After supper, each night, he would talk to her ramblingly until exhaustion sapped his scant vitality and he dropped into restless sleep.

"I was just thinking today," he would say, "I know where I can get some people with real money to go into the oil game down in Guatemala. And remember, if anything happens to me, that oil land down there is yours. But I'll get out of here yet and put it over . . ." and then he would swear with feeble virulence at his other backers for having abandoned the enterprise. Or: "I understand the Illinois Central's put my throttle on their Panama Limited, so it must be good, and if they don't pay us, we'll sue."

Guy Molony dropped in almost every day. Toward the last, Christmas had great difficulty in speaking at all, and there was a constant pain in his ear where an abscess had burst. He knew, then, that there was no longer any question of recovery.

He was given the rites of the Catholic Church a day or so before his death and, feeling that he had done all that could reasonably be demanded of him in this regard, became as violently angry as his bodily condition permitted the following afternoon, when two Sisters came to offer him spiritual solace, and he cursed those gentle nuns from his bed until his voice gave out. Guy Molony dropped in to see him that afternoon, and found him speechless. Mutely the General pointed to a few oranges on his bedside table, and to his mouth. Molony, understanding, cut one of the oranges and squeezed it so that a few drops of the juice could trickle upon and between the dry lips. There was a groan from an adjoining bed.

"Listen to — that old — son of a bitch!" gasped Christmas.

"Shhh! He can hear you, General," urged Molony.

"I want him to — hear me. All in the — world — that's wrong — with the old — bastard — is a — busted leg — and he takes on — like that. Tell him — shut his — god damned mouth and — leave me — die in peace."

"You ain't dying yet, *compadre.*"

"Like hell I ain't. — They don't know — what's wrong — with me, and — when I'm gone — tell 'em — cut me open — find out what's wrong — maybe — some other — have same — help somebody —"

The voice trailed away as Christmas passed into a doze and Molony tiptoed from the room. The General was still asleep when Ida came that night to relieve her sister who had been watching by the bedside.

By nine o'clock of January 24 — the time when, under the rules, visitors were required to leave for the night — he had not yet awakened, and the tray that Ida had brought to the bedside on her arrival was still untouched. There was a new floor nurse on duty that night. The others, more or less familiar with the situation, had always permitted Ida to stay beyond the stipulated time. But this nurse knew nothing of the case other than the routine information on the chart.

"Time's up for visitors," she announced.

"I haven't given the General his supper yet," said Ida, "and he won't take it from anybody but me."

"Oh, that's all right," the nurse assured her cheerily. "We'll feed him."

The talk evidently awakened Christmas.

"You will not feed me," he asserted abruptly, his voice stronger than it had been for days. "Ida, give me something to eat."

"It's past hours," objected the nurse, "and . . ."

"Man's dying," grumbled Christmas, "and they want to starve you on top of that."

"But the rules . . ."

Drawing upon some unsuspected reservoir of strength, Christmas half raised himself in his bed.

"God damn the rules!" he cried, and the words rang through the quiet hospital corridor. Thus, voicing a final revolt, he collapsed into the coma in which, a few hours later, he died.

There is, I think, to the story of Christmas, a —

Postscript

Guy Molony defrayed the expenses of the funeral and it was he who arranged matters so that a solemn cortege of mourners followed the General's garish red-white-and-blue casket to the grave. On the day of the burial Molony called up Col. John P. Sullivan, political leader of the old Third Ward and head of the faction which dominated the municipal administration at the time.

To Col. Sullivan, Molony explained the situation and the result was an immediate call upon the Sheriff of Orleans parish, whose patronage, by immutable custom, is a Third Ward perquisite.

Thus it happened that the casket that held all that was mortal of Lee Christmas was attended not only by relatives, but by a host of clerks and deputy sheriffs and deputy wardens — Third Ward folk — who had succeeded where Lee Christmas had failed; who had never gone brawling off into a whirling world of wonders, but had stuck to the old home ward; and who by consequence had won a place upon the city's payroll.

By their very presence they acknowledged him as one of their own. That had been his ambition at the beginning. It was gratified for him at

The End

APPENDICES

Appendix I

ONE OF the features of the yarns that were spun about Lee Christmas for popular consumption is the curious distortion to which the history of Honduras has been subjected in the process. At the time of the Soto revolution of 1897, Manuel and Policarpo Bonilla were still, personally and politically, cheek by jowl. Yet the newspaper accounts — published about 1911 when Lee Christmas was at the crest of his career — invariably made that poor little fortnight of revolution a revolt by Manuel against Policarpo. As an instance, the following is taken from one of Lee Christmas' scrapbooks. It is apparently from a Toledo newspaper, of January 29, 1911, although most of the identifying marks seem to have been cut from the clipping:

He loafed around the New Orleans harbor front for a while [*in the mental daze that followed the discovery of his color-blindness, that is*]. The aroma of bananas caught his nostrils. A steamer from which a cargo of bananas had just been unloaded was preparing to sail. Lee walked aboard, and didn't step ashore when the steamer backed away from the wharf.

"Give me a ticket for any old place," said Lee when the purser tapped him on the shoulder, and so they landed him at Puerto Cortez, Honduras.

A fresh revolution had just been started down there by the outs, who happened to be Manuel Bonilla's henchmen just then [*sic!*]. Both sides needed recruits but Manuel saw Lee Christmas first and made him a general — just like that!

At that time Policarpo Bonilla — not related to the other Bonilla — was in the president's palace at Tegucigalpa, the capital. Both of the Bonillas had been president and ex-president in turn several times [*sic!*]. When one was out he was busy starting another revolution to get in again. Any setting sun which saw no new revolution begun wasn't worth talking about.

Well, Lee started revolving in good earnest. He showed the Hondurans a few tricks in fighting they had never dreamed of. Policarpo was divorced from the President's palace, and allowed to ruminate in a four-by-four cell in the village lock-up for a while.

Another one of these remarkable synthetic biographies appeared in the *Railroad Man's Magazine* for May 1911, over the signature of one Thaddeus S. Drayton (p. 597 ff.). Mr. Drayton also pictures Christmas as contemplating suicide when it was discovered he was color-blind, and then walking aboard a steamer without realizing what he was doing, and being brought to himself by the purser's demand for a ticket. Let us quote verbatim from this point on:

"Where you headed for?" he [*Christmas*] asked.
"Puerto Cortez is our first stop, sir."
"That's in Honduras, isn't it?"
"Yes sir."
"Do they have the color test down there?"
"I don't know, sir," replied the purser, amazed. "The natives are pretty dark, if that's what you mean. Railroads? Yes sir. There's a little piece of a one."
Christmas paid his fare and went down to supper. By the time Puerto Cortez was reached, his plans were made. He spoke Louisiana French [*he did not, of course*] as fluently as he did English. He was confident that he could learn Spanish quickly. He would get a job on the railroad after he had looked about a bit.
On the evening that he landed, he was sitting at a sidewalk table of a cafe.* Christmas never touched intoxicants [*sic!*]. He ordered a bottle of soda, speaking in English. A man at the next table looked up, then leaned over with outstretched hand and called him by name. It was an engineer whom Christmas had known well, but whom he had not seen for more than a year. After their first greetings, Christmas explained how he happened to be in Puerto Cortez. He found that the other engineer had lost his job for the same reason — color blindness.
In the next half hour Christmas learned more about the seamy side of politics in Honduras than he had ever suspected before. A revolution was budding and was likely to burst into full bloom at any moment. Policarpio Bonilla was "in" and Manuel Bonilla was "out." The two Bonillas were in no way related and hated each other with the intensity of two opposing leaders in a Kentucky blood feud.

---

* Only one who knows the universal patio arrangement of Puerto Cortez and other similar Hispano-American cities can appreciate the absurdity of sidewalk cafés there, fronting on the railroad track of the Calle de Linea. But sidewalk cafés *do* lend a foreign touch, eh? — H. B. D.

Chance had sent Lee Christmas to Honduras. Chance was to determine his next step and to open to him the road to fame and fortune. As Christmas and his brother engineer chatted, a Honduran gentleman at a near-by table looked earnestly at Christmas. He was a secret agent of Manuel Bonilla.

He rose and moved out toward the pavement. As he did so, he dropped his cane in passing the two Americans. As he stooped to recover it, Christmas caught a muttered word in Spanish that appeared to be addressed to his companion. When the Honduran had disappeared, Christmas' companion suggested that they take a turn around the plaza.

In the course of their walk, Christmas learned that his companion was plotting with Manuel Bonilla to overthrow the existing government. It did not take much persuasion to induce Christmas to join him in the game.

There is a great deal more to the same effect, culminating in the " fact " that in six weeks Christmas had proved himself so efficient " that Bonilla made him his chief military adviser." All this, you must note, happened on the night when Christmas first came to the tropics — October 1894 — when Policarpo Bonilla had scarcely had time to warm the presidential chair, into which Manuel Bonilla and Terencio Sierra had helped to place him; long before Policarpo and Manuel fell out, and no less than nine counted years before Manuel led a revolution which, incidentally, was directed at Terencio Sierra and not at Policarpo.

However, the most elaborately detailed " description " of the battle of Laguna trestle is given in a syndicated article by " Captain Hermann Archer, U.S.A.," as published, among others, in the *New Orleans States* of August 7, 1927, three years after Christmas' death, by which time certainly there had been an opportunity to gather the facts with a reasonable degree of authenticity. This same article, incidentally, also reports that when Lee Christmas found out he was color-blind, he cast himself from the fourth floor window of a New Orleans oculist's office to end his life, and after recovering from this experience, it was listlessly and by chance that Christmas wandered upon a steamer about to sail. Then — as Captain Archer tells it —

At Porto Cortez, Honduras, they put him off.
No one would have thought that the quiet, humble human, who drifted into the office of the Honduran railroad — a line three or four hundred miles long, then [*How it has shrunk! For it is only sixty miles long now*], used mostly for transport of fruit and bullion from farm and mines — a few days later, was the future Lee Christmas. He

had been an engineer, he said, back in the States. Would they give him a job? Nobody, it appears, worried about color blindness in Honduras. Maybe they had never even heard of it. And so, in the end, Christmas was again allowed to climb into a cab . . .

Then the turn came. The revolution which Manuel Bonilla [*sic!*] had started against President Policarpo swept over the part of the country traversed by the little railroad. Government troops took a strong position along the line and one day a band of revolutionists boarded the train that Christmas was running and ordered him to take them to a point where they could attack the enemy. Christmas was disgusted; even on this dinky railroad fate wouldn't let him alone. He began driving the engine forward, probably cursing the luck, when all of a sudden the Government soldiers opened fire on the train.

Bullets spattered about the cab. Christmas, ducking, got "all-fired mad." He grabbed a rifle from one of the native soldiers and began firing. He had never before shot anything bigger than a squirrel, and he was amazed to see that he could shoot like a marksman. It was as if the spirit of his father suddenly took possession of him. The Government troops began to fall back.

Christmas leaped from the engine, and whipping the revolutionists into following him, drove that particular band of Federals into a mountain gully where they were faced with surrender or sure death. The Federals surrendered pronto. Christmas dropped his rifle, began mopping his face with the old red bandana he had brought from the States — a symbol of railroading he somehow loved — and ambled back to his engine.

When he got back, a small, fat vivacious man with heavy moustaches and a gaudy uniform ran to meet him. He was fairly bursting with eager enthusiasm. " Great," " glorious," " genius," " warrior supreme " — these were some of the things Lee Christmas heard himself called. He brushed the little man away, his engine was waiting. But when he learned the next instant that his admirer was none other than Manuel Bonilla, leader of the revolution, he stared.

" I'll make you an officer," Bonilla was saying. " A captain in my army. I will make you rich, give you place and power, once we have taken Tegucigalpa."

In amazement Lee Christmas looked into the avid bright little eyes, and the eyes changed. They became crafty, calculating, wheedling.

" You have killed government soldiers," whispered Manuel. " If they catch you, they will kill you as a traitor, an enemy. They will count you on my side anyway. You might as well go the rest of the way with me. You see."

Lee Christmas swore. By all that was holy, this Bonilla was right. He had killed Government soldiers, and aided in the capture of others, and the Government owned the railroad! He was a marked man, foredoomed to one of those firing squad parties, probably, if he was seized. Only by helping Bonilla, by changing the government, could Lee Christmas be sure of his life and his railroad job. Yes, he even thought of his job then! By Jove, Lee Christmas would fight. The next instant he was a captain in the army of Manuel Bonilla.

But the most amazing part of the situation was still to come. The little railroad became the key to the rest of that revolution. Battle after battle, skirmish after skirmish, was fought for possession of it, and Capt. Christmas discovered that for him fighting beat engine running all hollow. Planning attacks, rushing out ahead of his men and having them follow blindly through a hail of bullets, quelling incipient mutiny, snapping out orders to soldiers — all this was as simple as if he had studied and practiced it since babyhood. Bonilla kept saying that if he could win the railroad he could win the war. Christmas sputtered and swore and planned. Then one day he promised Bonilla he would "win the road."

Soon he had rigged up a traveling fort — a flat car with thick sandbag walls — and manned it with marksmen. He put this out in front of an engine and began shooting it back and forth along the right of way. Finally he had the company's other five engines bottled up at one end of the line. The railroad was paralyzed, the position of the government troops became untenable, and at last they were driven out. This proved the turning point. The victory brought the fickle people flocking to Manuel Bonilla's standard. Lee Christmas rode into Tegucigalpa at the head of Bonilla's men.

Apart from such addenda as the expansion of the railroad by more than 700 per cent, the transformation of Christmas into a "humble human being," bandanna kerchiefs and the like, let us recall that Manuel Bonilla was a spare little man who never wore a uniform in the field in his life, and would not even permit his officers to don uniforms for active service. There is something sublime in the effrontery which blandly pictures him as one who indulges in oglings and caperings, and hails a man of the Lee Christmas stripe as "genius." Under such a spell, the reader might almost be tempted to forget that the interchange here described between Bonilla and Christmas occurred no less than five years before the two men so much as met.

Appendix II

In spite of all the military gallantry and super-achievements later credited to him, it was as amorist rather than as sabreur that Lee Christmas first received publicity. The following account is taken from the New Orleans *Daily Picayune* of March 23, 1885:

BOLD LOCHINVAR

Steals His Young Bride From Her Mother and Speeds Away to Vicksburg

An Unwilling Parent But A Merry Christmas Pair

The Mississippi Valley Railroad depot was the scene of quite a romantic and exciting incident last Friday evening. Just as the seven o'clock through Memphis train was about leaving, cries of distress and calls for assistance were heard coming from the direction of the rear or sleeping coach. A crowd soon congregated and found that the cries came from the lips of an elderly woman who was accompanied by a boy. She was bewailing the anticipated loss of a daughter who stood on the front platform of the rear coach, and whom she had seized by the arm and was striving to drag from the train.

The young lady resisted and clasped tightly the hand rail to prevent her mother from taking her off the train. The bell rang and the train started, and the mother lost her grip on the arm of her daughter. She was however determined that the young lady should not leave without her and seized hold of the platform rail. She stumbled and fell and was dragged fully a square's distance when the train was stopped and the woman rescued from her perilous position.

The daughter alighted from the train but only remained on the depot platform long enough to ascertain that her mother had not been injured, and then boarded the train again accompanied by a young man. The mother called on the police for help to arrest her daughter, but the officer on duty would not interfere as the mother had no charge to make against her save that the young girl was about to elope with the young man who is a resident of Vicksburg, Mississippi.

The train again started and the mother again attempted to seize hold of the car, but was prevented by the bystanders. The officer then informed the woman, whose name is Mrs. Reed, that she might send a telegram and stop the runaway couple, and escorted her to the central station for that purpose. On arriving, however, Mrs. Reed concluded not to intercept the young people, who were en route to Vicksburg where they were to become man and wife.

From statements made by parties who profess to know, it appears that Mrs. Reed's daughter, Mamie, a most beautiful and amiable girl, had fallen in love with the young man, Lee Christmas, some time since, at McComb City, Miss., where the young man had been in the employ of the Illinois Central railroad company. The parents objected to the young man, and opposed the wishes of the young people.

Some time ago, the young man went to Vicksburg, where he purchased a property and made further preparation to receive his wife when he should have won her. All his plans having been arranged, he came to New Orleans two weeks ago, and held clandestine meetings with his lady love. Aware that they could never hope for her mother's consent to their marriage, an elopement was planned and on Friday night it was carried into effect. By some means or another, Mrs. Reed was informed of the arrangements made, and long before the hour advertised for the train to depart, she was at the depot looking for the young people — for she knew that they were meeting at the depot if they did not arrive together. She was not disappointed in this, and as soon as she espied her daughter, sought to compel her to go back to their home at No. 491 Chestnut street.

How vain her efforts were is told above, and doubtless Mr. and Mrs. Christmas, though they may regret the measures they were compelled to take to consummate their object, are now enjoying their honeymoon.

Appendix III

DURING his later years, when he was polishing up his past for public consumption, Christmas always gave reporters a version of the circumstances of the wreck in substantially these words:

"Yes sir, I was through a wreck one time, when I was a youngster, that like to killed me, but I was too tough for 'em. Ran my train into one coming the other way and scalded myself most to death. They'd 'a' fired anybody else that would 'a' had such a wreck; but when it come out that I went to sleep at the throttle because I had been on duty for 54 hours running without a wink of rest, they took me on again and gave me back my job. And it wasn't long after that when I went to the tropics."

That was the version of it which Lee Christmas gave the writer at the time of the Molony blood transfusion in New Orleans. At about this same time, the *Illinois Central Magazine,* a house organ published by the railroad's employes, who certainly could have had access to authentic sources, described the incident as follows in the issue of October 1823 (page 34):

It was in 1891 that Engineer Christmas left the service of the L. N. O. & T. He had been 54 hours on duty and then had been ordered back to his run without a rest; as a result, he went by a station asleep, and had a disastrous collision with another train. In the wreck, Engineer Christmas was seriously scalded and his right eye was knocked out — but that eye is still in use, although he says it has been knocked out three times, the first time when he was in a fight as a boy.

After the collision, Engineer Christmas was kept out of work, *although he was not discharged. His friends succeeded in getting him a chance to return to work.*

The wreck occurred on November 29, 1891. Accounts of it appear in both the New Orleans morning dailies of that time — *The Times-Democrat* and *The Picayune* — on December 2, but they deal with the circumstances of the wreck, not the events that led up to it. Conductor Butterworth, of the train Christmas was driving, resigned immediately upon his return to New Orleans.

Mrs. Hanson, in Memphis, gave the writer the following account, beginning with the search for Christmas about his customary haunts, when the emergency call for his services was made, and the discovery of him, far gone in liquor, as he was holding forth to a corner gathering.

"Mama begged him not to go," Mrs. Hanson continues. "She even told him she had a dream that if he took out that engine, he'd never take out another. But he was so drunk he didn't know what it was all about. The caller said the train had to go, and he thought Lee would get straightened up. Why he was so drunk he was staggering! They took him down to the station and hoisted him in his cab, and meanwhiles mama took and made a bucket of strong coffee, and give it to papa so he could run to the crossing and catch the train and give it to Lee to sober him up. Papa jumped on the engine at the crossing and give Lee the coffee and jumped off.

"Well, Arthur Butterworth was the conductor on the train, and there was a new fireman on the run that didn't know Lee, and sitting down the way he was in the cab I guess they couldn't tell the shape he was in. So what did he do but fall sound asleep up there at the throttle, and run through Kenner where there was orders for him to wait and let another train go by him the other way. Right through there he went and he met this other train near Laplace I think it was, and it was run by an engineer named Chippie Smith. And Lee told me afterwards that when he come to he was on the cross-ties underneath of the engine, and couldn't so much as move his head which was the first thing he remembered after he left out of New Orleans.

"We were living at Wilson then, and they sent for me up there. Little Ed was just a few weeks old. I come right down as far as the wreck, which was still blocking the track, and I had to walk around the wreck and get on another train the other side of it, and when I saw where they taken Lee out from I just knew right away he was dead. They all thought he was dead, too. Why they didn't hardly even look for him at first, they was that sure nobody could have been mashed under where he was at, with all that steam shooting around him and still be a-living.

"They taken him to the hospital, and nobody expected there he'd ever be able to live. But he made out to pull through. I asked him what he was going to do when he got well. He said he would go back railroadin'. I didn't say nothing. What would be the use? But we come on up to Memphis after he got so's he could travel, and he went to see Captain Sharp. That was the Division Superintendent, or some such official, I don't rightly remember just which. I was with him when he went to talk to Captain Sharp.

" Captain Sharp, he looked Lee up and he looked him down, and he asked him what did he figure to do now. Lee said he wanted to keep right on railroading. 'You're the man got drunk and had the wreck, ain't you?' Captain Sharp asked, and Lee said yes, he was the man. 'Well,' said Captain Sharp, 'all I got to say is it's a pity they ever got you out from underneath of that engine, and let you wake up. That's all I got to say to you. You couldn't get another engine on this railroad no matter what, and I don't want to see you, no, not ever again.' And then — well, for most three years after that Lee wasn't nothing more nor less'n a tramp. He'd be gone months on end, and times I'd be living with my sister in Memphis, and times I'd be living with papa and mama. He'd turn up now and again. Sometimes he'd have a little money with him, and sometimes not."

Christmas was never again at the throttle of a railroad locomotive in the United States.

Appendix IV

The following excerpt is from the syndicated article by " Capt. Herman Archer, U.S.A." :

He went to the railroad doctor for the examination customary after accidents, and it was decided he was color blind, no longer fit to drive an engine. They offered him a "dead man's job" in the yards. But Christmas shook his head. He walked into the hall, and with wet, dazed eyes stopped before one of the windows that looked down into the street far below. Life seemed suddenly to have turned to ashes. Christmas climbed upon the window ledge and stepped off.

He fell several stories to the busy street. But he did not die — fate wanted him for wars.

When he recovered from his injuries, Lee Christmas was, in that moment, probably more utterly beaten than ever again. He wandered down to the wharves, boarded a steamer about to sail, and as she went out, stood at the rail, saying good-bye to the scene of his failures, unknowing the glamour that awaited at the end of the voyage. The purser asked him for his ticket, and in turn he asked listlessly where the ship was going.

At Porto Cortez, Honduras, they put him off.

Pray let the reader recall that the " accident " so feelingly referred to above was the fact that Christmas got drunk, went to sleep at the throttle and wrecked his train; that he took this examination in a railroad testing car, from no window of which, with wet, dazed eyes or otherwise, could he have leaped more than four feet to the ground that was " many stories below."

Appendix V

THOSE who are not familiar with the endless series of bloody revolutions which characterized, in practically every instance, the succession of one administration by another in Honduras during the closing half of the nineteenth century, can hardly appreciate what an epochal event the peaceful transfer of the reins from Policarpo Bonilla to Terencio Sierra was.

Dr. Félix Salgado's " Compendio de Historia de Honduras," published in Comayaguela in 1928 as part of the " Biblioteca de la Sociedad de Geografía e Historia de Honduras " (Section 90, p. 210) gives an account of the Sierra inauguration, and quotes the outgoing President, Pilacarpo Bonilla, as saying:

In the history of Honduras, and in general among Hispano-American peoples, it is phenomenal that an occasion arises when a governor voluntarily transfers his command, it being the ordinary thing that a revolution ousts him before the end of his term, or afterwards, because he has sought to perpetuate himself in power, when he does not pay forfeit with his life which is plucked from him by the dagger of an assassin or of a patriot . . . no acts of fraud or violence have brought about the triumph of your election, and *this is the first time in Honduras,* when the parties could say, on learning the result, as do those in the United States: " The candidate is dead! Long live the President! " . . Receive, sir, this copy of the Constitution as a symbol of the sacred trust placed in my hands by the Assembly of 1894, and which I have the satisfaction of having passed intact on to you, confident, as are the Honduranean people with me, that in the same fashion you will give it to your lawful successor on February 1, 1903.

To which Sierra replied:

Profoundly moved, I have heard the noble and sincere phrases which have just been addressed to me on the occasion of taking possession of the presidency of the Republic. . . Always the transfer of the governmental power has taken place in Honduras under such abnormal conditions, *that it should be considered an extraordinary thing that in this act the outgoing and incoming Presidents should meet each other . . .* upon receiving from your hands a copy of the Constitution as a symbol of the depositing of the supreme power, I express my firm determination to transfer it just so to my lawful successor on February 1, 1903.

Of course, it was too good to last. The reader knows by this time just what happened on February 1, 1903.

Appendix VI

La Gaceta, the official government journal published at Tegucigalpa, prints the annual message of President Sierra to his Congress, in the issue of January 17, 1903 (Serie 225, Numero 2249), as a formal *Meñsage dirígido al Soberano Congreso National.* Both it and the annual report of the *Ministro de Gobernación,* R. Alvarado Guerrera, published in *La Gaceta* of the following week, make references to the appointment of Christmas as police chief at Tegucigalpa.

The President informed Congress that:

The police force is divided into two sections to serve in the towns of Tegucigalpa and Comayagüela, which together form the capital; the director, *don* Lee Christmas, a person of honor and ability, has organized it well, and as a matter of fact, it is now adequate to the needs of the community as a proper safeguard for the citizens and for the maintenance of order.

Señor Alvarado Guerrera's report remarks:

After the acceptance of the resignation of Lt. Col. Dolores Cuadra Perez as director of the police force, *don* Lee Christmas was appointed to take his place May 24 (1902) last, who, known for his honor, energy, impartiality and other qualifications which characterize him, has understood how to bring about a good organization in the said police force, developing it into a safeguard for the community and for the public peace.

Appendix VII

AMONG the strange versions of the "Don't Bury Me" incident is the following from the New York *Times* of Sunday, January 15, 1911:

He [*Christmas*] became a prisoner of the Nicaraguans, in Tegucigalpa, and realized that he would be sentenced to death.

A few mornings later he was not surprised when he was marched out and told he would be "stood up against the wall " . . and he planned to hurl insult at his enemies in true Latin way [*sic!*] just before the firing squad got down to business.

On being asked if he had anything to say before the order to fire was given, he replied "Yes, I do not want to be buried. I want my body to remain above ground." This strange request excited the curiosity of his enemies and they inquired why. This was the very question he had planned to induce his jailers to ask, and he hissed back: "Because I want the buzzards to eat me and then scatter my remains all over every one of you."

This insult, terrible to the ears of the Nicaraguans, so angered and enraged them that they decided to retaliate with some strange and extraordinary punishment on Christmas before they killed him, but could not agree among themselves what form it should take. Some wanted to punch out his eyes. Others wanted to peel his skin off in small strips. They wrangled and quarreled and lost time, and while they wrangled a party of Hondurans arrived, fell upon them, drove them away and rescued the hard-pressed soldier of fortune.

In substantially the same form this account was published in the New Orleans *Daily Picayune* of January 9, 1911, and elsewhere. A far more bizarre description — and one far more replete with " detail " — is embodied in the syndicate article by " Capt. Hermann Archer, U.S.A." which was published some years after the General's death, and printed, among others, by the *New Orleans States* under date of August 7, 1927. The Archer account would have it that —

The next morning he was marched out to the old wall where losing warriors and Presidents were usually shot [*Within the past half century or more I do not believe there is a record of a single ex-president having been shot or otherwise executed in Honduras*]. A climax for motion pictures ensued. During the night Christmas managed to get word to Guy Molony [*which was quite a feat, since Molony was somewhere in the Philippines*] who had served with him through several battles [*sic!*]. When dawn came it appeared that even this friend had failed him or else could do nothing to save him. Still Christmas fought on, with surprising subtlety and craft. He hit upon the idea of insulting his captors, of enraging them in the hope of delay.

The firing squad drew up. The ironical Nicaraguan Captain asked him if he wanted his body shipped back home. Christmas began his stream of insults. He called the captain and his men, with deep calculation, all the vile things he could think of. He insulted their intelligence as soldiers, their church, their women, their country. The Nicaraguans — in their hearts the subtle savagery of an Indian ancestry blended with the fierce pride of Spanish blood that also ran in their veins — became frantic. They pounded his face while his hands were bound and he laughed at them and continued his taunts. They drew away to consider what tortures would wash away this gringo's insulting epithets. They glared, sneered, told him in detail all the cruel things they intended doing to him. They whetted knives and brought in braziers of burning coal. Christmas talked on, grimly, hopelessly.

Just in time Molony and a band of American soldiers of fortune smashed their way into the place, bested the surprised firing squad, and fled that night safely into Guatemala.

Off hand, one would imagine that this version, supported by such an astonishing wealth of corroborative detail, would have exhausted the possibilities in chronicling the incident. In that event one must read what Thaddeus S. Dayton, writing in the *Railroad Man's Magazine* for May, 1911 (pp. 597 ff.) has to offer; namely —

One morning Christmas was summoned from his cell. His arms were bound behind his back, and he was marched out under a heavy guard to a place in the edge of Tegucigalpa. He was made to stand against the wall of his own official residence [*sic!*]. He realized that the end was near. But still he couldn't tell the difference between the danger and the safety signals.

He was not afraid. His first thought was that it was a shame to spatter up the new wall with a lot of blood and bullets. He was rather proud of that wall, for he had superintended the building of it himself [*sic!*]. He wasn't frightened — "peeved" is nearer the word to express his feelings.

Christmas knew exactly the formalities that would precede his execution. He would be asked politely if there was anything he wished to say before the firing squad would riddle his breast with their bullets. He would be expected to say: "*Adios, amigos. Viva el Presidente*

Manuel Bonilla!" Then the captain's raised hand would fall, and that would be the end.

Before the firing squad got down to business he was asked the usual question. His reply threw consternation into the hearts of President Zelaya's followers who had gathered to see the taking off of "*el diabolo Americano.*" What Christmas said in fluent Spanish had a sting, an insult that is untranslatable. It drove Zelaya's men into a rage. Some of them wept in their frenzy. Here is the English of it:

"Yes, I've something to say to you swine," sneered Christmas, and he spat upon the man who stood nearest to him, a cabinet minister [*sic!*]. After you kill me I don't want my body to rest within the earth of this country that I have made my own and which I love. I want it to remain above ground. I want the buzzards to eat me and scatter my remains over every one of you. Now fire, you mangy curs!"

General Christmas' remarks are much expurgated . . . This speech, so superlatively insulting, so angered and enraged his captors that they decided at once that shooting or hanging was too good for him. The firing squad squatted on the ground and smoked cigarettes, while the government officials quarreled among themselves trying to decide on some cruel and unusual form of torture.

Some wanted to tear out his eyes and then turn him loose among a herd of horses and let him be trampled to death. Others favored flaying him alive, bit by bit. The contestants waxed so warm in their altercation that they did not hear the approach of armed men. Suddenly there was a crash of rifles. Half a score of men lay dead. The rest ran away. Manuel Bonilla himself cut Christmas' bonds and offered him a cigarette [*sic!*]. Manuel Bonilla was again in the saddle temporarily.

Lee Christmas never did make Honduras his own country. He remained always a citizen of the United States. Even had he become a Central American by naturalization, it would be difficult to discover how Manuel Bonilla got into the saddle again while fleeing in a foreign warship to Guatemala.

IN THE circumstances, it is no more than fair to show that the Christmas version of the battle itself — not of the circumstances from which sprang the "Don't bury me episode" — varies from that given in one of the detailed histories of Honduras, whose author, Lic. Félix Salgado, on pages 257 and 258 of his *Compendio de Historia de Honduras,* writes:

Tomadas las posiciones de "El Lindero" por el enemigo, a las tres de la tarde, muy immediato al Campamento General, fueron convocados la mayor parte de los Jefes, por el Gral. Barahona, a Consejo, y todos estuvieron de acuerdo en hacer la retirada, rompiendo para ésto las líneas enemigas por el llano de Lizapa, encargo que el Gral. Barahona, después de arreglarlo todo, dió a los Coroneles Encarnación Paniagua, Maximiliano Ferrary y otros Jefes, quienes efectivamente abrieron brecha, in las líneas enemigas en el punto señalado, después de las cinco de la tarde, por donde pasó la mayor parte de los que, momentos antes, formaban el Ejército de Oriente; pero no la retaguardia donde estaba el General en Jefe, acompañado de un grupo de jefes y officiales. El Gral. Barahona pretendió salvar el tren de guerra, pero llegó un momento crítico, en que por el fuego convergente del enemigo no se esparaba salvarlo. En esta situación, algunos jefes manifestaron al Gral. Barahona, la necesidad que había de que se salvara él, ya fuera refugiándose en las sinuosidades del terreno, o aprovechando el avance mayor sobre las líneas enemigas, que se iban rompiendo; pero a todo ésto se opuso aquél, manifestando: que su honor no lo dejaria nunca manchado con la cobardia; and con la calma que le era peculiar, siguió su marcha paso a paso, como dando tiempo a que todos se salvaran. Al concluir el descenso del cerro "Los Coyotes" y principiar a recorrer la pequeña llanura de lizapa, el Gral. Barahona cayó herido de las extremidades inferiores, safándose de la bestia que montaba y una vez en el suelo, al ser reconocido por los enemigos que lo rodearon immediatamente, uno de éstos — José de la Crez García — por sobre el grupo hizo un disparo de rifle, hiriendo mortalmente al Gral. Barahona en el costado derecho, por lo cual exclamó más o menos, estas palabras: "Mátenme traidores, que no saben lo que han hecho." Esto ocurrió entre las cico y las seis de la tarde. El Gral. Barahona fué recogido por los revolucionarios, quienes deseaban que se calvara; pero aquél se oponía a que se le hiciese curación alguna y decía: "Todo es inútil, mis horas están contadas." Efectivamente, en la noche del 22 al 23 de Marzo, murió el Gral. Barahona, en medio de sus enemigos, quienes pesarosos le enterraron en Galeras, en la orilla del camino real, que conduce de San Antonio a Güinope, dentro de un cerco de doña María del Carmen Morazán, donde pocos meses después su viuda, hizo construir un modesto mausoleo. El 8 de Abril de 1914, el Gobierno del Dr. Francisco Bertrand, hizo exhumar los restos del Gral. Barahona y depositados con gran solemnidad en unión de otros héroes, en el mausoleo que el estado mandó construir en el Cementerio de la capital, donde descansen definativamente.

Cuando el Coronel don Florencio Tejeda Reyes, que ya estaba fuero del peligro, se dió cuenta de que el Gral. Barahona quedaba en medio de las filas enemigas, volvió atrás para defenderlo o morir con él, como en efecto así sucedió, habiendo recibido un balazo en la cabeza, que le hizo victima immediatamente, a poca distancia y casi al mismo tiempo en que su jefe caía herido. Asimismo cayeron heridos, el Gral. Lee Christmas, el Alférez Andrés Avelino Díaz, quien fué salvado por un compañero y algunos otros cadetes y oficiales, que defendían a su Jefe en aquella luctuosa jornada.

Appendix VIII

INDICTMENTS were lodged in the United States District Court for Eastern Louisiana by a grand jury on February 18, 1911, against Manuel Bonilla, Lee Christmas, Joseph Beer, Florian Dávadi and Captain Charles Johnson (master and navigator of the *Hornet*). Two indictments were brought in this case, both at the instance of the late Charlton W. Beattie, then federal district attorney. The cases were tried before Rufus E. Foster, now judge of the United States Circuit Court of Appeals.

The first indictment was withdrawn, because District Attorney Beattie felt it would be difficult to make out the *Hornet* and her cargo of coal and her passenger list of five men as a military expedition. Two new indictments were then filed, the first of which (Case No. 2741) charges that the five accused

did unlawfully, knowingly, wilfully and feloniously fit out, arm, and procure to be fitted out and armed, and were unlawfully, knowingly, feloniously concerned in the fitting out and arming of a certain American steamship called "*Hornet*," which said steamship had American registry and sailed under the flag of the United States with the intent then and there that said vessel should be employed in the service of a certain party; that is, one Manuel Bonilla, then and there claiming to be president of the republic of Spanish Honduras but not the de facto president of said Republic, though aspiring so to be, and intending to lead an armed revolution and insurrection to accomplish this aspiration . . . to cruise and commit hostilities against the subjects and citizens and property of the said de facto government of the Republic of Spanish Honduras, with whom the United States were then and there and still are at peace.

The companion indictment (case 2742) charges that the same defendants did, under the same circumstances, conspire to

prepare the means for a certain military expedition to be carried out from the United States against the territory and people and dominions of the Republic of Spanish Honduras with whom the United States were then and there at peace.

Only two of the " culprits " were within the jurisdiction of the court at the time these indictments were filed, for Bonilla and Christmas had won their revolution by then and were busily occupied in Honduras. However, Captain Johnson and Joseph Beer were in New Orleans. They were brought to trial on April 6. Drew Linard, the reporter-diplomat, was one of the principal witnesses.

A mistrial was entered, and the charges were tried anew, before another jury, on April 17 and 18, when both defendants were found not guilty.

Some of the special charges read to the jury by the court on this occasion set forth that " it is not a crime against the neutrality laws of the United States for individuals to leave this country to enlist in a foreign military service," and that " if the prohibited intent does not exist, a citizen of the United States may not only sell a fully armed vessel in a port of the United States to a belligerent power or to a subject or citizen of such a power, but may also send a fully armed vessel to a foreign port for sale, as a purely commercial venture, accepting the risk of loss by seizure, capture, and confiscation in transit."

As soon as the charges against Johnson and Beer had been decided by verdicts of " not guilty," the indictments pending against Bonilla, Christmas and Dávadi were nolle prossed.

Appendix IX

THE veiled and unveiled charge that throughout the early days of 1911 the United States kept hands off the revolution as a cudgel to be held over President Dávila to bludgeon him entering into the "dollar diplomacy" treaty were freely printed and voiced not only in Honduras but in the United States as well. The publications which sponsored such charges naturally found a toothsome morsel in the *Hornet's* ultimate seizure, declaring that this step had been taken because Morgan & Co. had come to so thorough an understanding with Dávila that they could afford now to see the Bonilla-Christmas revolution smashed.

The following Washington Dispatch to the New Orleans *Times-Democrat* of January 25, 1911, is an instance in point:

WAS LESE MAJESTE
HORNET OPERATED CONTRARY TO WISHES
OF J. P. MORGAN

Washington, D. C., Jan. 25 — Accusation by intimation that what is known as "double crossing" has become one of the means for the furtherance of dollar diplomacy is made in connection with the seizure of the *Hornet* — the "navy" of the Bonilla revolutionists in Honduras. Alberto Membreno, the representative of the Honduran revolutionists, and his attorney, have suggested to Senators who, sooner or later, will have to deal with the Honduras matter, that Morgan & Co., and other financiers who have been trying to make a loan of $12,000,000 to Honduras, have come to such a degree of understanding with President Dávila that they are now ready to have the Bonilla revolution smashed by the United States.

The seizure of the *Hornet,* said to be in defiant violation of the rule laid down by Chief Justice Marshall in the case of Rose against Himley, is the easiest way to smash it. Membreno, having no standing here before the State Department, is forced to discreetly communicate his suspicion that that is the reason for the seizure of the *Hornet.*

The indirect accusation is that the State Department is being used for the furthering of the plans made by the financiers called in to help make the dollar diplomacy effective, regardless of what the law may be and regardless of the implied obligation assumed by the State Department in countenancing the revolution . . .

Secretary Knox' close personal relations with H. G. Frick, who is naturally in close business relations with Morgan & Co. . . gives the Central Americans what they deem ground for suggesting that even if Morgan & Co. needed a way for getting their views before the State Department, other than by direct correspondence, Mr. Frick would be the natural avenue of communication for anything indicating that it would please the financiers to have Bonilla stopped because Dávila has given assurance that satisfied the money lenders they can do business more satisfactorily with the existing than with the proposed government.

The fact that the *Hornet* was permitted to steam around on warlike errands for many days before there was any suggestion that she could be seized for violating the neutrality laws of the United States is pointed to as indicating that a change of view took place among the money lenders.

Appendix X

PRESIDENT DÁVILA sent his cabled plea for intervention to President Taft on January 28, 1911. The next day he published a resolution embodying approval of the Paredes-Knox treaty. In due form, this resolution was turned over to the Congress for action on the morning of January 31. What happened in the *salón de sesiones* is here related by Dr. Rómulo E. Durón, one of the nation's leading scholars and statesmen, whose work on the history of Honduras is the standard volume of reference in this field. Dr. Durón was one of the deputies in the Congress to which President Dávila submitted his treaty.

Our first intimation [he recalls] that the treaty was being submitted to us came in the form of a request that we, the Congress, go into executive session. None of us knew for certain what the subject of discussion behind the closed doors was to be, but all of us naturally suspected it would be the Morgan Loan. As soon as the treaty had been read to us, a long discussion was held, the upshot of which was that a committee should be appointed to study the provisions of the treaty, and report back to the Congress the next day. This procedure was modified by the suggestion that since the treaty was a matter so vital, leading men of the nation, even though they were not members of Congress, should also be asked to serve on that committee. This suggestion was adopted, and it was decided that Policarpo Bonilla, Angel Ugarte, Pedro J. Bustillo, Rafael Alvarado Manzano, Saturnino Medal, Miguel Oquelí Bustillo, Dionisio Gutiérrez, Alberto A. Rodríguez, Antonio R. Vallejo, César Bonilla, Jerónimo Zelaya, Máximo B. Rosales, and a number of others be appointed. Congress then adjourned to give the committee time to deliberate.

Just as the deputies were ready to leave, an officer came from the President to invite the entire Congress to pass into the President's reception chamber. When we entered this hall, he seated us all around the walls, and then the president made a long and impassioned address, in which he declared that Providence had offered Honduras this opportunity to secure the help of the United States, and he urged us not to adjourn, but to take action that same day and to make that action favorable. Nobody said so much as half a word when the President had finished. There was no applause, not a sound, nothing.

The deputies returned to the chamber just the same as if no adjournment had been taken, and a resolution was adopted to remain in permanent session until the treaty was disposed of. That was about one o'clock in the afternoon. There was discussion for nearly two hours, at the climax of which the treaty vote was taken. Thirty-two members voted to disapprove the treaty and four voted to ratify it. The President of the Congress, Dr. Francisco Escobar, appointed me as a committee of one to draw up the decree of disapprobation, and I did so at once. The decree was adopted.

This decree would not become effective as law until the minutes of that session had been read and approved at the next sitting of Congress. The following morning word got about that some of the deputies had been asked not to attend, so that it would be impossible to adopt the minutes of the previous day's session, and thus impossible to give the decree of disapprobation the force and effect of law. It was even rumored the deputies would be arrested if they tried to meet. Hearing this I personally went about to all the members, and requested them to attend the session with me. There was a quorum present, the minutes were adopted, and the decree of disapprobation was promulgated.

The Congress later issued a printed statement to the people of Honduras, in pamphlet form, in which were set forth the text of the Paredes-Knox treaty, a statement of the motives which impelled Congress to disapprove the *convención,* and the minutes of the various sessions at which this action was discussed and taken (*Manifiesto del Congreso Nacional al Pueblo Hondureño, Tipografía Nacional, Tegucigalpa,* 1911). A perusal of it does much to clear up the fog of chauvinistic and political hokum in which the entire question of " dollar diplomacy " was enveloped at home and abroad, and to reveal very clearly just what the source of the intense bitterness over the proposed Morgan Loan in Honduras was.

Article IV of the Knox-Paredes treaty provided that the customs moneys of Honduras, during the term of the treaty, should be administered by an *Administrador General de Aduanas* who should be selected from a list of names submitted to the government of Honduras by the Fiscal Agent of the lenders. This official would have complete supervision over the collection and disbursement of the customs moneys, and would make annual statements to the governments both of Honduras and of the United States (oftener, if required) giving the exact account and audit of these funds.

Now there was, of course, a good deal of talk about such a procedure violating the Constitution of Honduras. As a matter of fact, it probably did. But the crux of the matter, as pointed out in the *Manifiesto*, was this:

Apart from the illegality of a Fiscal Agent concerning whose appointment nothing is known, and of an Administrator of Customs appointed in the fashion prescribed in the treaty, it remains a fact that the clauses which refer thereto constitute an insult to the Honduraneans, regarding them as incapable, morally and intellectually, of administering their revenues, of fulfilling their promises, and of respecting their laws.

Gloss this over as you please, that was the key to the intense feeling in Honduras concerning the *" convención Paredes-Knox."*

Appendix XI

J. H. BURTON, head of the New York lumber firm that bears his name, writes me that:

During the last half of the year 1917, J. H. Burton and Company, Inc., were engaged in the manufacture and delivery of several thousand portable barracks for the United States Government for shipment to France. This contract was completed in December, 1917, and the barracks, I understand, were used by our troops at the front. They were so constructed that the troops erected them themselves, dismantled them and again re-erected them as the position of the lines changed. In other words, moving them back and forward, principally forward, as action required.

As I recall it, Guatemala City was visited by two earthquakes, the first on Christmas Day, 1917 and the second in January 1918. These earthquakes were very severe. Guatemala City at that time had a population of about 125,000. After the earthquakes there were only about four or five buildings standing undamaged and these were of steel and concrete construction.

The Government of Guatemala made inquiries through their representative at New Orleans with instructions that he immediately get in touch with United States firms competent to promptly manufacture and ship several thousand portable wooden houses, which he stated would be paid for by the Guatemalan Government and used as, more or less, temporary housing during the rehabilitation and rebuilding of the city.

This Guatemalan official at New Orleans got in touch with the writer at our New Orleans office and opened negotiations. He suggested that our Company immediately send its representative to Guatemala, for the purpose of conducting negotiations directly with President Cabrera, and assured us that the Guatemalan Government was prepared to purchase and pay cash for buildings to the extent of $3,000,000 if necessary. Our experience with Latin-American countries had taught us that irrespective of the urgency of any situation, such negotiations were usually subject to procrastination, delays and all sorts of uncertainties. Therefore I made the following suggestion to the Consul: that we were very busily engaged and could not afford to send representatives to Guatemala except and unless we were assured the inquiry was sincere; that cash credits would be established in case an agreement was reached as to prices, quantities and times of delivery, and finally, that we receive from President Cabrera a cable invitation to send our representative there, with the understanding that if plans, specifications, terms and times of shipment could be arranged on a mutually satisfactory basis, a contract would be entered into and credits furnished. The Consul told me that in his opinion no such invitation or assurance could or would be given as it would be contrary to all precedent. I told him I was sorry, but those were the only conditions under which I would entertain the proposition. Thereupon he informed me that he would immediately cable my decision to his Government, and would acquaint me of its reply. Two or three days later, he informed me that he had received the necessary invitation and assurances issued by President Cabrera.

Promptly thereafter, we proceeded to Guatemala via the United Fruit line steamer from New Orleans to Puerto Barrios. Our party consisted of Mr. F. A. Palen, engineer and designer of the Burpal portable buildings, Mr. R. A. McDonnell, an architect and draftsman whose name I have now forgotten, and the writer. General Christmas boarded the steamer at Puerto Cortez, bound for Guatemala City via Puerto Barrios. Mr. McDonnell met and engaged him in conversation and later introduced him to me. We needed an interpreter, preferably a man who was persona grata with the Guatemalan government. Mr. McDonnell suggested that General Christmas might be of service to us in that connection. He — General Christmas — intimated that his services were available.

On arrival at Puerto Barrios, I made certain confidential inquiries of people who were in position to know and on whose judgment I felt I could rely and to whom I frankly outlined the purpose of our visit and our need for an interpreter and confidential man, who had a satisfactory standing with President Cabrera and the Guatemalan government. Their advice was that we employ General Christmas and that while he was irresponsible so far as money matters were concerned, once his services were engaged he stayed bought and at that particular time he enjoyed the confidence of President Cabrera and the Guatemalan government. I thereupon closed with General Christmas at a salary, as I recall it, possibly $200 or $250 a month to work with us and represent our company under my direction during the course of the proposed negotiations.

We then proceeded to Guatemala City via railroad. On arrival we found the City in a most deplorable condition. The buildings that were not totally demolished were damaged to an extent that they were unsafe for habitation. The only accommodation we could secure was in the

City Park in a shack built of dry goods boxes and old lumber with a temporary metal roof. In this shack were placed five army cots secured from the Red Cross and there we lived for about ten days or until we had secured a location and erected our own portable house, after which we lived for an additional five or six weeks in reasonable comfort in our own building, attended by a Chinese cook and general servant, who served us well. Shortly after our arrival, General Christmas arranged an interview for the writer with President Cabrera, who was living in a temporary building on what was known as " The Hill," being about one and a half or two miles from the center of the city. In this preliminary interview, general details were discussed and a memorandum was made of various and sundry matters on which President Cabrera desired information. Two or three subsequent interviews were had, the details of which are unnecessary to recite at this time, except to say that in the final analysis it developed that President Cabrera, while desiring to purchase buildings was either unable to or unwilling to establish the necessary credits, and while his attitude toward us was courteous and cordial, because of his inability or unwillingness to establish credit, that particular project was dropped.

In the meantime, we were making a survey and analysis of conditions in Guatemala. We finally decided it might be a good plan to establish a lumber yard which we subsequently did, appointing General Christmas as our manager, arranging that all sales were to be made on a cash basis with invoicing through and payments to be made to a certain bank in Guatemala, whom we appointed as our fiscal agents. This arrangement worked out satisfactorily and profitably for a period of, I should say, perhaps a year, after which the business became unprofitable and we decided to liquidate. General Christmas did not like the idea of liquidation as it would mean as soon as the business was wound up, his connections with us would cease and we soon began to sense that our interests were suffering. We had no open disagreement with him, but frankly we felt that he did not like the idea of winding up the business. We were insistent, however, and suggested that we send a Captain West, who was in our employ in New Orleans, to Guatemala City, for the purpose of co-operating with General Christmas in the liquidation of the company's affairs and to this General Christmas agreed. Captain West and General Christmas did not get along any too well together, as was natural in the circumstances, but through Captain West's diplomacy and the occasional exercise of his authority, the business was finally wound up with little or no loss.

In the meantime, during the latter part of 1918 and the year 1919, as I recall it, General Christmas, with our consent, was acting as secret agent in Guatemala for the State Department of the United States government and during that period, many cabled messages of the State Department were relayed through our New York Office and received by our New York office covering negotiations that General Christmas was conducting under instructions of the State Department.

The above covers in a general way the relations of General Christmas with our company.

Briefly stated, the General of course was no business man. He was a man of unquestioned courage, feared no one, loved intrigue, had his own standards of honor which while peculiar one could not help but admire and our experience was that once his services were engaged he remained loyal, according to his sense of values. Until he knew one, he was very suspicious and secretive, but once you gained his confidence, he was very frank. Of course you know that he was associated and more or less intimate with all sorts and conditions of men and women. He was one of the most nearly unique characters I have ever met and while our relations with him from a business standpoint were not as profitable as they would have been had he been a business man, yet if he had been a business man, he never would have been the character he was. One connection with him from a money standpoint was unprofitable, but from the viewpoint of experience, it was certainly very interesting.

Appendix XII

MAX M. SCHAUMBURGER has turned over to me the following copy of his diary entry for April 8, 1920.

Great excitement prevailed at the Hall of the National Legislative Assembly in Guatemala City on this date. A large crowd was gathered on the outside — filling the street, as well as the roofs of the adjacent buildings, and people were clinging to the barred windows of the Legislative Hall itself. It was a difficult matter to get through the guard and inside of the small meeting hall — which was soon filled by the members of the Legislative and Special Commissions of the Unionistas party. For a while inconsequential routine was taken up, and it was only when General José María Letona, a member of the Assembly and ex-Sub-secretary of War arose and began to speak that it became apparent that something of more than ordinary nature was about to transpire.

General Letona made the specific charges that President Manuel Estrada Cabrera was a sick and crazy man, suffering from a monomania of persecution, weeping before images, holding witchcraft sessions and often breaking into a raging fury, during which no one close to him was safe; in other words, said Gen. Letona, the President is a madman, a constant danger to the lives and liberties of the people of Guatemala and unfit to continue as head of the government, the helm of which he had had for twenty-two years. The applause inside and outside, which was provoked by this subject, was thrilling, to say the least. Next arose Deputy Vidauure, who also made a stirring talk, in which he accentuated what had already been stated by Letona, and suggested that if a committee of medical experts considering the situation would declare the president as sick and unfit to govern, this would be an easy way out of what would otherwise be a disgraceful situation of trying the president for the many crimes of which he doubtlessly was guilty. In accordance with this suggestion, a meeting of medical men, who also happened to be members of the Congress, was convoked and after a short consultation they then and there issued a statement, declaring President Cabrera as mentally unfit to continue as head of the Government; thereupon, a decree of the Assembly was passed to the effect that

Manuel Estrada Cabrera be relieved of the Presidency, given license to leave the country, and that a provisional president be named *ad interim*. Just at this point things inside of the meeting hall became very uncomfortable, as those on the outside, clinging to the bars of the windows, shouted a warning that Cabrera's troops were approaching; in view of the fact that there was no organized force to repel these troops, the situation at this moment was very dangerous to all of those inside of the meeting room. Luck was with the Unionistas, however, as a committee of the members of Congress who happened also to be ranking officers of the army went out and were able to persuade the officers commanding the troops to retire from the scene. It was evident that these troops came without any specific or definite orders, as, if they had made an attack on the crowd and the Assembly room at that time, the whole plans of the revolution would have gone up in smoke and bloodshed.

When the Commission of Generals returned and advised that the troops had retired, a great sigh of relief went up throughout the meeting hall. A vote was then taken and out of 41 members of Congress present, 39 voted for Carlos Herrera, 1 for General Fuentes and 1 for A. Sarvia. Immediately Carlos Herrera took the oath of office, as President, and after all the members of Congress had signed the decrees, the Assembly broke up amidst great confusion and applause from the people on the outside, as well as on the inside.

Immediately thereafter, great excitement prevailed throughout the City; two of Cabrera's henchmen, who were found in the vicinity, were badly beaten and almost killed; all houses of business closed, whistles blew and the Unionistas headquarters were surrounded by a seething mass. The American Legation was immediately informed of what had transpired and a cable was sent to Washington. The excitement throughout of the city became greater and greater and when, after dark, great fear prevailed that Cabrera's troops, stationed in the outlying forts and barracks, would raid the city; all during the afternoon old army officers, as well as civilians, presented themselves at the temporary Presidential Headquarters of Herrera, which had been established at the Mexican Legation. On the other hand, all Cabrera agents and henchmen who were found on the streets, were badly beaten and even killed, particularly, while the writer was at General Calderón's home, several shots were heard in the street and upon rushing out, we found the lifeless body of Captain Anguiano, one of Cabrera's henchmen who, it was charged, had fired on the Unionista parade on March 11, when many civilians were killed in front of the Military Academy by the Cabrera troops and police. Anguiano had evidently been caught unawares on the street and had been made the target for a general fusillade of shots, as his body seemed to have been pierced by no less than twenty bullets.

The excitement that prevailed in the City during the night is very difficult to describe; General José María Lima had established head-quarters at the Plaza and those headquarters were besieged by great crowds of citizens and students clamoring for arms. The whole city was immediately converted into an armed camp, volunteers armed with rifles, machetes, or even pieces of pipe and sticks challenged every passer-by; and when the bomb from Fort Matomoros exploded in the heart of the city towards midnight, killing several civilians, every one was looking for shelter. Why this shot was fired at that time was never explained, unless it was merely a signal to the other forts that everything was in readiness for the general bombardment on the city, which was to open at five o'clock the next morning, April 9.

At the Plaza things were in a terrible state of confusion. The only troop of soldiers which the Unionistas had succeeded in winning over to their side were sleeping around the Plaza benches; an attempt at organization and discipline was made, rations were ordered and the erection of temporary barricades and machine gun nests was begun. At 2 o'clock A.M., the writer returned to the American Legation, and found the secretaries, Scotten and McFadden, moving in with their mattresses and other personal belongings.

On April 9, as previously stated, the general bombardment of the city was begun at five o'clock this morning and lasted with intervals from April 9 to the morning of April 14 inclusive, finally resulting in the unconditional surrender of Cabrera.

Appendix XIII

THE following note from A. Bruce Bielaski, of New York, throws some interesting sidelights upon the oil concessions General Christmas was seeking to promote when he was overtaken by the illness to which he ultimately succumbed. Mr. Bielaski writes:

My first acquaintance with the General grew out of investigations and prosecutions of our neutrality statutes when I was in the Department of Justice and later on when the World War broke out when he was trying to secure a commission for service in our Army. He did some work, I believe, for the State Department which pleased them quite a bit, and after I left the Government service the Company with which I was then connected employed him to obtain an oil concession in Guatemala.

When General Christmas was originally engaged, it was with the thought and the assurance that the enterprise would require but a very short time, although we made due allowance for the fact that nothing is done in Central America within the time set. Difficulties of one kind or another developed which largely through General Christmas' efforts were gradually overcome and finally it seemed legally possible to get the sort of a concession which would be workable and worth while.

General Christmas had always had assurances of priority in certain territory, although he knew it was common practice for individuals close to the government to file claims without specifications which would be found to have a very slightly earlier date than plans filed by legitimate companies or genuinely interested individuals and later on the specifications would be copied and made a part of the favored individual's claim.

In the final show-down, it devolped that while the government had assured General Christmas that the selections he had made on behalf of the Company were first claims, there were, in fact, a number of claims filed by favored native individuals which while not at the time effective, could under the law be made effective, and then take priority over the claims General Christmas had made on behalf of our company. It was apparent, of course, that these individuals did not intend in good faith to go ahead with any development work, but merely wanted to be bought out, and, in fact, a number of them approached General Christmas and made propositions of this kind to him. It seemed to us a plain hold-up game and made the venture not worth the risk. Finding that we could not get a clean-cut bona fide concession on workable terms, we abandoned the enterprise. We felt that the General did about as well as could be expected under the circumstances, but was imposed upon by numerous people in whom he put some reliance.

You are doubtless familiar with the difficulties that are always present in doing business with the governments in many of the Latin-American countries and we had expected a great deal of the sort of thing which General Christmas encountered. There was too much of it, however, in this particular instance and the absence of good faith on the part of some individuals was so apparent that we gave the matter up as hopeless.

I would not have you feel that we hold too low an estimate of Latin-Americans, for we have numerous friends in Latin-America and know that many of them are just as dependable as persons to be found anywhere else; but you also know that the methods and standards of doing business in many places are, whether better or worse than ours, at least very different.